Bringing Your
FAMILY
HISTORY
to LIFE through social history

WITHDRAWN

Katherine Scott Sturdevant

BETTERWAY BOOKS
CINCINNATI, OHIO

www.familytreemagazine.com

About the Author

Katherine Scott Sturdevant is a social historian with the B.A., M.A. and Ph.D. candidacy in American history. She has taught college-level American history courses for more than sixteen years, including regional, community, women's, immigrant, and minority history. A popular speaker for historical and genealogical organizations, Kathy is also a professional editor. As an innovator of the idea that genealogists should research and write their family histories in the context of social history, she team-teaches with Sharon Carmack college courses in family history and genealogy, as well as an online course for Writer's Digest School. Kathy lives in Colorado Springs with her husband, Rick, who is a historian for Air Force Space Command.

929.1072
S9356
2000

Bringing Your Family History to Life Through Social History. Copyright © 2000 by Katherine Scott Sturdevant. Manufactured in the United States of America. All rights reserved. No part of this book may be reproduced in any form or by any electronic or mechanical means including information storage and retrieval systems without permission in writing from the publisher, except by a reviewer, who may quote brief passages in a review. Published by Betterway Books, an imprint of F&W Publications, Inc., 1507 Dana Ave., Cincinnati, Ohio 45207. (800) 289-0963. First edition.

Other fine Betterway Books are available from your local bookstore or on our Web site at www.familytreemagazine.com.

04   03   02   01   00   5   4   3   2   1

Library of Congress Cataloging-in-Publication Data

Sturdevant, Katherine Scott
   Bringing your family history to life through social history / by Katherine Scott Sturdevant.—1st ed.
     p.   cm.
   Includes bibliographical references and index.
   ISBN 1-55870-510-4
     1. Genealogy. 2. Local history. 3. Material culture. I. Title.

CS16 S862 2000
929'.1'072073—dc21   00-044505
                                                                        CIP

Editor: Sharon DeBartolo Carmack, CG
Production editor: Brad Crawford
Production coordinator: Emily Gross
Interior designer: Sandy Conopeotis Kent
Cover designer: Wendy Dunning
Icon designer: Cindy Beckmeyer
Cover photograph by Underwood Photo Archives/Superstock

DEDICATION

This book is dedicated to my parents,

BARBARA HARPER SCOTT
(1917–1999)

and

JAMES ALEXANDER SCOTT
(1915–1999)

for giving me a family history,

and to my husband,

RICK WILLARD STURDEVANT

for sharing his and mine with me.

Acknowledgments

Most authors save thanking their spouses for the end of their acknowledgments. I must diverge. Thank you, Rick, for being my loving partner, best friend, toughest critic, most trusted adviser, and even a "character" in this book. Thank you also for being the first reader of this book to apply its principles to a newly rejuvenated interest in family history.

It is strange and sad that both of my parents, James and Barbara Scott, died the year this book was born. Thanks to them for their eternal support and to my parents-in-law, Wendell and Carol Sturdevant, for theirs. I am grateful to Wendell and Rick for their permission to use photographs and stories from the Sturdevant family. Thanks go also to all of the relatives who have assisted my family history efforts and thus have contributed to this book.

All of my professors helped me to be a better historian. I am especially grateful to Jerald Combs of San Francisco State University, who introduced me to the "new" social history and who convinced me that I could build a career as a historian. Moses Rischin, also of San Francisco State University, assigned me to write my family history in historical context, and look what happened! My doctoral program at the University of California, Santa Barbara, introduced me to the general public history perspective that I apply here. Thanks to the faculty there, particularly Carl Harris for teaching community history and Patricia Cline Cohen for reading this manuscript (under extreme time constraints) and responding with such meaningful encouragement.

I am grateful to all of my students for teaching me so much. In this instance, I owe special thanks to those who allowed me to use excerpts from their family histories in historical context: Mary Weber, Bob Fineberg, Sharon Swint, Sherry Walker, Muriel Haase, Joanne Ellenberger, and Rose Keefe. Thanks also to those colleagues who provided such wonderful case studies for me: Betsy Jameson, Roger Joslyn, Mary Ann Tabor, and my special Historian Everymen, Marion Parker and Mary Tabor.

For taking the time to read some or all of the manuscript and offer helpful advice, I thank genealogist Suzanne McVetty, historian Pat Cohen, Colorado State Folklorist Bea Roeder, and of course historian Rick Sturdevant and genealogical author Sharon Carmack. Any errors that remain are my responsibility.

Many librarians and archivists assisted along the way with specific information. Thanks to the staff of the State Historical Society of Iowa for introducing me to professional methods in conservation, photograph archiving, and historical societies generally. Other librarian colleagues who have contributed to this book include Judy Rice-Jones of the University of Colorado at Colorado Springs and Mary Davis of Pikes Peak Library District. A professional in another category also helped greatly: Thank you, copyright attorney Brenda Speer, for guarding my book as your own.

I shall never forget the day when, at a national genealogical conference, then-editor in chief David Lewis of Betterway Books approached me after one of my presentations and asked me to write a book. Thank you, David, for initiating this project and doing inestimable good for my self-esteem. Editorial director Bill Brohaugh followed up on both projects—my book and me. Thank you, Bill, for your kindness, patience, and faith when crises in my life, especially the political ones, coincided with this project.

Finally, Sharon DeBartolo Carmack has helped me at almost every step. I might never have thought to write a book on this topic had not Sharon been my student, team teacher, friend and, now, editor. So, thank you, Sharon. Is there any more gratifying experience than to open new doors for someone, watch them rush through, and then see them stop, turn around, and open new doors for you?

— Katherine Scott Sturdevant
Colorado Springs, Colorado

Icons Used in This Book

Case Study

Examples of this book's advice at work

Oral History

Techniques for getting family stories

Citing Sources

Reminders and methods for documenting information

Printed Source

Directories, books, pamphlets and other paper archives

\di'fin\ *vb*
Definitions

Terminology and jargon explained

Reminder

"Don't-Forget" items to keep in mind

For More Info

Where to turn for more in-depth coverage

Research Tip

Ways to make research more efficient

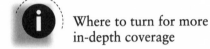
Hidden Treasures

Family papers and home sources

See Also

Where in this book to find related information

Idea Generator

Techniques and prods for further thinking

Sources

Where to go for information, supplies, etc.

Important

Information and tips you can't overlook

Step By Step

Walkthroughs of important procedures

Internet Source

Where on the web to find what you need

Supplies

Advice on day-to-day office tools

Library/Archive Source

Repositories that might have the information you need

Technique

How to conduct research, solve problems, and get answers

Microfilm Source

Information available on microfilm

Tip

Ways to make research more efficient

Money Saver

Getting the most out of research dollars

Warning

Stop before you make a mistake

Notes

Thoughts, ideas and related insights

Table of Contents At a Glance

Table of Contents

1   Social History: Your Ancestors' World, *4*

Train yourself to view everything about your family in social history context. The Elements of Social History will guide you, and examples will show how meaningful family history can become.

2   A Historian's Approach to Home Sources: Artifacts, *24*

As you locate nearby family and social history sources, you will learn how to view even the most ordinary things as artifacts and draw history from them the way that professionals do. Analyzing a simple recipe collection teaches methods for recapturing the lives and even the thoughts of an ancestor. Recommended sources, examples, and forms assist you with analyzing your own artifacts.

3   Artifacts II: Culture, Citing, and Caring, *56*

If we take good care of our artifacts, they can write tomorrow's family and social history. Using some of the methods and resources of folklorists, you can extract revealing colorful folk life from your home sources. Taking family artifacts seriously as sources means citing them properly and caring for them as archivists and curators do. You'll find practical advice for rescuing artifacts and storing, displaying, and using them.

4   A Historian's Approach to Family Photographs, *85*

Get out those pictures! Here are a historian's methods for identifying and analyzing what you see. You can develop a sixth sense for recognizing mysterious, unidentified relatives. Charts, examples, and a form will help you determine the historical meaning of your photographs. Learn how to find and acquire more photos from your family, how to cite them in your history, and how to care for them, copy them, and display them.

5   Relative Talk: Oral History and Oral Tradition, *123*

Historians interview people for the stories, descriptions, and feelings of what life was like "back then." Using simple guidelines, learn the methods of oral historians and practical ways to apply them to your own research.

A complete checklist of interview equipment and suggested questions for establishing social history context will ensure you are prepared. Charts, examples, and a sample form give you realistic advice on how to maintain professional standards.

6   Recapturing a Dying Art: Correspondence, *144*

Out there somewhere may be folks—relatives or archivists—who still retain your family history through memories, documents, artifacts, photographs, and local history sources. A primer on the art of historical letter writing will help you lay a solid document base for your progeny. If you don't know of any relatives in the old family home, you can find a gold mine of information by writing to a local or state institution, or to the small town itself. And you might find a Historian Everyman who knows all and is eager to help.

7   "Here Come the Genies":
     Braving the College Library, *166*

Get ready to do some serious historical research to flesh out your family history by describing the context in which your ancestors really lived. These guidelines will ease you into using university libraries the way historians do. You should know that some genealogists have created an unpleasant stereotype this chapter will tell you how to avoid. Guidelines will help you choose the best libraries, ask the best questions, and find the best sources for your family history. You'll also find practical adaptations of historical methods for researching, note taking, organizing, and evaluating your sources.

8   My Conclusion Is Your Beginning:
     Writing Family History, *197*

It's time to start writing your family history in historical context. Here are guidelines and tips adapted for all of us based on historians' methods. Try the idea of a conceptual framework, such as describing the lives of your family within the larger community of their hometown or neighborhood. Following easy guidelines and examples, learn to make the transitions in your writing from specific family information to general historical background and back again. In the end, a historical perspective will not only offer you new sources and ways to write a more fulfilling family history, but it will also help you deal with family skeletons in the closet and with delicate, controversial matters.

Foreword

> The genealogist needs the historian to broaden his perspective and deepen his comprehension of the ultimate objectives. By the same token the genealogist is useful to the historian, lest he underrate the personal element in his narrative.
>
> —*Lester J. Cappon*

Notes

Endnotes for foreword begin on page 219.

T rust me. You are not alone. I felt exactly the same way you do. Names and dates on genealogical charts were fun—for a while. Then I remember thinking, "Is this all there is to genealogy? But I want to know more about my ancestors than the dates things happened. What were their lives like? How did they dress? What did they eat? How did they behave?" I was craving something more than sterile facts. Surely others before me must have wondered the same things about their ancestors. How did they find the answers? History textbooks didn't offer any clues, so I began scouring genealogical guides.

The few genealogical guidebooks of the early 1980s offered very little, if anything, about putting ancestors into historical perspective and learning about their daily lives. The only available genealogical writing manual, Donald R. Barnes and Richard S. Lackey's 1983 book, *Write It Right: A Manual for Writing Family Histories and Genealogies*, devoted a page and a quarter of its 124 pages to "Historical Events and Perspective," stating that "knowing major historical events is a must for a good genealogical writer. . . . Your ancestors will cease to be names and dates. They will be lifted off the pages of forgotten history. . . ."[1] Great! This was exactly what I was looking for. But how would I do that?

I next turned to past issues of genealogical journals. In 1957, Lester J. Cappon published an article titled "Genealogy, Handmaid of History" in the *National Genealogical Society Quarterly* based on his presentation to the society in 1955. Although the article is largely about the history of genealogy in America and the shift from documenting prestigious pedigrees to those of common folk, Cappon seemed to be headed in the direction I was seeking: "Thus the study of genealogy is something larger than the particular genealogy itself: it is the history of a family in both its immediate relationships and its wider impact on society." He called this method "historical genealogy" and continued to say that "when the genealogist interprets his lineage of begats and begottens with perspective and presents it in forceful literary style, he begins to delve into the meaning of the past and to earn the richer rewards of historical genealogy."[2]

While it is apparent that some savvy genealogists of the 1950s realized the value of combining history and genealogy, it was not until the "new social history" appeared on the horizon in the 1970s that genealogists really started taking notice. Prior to the debut of social history—the history of ordinary folks in ordinary society—it was difficult for many genealogists like me to see a relationship between traditional history—politics and military campaigns—to their own families. As I was searching for the key to unlock information about my ancestors' daily lives, I found a surprising disharmony between genealogists and historians.

In 1975, historian and amateur genealogist Samuel P. Hays published a three-part article, "History and Genealogy: Patterns and Change and Prospects for Cooperation," in *Prologue*, the magazine of the National Archives. Professor Hays's article was not an attempt to show genealogists how useful social history could be in their family history research, but to enlighten historians about genealogists' noble efforts beneficial to social historians—that is, indexing projects and public records preservation.[3]

Not only were some historians attempting to persuade other historians that genealogists really were nice people, but the same thing was happening in the genealogical field as well. In 1983 Elizabeth Shown Mills published "Academia vs. Genealogy: Prospects for Reconciliation and Progress" in *National Genealogical Society Quarterly*. Mills stressed the importance of high standards in genealogy, which would help bridge the gap between historians and genealogists.[4]

Even as recently as 1997, the fields of genealogy and history had not quite developed the symbiotic relationship that many had hoped for, although we are certainly much closer today than half a century ago. David Hackett Fischer, historian and author of *Albion's Seed*, discussed in these pages, published his presentation to the New England Historic Genealogical Society, "Genealogy and History: The Leah and Rachel of Learned Disciplines," in *The American Genealogist*. Fischer showed how the origins of history and genealogy, "the two sister disciplines," moved along parallel lines in their development, trends and standards—but showed that history took an academic turn, causing estrangement between the disciplines. Fischer remarked, however, that "genealogy and history have been coming closer together in recent years."[5]

All of these articles, and a few others published in between, had excellent messages and acquainted me with this new field called "social history." Yet I still hadn't found the answers I was looking for: How do I apply this to my family? How will this tell me what my ancestors did and felt, and how they behaved? Something was missing from all the hype that "history and genealogy can no longer be separated," as Mills proclaimed. I couldn't have agreed more with the premise. The newer genealogical guides were even beginning to extol the idea of doing "family history" and "putting your ancestors into historical perspective." The Board for Certification of Genealogists made historical perspective part of its requirement for one of the certification categories. Everyone seemed to be saying to do it, but no one was saying *how* to do it.

In the pathbreaking book you now hold, Katherine Scott Sturdevant, a social historian and instructor, at last bridges the gap between the genealogist and the historian, making history and genealogy a whole as other scholars have been urging us to do. She shows you why social history is important to your research as a family historian, how to find social histories, how to determine what life was probably like for *your* ancestors, and how to combine social history research with your own family history—also known as putting your ancestors into historical perspective.

I met Kathy in 1989 when I was a "female reentry student" at Pikes Peak Community College in Colorado Springs, Colorado. Having just embarked on a career as a professional genealogist, I decided to get an academic degree in history. Unfortunately, the first U.S. History survey course I took at the college level was no different from the history classes I remembered in high school—boring—which is why in high school I flunked one semester of the subject and had to repeat it. But this time I was determined. I tried a different instructor. It was Kathy Sturdevant's history class, and through her instruction and mentorship, the proverbial light bulb went on for me.

As you will read in these pages, Kathy and I became fast friends despite the snobbery between most historians and genealogists in the real world. I introduced her to scholarly genealogy, and she introduced me to scholarly social history. Together we began teaching courses in combining social history with family history, and there I found many students who had the same desire I did when I was a "baby genealogist": to know our ancestors more intimately.

There is a reason students don't take just one course, but *every* course taught by Kathy Sturdevant. She teaches in a friendly, witty, down-to-earth, and unintimidating manner, qualities she successfully brings to this book. In *Bringing Your Family History to Life Through Social History*, you will learn how to research and discover what your ancestors' lives were like. Kathy shows you how historians explore, analyze and use oral history, home sources, photographs and artifacts so you can apply the same techniques to your own family history. She opens up the world of social history, offering guidance and suggestions for accessing this largely untapped resource for genealogists. She shows you how to converse and correspond with those in academic and historical institutions to get information you might otherwise miss. Kathy acknowledges the haughtiness that has separated genealogists from historians and librarians for far too long. She explains how this unfortunate atmosphere developed and how we can help tear down these walls because, after all, historians and genealogists are seeking the same records, though our goals might be different.

Kathy also shows you how to bring all of your research together to write an engaging, dramatic account of your family history in historical perspective, encouraging you to strive for the high quality that your family history so richly deserves, an account that would be accepted by genealogists and historians alike. Even if writing your family history is not your ultimate goal, with the methods and sources taught in this book, your ancestors will become for you the thinking, feeling human beings they once were.

You are not alone in quickly becoming dissatisfied with names and dates on charts and wanting to satisfy your curiosity about your ancestors' lives. Whether you are new to the world of genealogy or someone who has been researching for decades, this book will give you new resources to check and new avenues to take, enriching your family history search. You will gain new perspectives on several sources, which you may have thought you had already exhausted for family history information. Whether it's a photograph, an interview with a relative or that old recipe box you inherited, you will soon discover that you are surrounded with social history.

—Sharon DeBartolo Carmack, CG

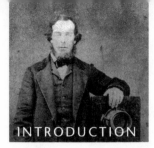
Discovering Scholarly Family History and Having Great Fun With It

Y our assignment is to write your own family history in historical context," said Moses Rischin, a well-published immigration historian and one of my history professors at San Francisco State University. It was 1975 and I was an undergraduate history major taking History 300, a junior seminar in historiography. Unless you are a historian, that class may sound about as boring and irrelevant to life as a class might be. I must confess that the only in-class revelation I recall from that particular class—due to my own attentions, not the professor's—was that I did not care to become a Marxist or determinist historian. The remarkable assignment, however, started me on that fulfilling, lifelong pursuit of being a family historian.

My parents' family histories had always fascinated me without my ever seeing them as relevant to schoolwork. My grandparents, two of whom I had met and two I had not, were my heroes and role models. My mother steeped me in oral tradition from her family and my father told World War II stories so much that I forgot I was born a decade after the war ended. So I knew I was equipped to write a family history paper. I researched the families and their surrounding history for months, unknowingly retracing the steps so many genealogists and historians had taken. I interviewed relatives and gathered home sources. I wrote letters across the country, to Canada, to Scotland, and to Wales. I researched genealogical sources at San Francisco's Sutro Library. My college library had already become my home away from home. Now I was locating books on such diverse topics as the Outer Hebrides and Quantrill's Raiders during the American Civil War.

THE *ROOTS* OF AN IDEA

Professor Rischin had explained that the recent success of Alex Haley's *Roots* had inspired him to make this assignment. I did not read or watch *Roots* myself at the time. I simply approached the assignment as I did all of my history work.

Being more a student than anything else, I was unaware that I had stepped into a fad that was rapidly becoming a movement. I traveled to the San Bruno, California, branch of the National Archives and studied my first census microfilm. I recall noticing that the other folks waiting in line ahead of me for microfilm readers all had gray hair and that most seemed to be married couples. I remember telling one of the archival employees that I was surprised to see so many people doing research. He said, "It's been this way ever since *Roots*."

I compiled a lengthy narrative paper to turn in at the end of that 1975 semester. I already believed that one could tell a story with meticulous historical accuracy, scholarly documentation, and yet with drama, humor, suspense, and inspiration. People's lives were like that. I always enjoyed movies most if they were based on true stories. My second field of study was American and English literature. My standards were high: discovering historical inaccuracies in films or novels often caused me to reject the whole works mercilessly. So I wrote this family history paper with feeling, calling attention to natural drama or human interest wherever I found it, but was just as careful as ever with research results and documentation. Professor Rischin commented that the paper was A+ and publishable, with a remarkable sensitivity for how ancestors must have felt during their struggles. I can even remember his marginal notes. He was struck to learn that my Hebridean ancestors probably drank sheep blood and that my great-grandfather had been a Quantrill Confederate until Bloody Bill Anderson scared him away.

LITTLE HISTORIAN ON THE PRAIRIE

I continued on through my three history degree programs and the equivalent of master's degree work in literature, writing many scholarly theses, none of which had to do with my family. My history professors were traditional political historians in their training, so I was as well. The 1970s, however, was also a time when professors were excited about "the new social history." I was too. Professors such as Jerald Combs and Joseph Illick validated for me that historians could study and write about the everyday lives of ordinary folks. Monographs proliferated on subjects such as community life—especially in the Puritan New England towns—or private life—especially women's. Robert Kelley's *The Cultural Pattern in American Politics* introduced me to the idea that even political history might be socially driven. The 1976 bicentennial celebration in the United States—every moment of which, during my undergraduate years, I must have viewed on television—brought home that there is historical drama and inspiration available around us, all of the time, everywhere. History was alive for me and enriched every aspect of my life.

I learned in graduate school that I would face skeptics in pursuit of my dream to be both scholarly and literary about history. My favorite history professor disappointed me once. In his graduate seminar on early American history he asked each of us to introduce ourselves by discussing our goals. I said I hoped someday to write history with the accuracy of a historian and the readability of fine literature. I said that I was working with my grandmother's memoirs about growing up on a Kansas homestead in the 1880s and 1890s. His response: "You mean you want to write *Little House on the Prairie*?" (That television show was popular then too.) I knew he meant this as a put-down, but I should have taken it as a compliment. Who has reached more audiences with more authentic and inspirational history: the average scholarly historian or Laura Ingalls Wilder?

MAKING FAMILY HISTORY COME ALIVE

Training and a career in history have taken me in many directions. Little did I know that someday I would teach American history—many sections of it, year after year, to hundreds of students. Indeed, until I started work on my doctorate, I thought I would be exclusively a professional writer because I was too shy to speak before audiences. Now I even teach on television! Whenever I assign a paper, I suggest that students choose to research and write about their own family histories. I once made this suggestion to a class that included Sharon Carmack, a professional genealogist. The rest is history—family history in historical context. As soon as I taught my approach to Sharon, we started to plan how to teach it together with genealogy, as I explain in chapter one.

"She makes history come alive!" is the most common remark students and audiences have made in praise of my teaching and speaking. Some of my friends and I have even laughed at how predictably people say this. Yet it is no joke. People mistakenly assume history is boring, trivial, or irrelevant to them. If I help convince them otherwise, I am a success. Of course, you already know how fascinating history can be, or you would not have picked up this book. You certainly would not have read this introduction! So let's see whether we can unlock some of those doors to bringing your family history to life through social history context.

ONE

Social History: Your Ancestors' World

But why, one might ask, recount the lives of anonymous Americans . . . when there were giants . . . in those days? . . . Surely the best answers . . . rest not in what the nation's leaders, the century's giants, said the promise of American life was but in what the common folk found it to be.

—Gerald McFarland in *A Scattered People: An American Family Moves West*[1]

Notes

Endnotes for this chapter begin on page 219.

It seemed obvious to me. "Write your family history in historical context," I would say to my students through my years of college history teaching, be they neophytes or genealogists. Somehow I had known what that meant when a professor said it to me in 1975. I discovered soon enough that people do not know how to do this automatically. Then I discovered that even experienced genealogists who wanted to graduate from charting names and dates to writing narrative either did not know how to do it, wrote genealogical narrative (more technical than historical), or would attempt historical narrative in less than desirable ways. So I began teaching individual students how to write family history in historical context and, ultimately, these lessons became several separate courses in several colleges and programs.

One of my students was professional genealogist Sharon Carmack, who took my U.S. history survey class when not yet aware of what social history context could do for family history. She caught on fast and has run with it ever since. She wanted to teach genealogy classes at our college, but the division director (another historian) would not hire someone based solely on genealogical credentials, no matter how good those credentials were. I had history degrees and had always wanted to teach a class in how to do family history. Yet I was no expert in genealogical methods or sources. Joining forces seemed natural. We developed a team-taught course, then called "Your Family in U.S. History," and began teaching it with great success in 1990. We were both surprised at how many people wanted the class, how few understood the approach automatically, and how well most people could do family history in historical context once they became experienced. On the genealogical lecture circuit and in publications, Sharon has attracted enthusiastic audiences with topics stemming from this approach, and I have followed suit. This book is my response to many requests that I write the advice I have been giving on how to do family history in a social history context.

Clearly many genealogists want to make this connection. At genealogical conferences, in genealogical publications, through book-publishing and book-purchasing trends, in local genealogical communities, and in my classes I have heard a clamor for "social history" and "historical context." The lectures we offer on this topic are in demand and well received. Surveys by Betterway Books of what genealogists would buy brought this topic to the top of the list. Often, inspired genealogical faces gaze up and say of social history context: "This is exactly what I've been looking for!" Yet my classes with Sharon Carmack have been almost unique. It is unusual to bring together a historian and a genealogist who have the perfect blend of expertise and interests to spread this method to other family historians.

The purpose of this book is to introduce genealogists (family historians) to the ideas, methods, and sources for building appropriate historical context around their genealogical information. The book will convey the knowledge, skills, approaches, and resources of historians—especially social historians—in lay terms. In this manner I hope to make it more accessible and understandable for as many family historians as possible. To keep us all on the straight and narrow, this book will also address standards for proper use and documentation of sources, for care of artifacts, and even for speaking the right language when acting on the historian's stage. Often it will not just be historians' sources but the viewpoints and perspectives of historians themselves that help a genealogist. So I will occasionally exhort: think like a historian!

A note to history teachers: a second possible audience for this book is students, undergraduate or graduate, in college history programs. History professors tend to make the same mistaken assumption I did. "Write a ten-page analytical research paper," we will pronounce, "using scholarly secondary and primary sources." We often do not think about whether the students know where or how to begin. Sometimes it is even the senior or master's thesis—or worse yet, the doctoral dissertation—that the student faces with less than adequate training. I have had seniors and graduate students from the nearby four-year colleges contact me at my community college office to seek my help with how to do their theses. Each student confesses a fear of asking the assigned professor one of those proverbial stupid questions, such as "Where would I find a source like that, and how would I look it up?" If you are that student, or the history instructor looking for a beginner's guidebook, please consider this one!

Indeed, I have assisted in several cases when a student used part of his or her own family history as a thesis. Initially, the proposal to do so may alarm the professor. A historian might suppose that such a thesis would be too individualized, too motivated by vanity, too difficult to research, or not revealing enough of what the student has learned about historical thought. Done by the method I am recommending, however, family history in historical context makes an excellent thesis topic. One important goal in writing a senior thesis, let alone a master's thesis or doctoral dissertation, is to demonstrate the ability to locate, extract, and analyze primary sources. These are the stuff of genealogy: censuses, county courthouse records, etc. Then, to develop social history context, the writer must

Important

Idea Generator

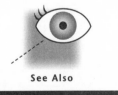

See Also

The purpose of this book is NOT to serve as a beginner's guidebook to the basic methods of *genealogical research*. There are many excellent books by skilled professional genealogists and teachers to do that for you. See the general bibliography at the end of this book.

familiarize herself with the secondary literature—published history books—another important goal of any thesis project. The proper family history in historical context will serve as a case study in which one family's history illustrates larger trends. It should draw some analytical conclusions and cite its sources thoroughly. This kind of family history writing may open the door to hundreds of possible thesis topics for students. Writing a paper relevant to one's own family can be a way for the student to feel much more invested in and excited about that project.

On the next page is an example of how history student Mary Weber used her grandmother, Ellen Ayer, as a case study of rural Colorado women for a senior thesis. Note how Mary integrated her specific family information from an interview with general women's history information from a published historical monograph. The following style can serve your needs whether you are attempting to illustrate a larger historical point (as in a thesis like this) or write narrative family history for the sake of the family. In this case, the author could write a family history for relatives and complete her degree with the same project!

WHAT IS SOCIAL HISTORY?

Definitions

Social history is the study of ordinary people's everyday lives. It is history from the bottom up instead of the top down, not focusing exclusively or primarily on the elite and famous. Social historians tend to identify something's importance by how many people it affected more than by how singular it was. We even organize history differently: by trends rather than by just the actions of "great men." Having a social history perspective means that one sees historical events as they affected groups collectively, not just as they affected exceptional people individually. We study the common people and the frameworks within which they lived. Social history is much more inclusive of ethnic minorities, women, and age groups than is traditional political history. But social history is not "history with the politics left out," as some have accused. Instead, social historians will tend to look at the people side of politics: grass roots campaigns, local politics, the formation of parties, and reform movements. Again, this is a help to the family historian. Your ancestors were more liable to participate in politics at these levels than as presidents of the United States.

Social historians borrow from social sciences such as psychology, sociology, anthropology, and geography to gain additional tools with which to analyze group and individual behavior. We also help ourselves to the methods of folklore studies to be able to hear the voices of ordinary people. The common folk were not as articulate or literate as the elite and so did not leave us as many obvious sources. Indeed, to conduct research on mass societies, social historians develop statistics from the same types of records that genealogists use when they research individual families—censuses, town and church records, wills and deeds—but the historians usually are thinking about society collectively and watching for group patterns.

Social history has an interesting history of its own. Its roots are in the work of historians in Europe. In America, the field developed among scholars in the

Women's lives centered on home and family, and their common experiences were demonstrated through the remarkable similarity in their journals, letters, memoirs, and reminiscences.[34] In Ellen Moberly Ayer, one can find the uniqueness and the commonality that bound these women. Ellen began her life August 10, 1912, in a soddie, or a sod house, near Saint Francis, Kansas. She was the second child of German immigrant parents from Nebraska. . . .[35] Ellen's mother died after delivering her fourth child in February 1917, when Ellen was four years old. When the afterbirth would not come properly "Papa Earl," Ellen's father went to get help, but it was too late. Quite often many women did not know the importance of regular doctor visits when they were pregnant. In keeping with their independent and self-sufficient nature, it was common for women to give birth at home with only husbands or neighbor women attending. The frequency of births quite often led to a matter-of-fact attitude regarding birth.[36] In this case, however, Ellen's father blamed the death of his beloved wife on his mother since it was she who did not believe that a doctor was necessary at birthing. Knowing he could not properly care for an infant son, he gave the newborn to his parents to raise, and they adopted the boy as their own.[37]

Ellen's father, now a young widower, had three other children ages two, four, and six who needed attention and motherly care. His solution was to marry again soon. He met his second wife that same year in Saint Francis. They were married in September 1917.[38] Such hasty remarriages were for practical reasons. The willingness of women to accept such arrangements illustrates once more their ideals of social and familial responsibility. . . . By the age of nine, Ellen had begun to assume adult responsibilities. She soon learned to make bread and noodles. She and her sister helped cook for harvesting crews during the autumn season.[39] Likewise, young girls in rural Western Colorado families were taught at an early age how to cook and care for families, since the assumption was that they would have families of their own soon after their teen years. Brides . . . could observe family units and their society around them to realize that home, marriage, and children were the focal point of women's lives.[40]

[34] Glenda Riley, *The Female Frontier* (Lawrence: University Press of Kansas, 1988), 4.

[35] Ellen M. Ayer, Interview by Mary A. Weber, 7 April 1987, Colorado Springs, Colorado.

[36] Riley, 51.

[37] Ayer Interview.

[38] Ibid.

[39] Ibid.

[40] Riley, 42.

Quoted with permission from Mary A. Weber, "Women of the Western Slope of Colorado, 1930–1960," unpublished senior thesis for the bachelor's degree in history, 27 July 1994, University of Colorado at Colorado Springs, copy in author's possession, page 8.

late 1960s. Starting in the 1970s, it spread in college courses more through special topics, such as women's history or ethnic history, than in surveys of American history. "The strength of social history," wrote Peter Stearns, the pathbreaking European and world historian from Carnegie Mellon University, "remains in research." If the field continues to have novelty, Stearns determined, it is in its "continually exploring new facets of the social past—generating topics . . . and responding to new demands."[2] Genealogists embarking on social history research about their families can take heart that the discovery of new topics will continue and increase. It is a happy fact that historians and graduate students *must* research and write about new topics and new case studies for their work to earn them academic degrees or publication. Thus there will be new materials for you to utilize as long as there are historians and history students!

Social history is so hot that it has met with political controversy in recent years. Many of us teaching history at all levels try to integrate social history with all of the traditional history we still must teach. We try to do so without just relegating social history to "snippets," as Peter Stearns called them.[3] In the 1990s, hundreds of historians and teachers participated in the development of the National History Standards for presentation to Congress, and then in the development of state and local standards. I worked on the Colorado history standards and in a State Board of Education project to teach elementary and secondary teachers how to implement those standards. Naturally, we all included social history in these efforts. Historians were trying to remedy the general ignorance that American students have about their own history. At the top of the effort was historian Gary B. Nash of the University of California, Los Angeles, author of several books on topics such as freed slaves and Quaker politics in Pennsylvania history.

Unfortunately, these well-intended history advocates met with dramatic resistance from high-profile politicos like Newt Gingrich and Rush Limbaugh! The opponents said that they feared the teaching of social history would ignore the founding fathers for the sake of political correctness; that we were sacrificing great men and events for minorities and women. Fortunately for all of us, social history is by nature inclusive—everyone counts. We do not ignore Abraham Lincoln, but we interpret him as a man of his times and we add in how the masses mourned him. We cannot describe the social history of Scotch-Irish immigrants without using Andrew Jackson as a favorite example. As a genealogist or family historian, your research will benefit greatly from the continuing enthusiasm of social historians who will write about your ancestors regardless of political slings and arrows.[4] Be aware, however, that for much of America, social history is still on the cutting edge. When you use social history for family history writing, you will be on a cutting edge, too.

Social history is the best tool for reconstructing your ancestors' entire world. Some historians realized the value of writing family history in historical context in the mid to late 1970s. Two pairs of them wrote workbooks for college students to use with family history as a class project. In 1974, Jim Watts and Allen F. Davis wrote *Generations: Your Family in Modern American History* based on their experiences teaching at City College of New York and Temple University, respectively. Both saw a family history project as good training for history students. This book consists primarily of firsthand accounts by individuals, many of them famous, of their family lives. It was not a detailed how-to guide, nor could one expect it to be, then. It did suggest, through many examples, how collecting oral and written memoirs of life in various times and circumstances was a way to do one's family history.

David Kyvig and Myron Marty wrote *Your Family History: A Handbook for Research and Writing* in 1978, a brief introduction for students that has also been useful for family historians writing in historical context. In particular, it introduces beginners to writing family history by historical themes, and because it is so brief a book, has been useful in classes where the family history paper is a smaller feature of a larger class, such as in a U.S. history survey. Kyvig and Marty also wrote *Nearby History*, an admirable effort to awaken students to some of the kinds of research I will recommend, such as oral history and material culture studies. These four historians could see family history papers as a useful way for their students to learn historical skills. Kyvig and Marty were also active in the field called public history, another late-1970s variation of traditional history.

Public history is the practice of history—its subjects and skills—in environments beyond academic (teaching) institutions, such as government agencies and private or public institutions. For example, we advocates say someone is practicing public history by serving as a researcher, writer, archivist, curator, multimedia producer, or in any way an interpreter of history for people other than just students in school. Public historians work in military, government, and corporate offices, museums, libraries, archives, and historic sites. Public historians (of which I am one) are particularly equipped to face genealogy with interest and open minds.[5] In 1983, the first comprehensive bibliography of public history sources, *The Craft of Public History: An Annotated Select Bibliography*, became available. Its editors, David F. Trask and Robert W. Pomeroy III, dedicated a separate chapter to "Genealogy and Family History." The editor of that chapter, Glen M. Leonard, noted that genealogy and family history had become popular and were tied to professional historians' increasing interest in demography, also known as population studies. Thus experts were coming close to the combining of social history and genealogy. In *The Craft of Public History*'s annotations, it became clear that professional genealogists were trying to overcome historians' snobbery toward their work and cooperate with historians toward productive use of the same sources.

In 1986, an anthology called *Generations and Change: Genealogical Perspectives in Social History* was the "first effort to produce . . . a conversation" among genealogists, historians, and others about the common ground between genealogy and social history. The book's articles, all of a scholarly quality, displayed the relationship for the reader to note by comparison, but it still did not offer guidelines for the ordinary genealogist to make use of both fields together. A key paragraph by editors Robert M. Taylor Jr. and Ralph S. Crandall "spoke to my condition," however, as the Quakers say.

> Also important, finally, is that genealogists be encouraged to write family-history narratives, to take that pedigree chart and expand it into a full-scale group biography. . . . It would be of inestimable value to the professional historian. When composing these narratives genealogists should be encouraged

\di'fin\ *vb*

Definitions

to mine the relevant historical literature, to become acquainted with recent data relative to community, family, and kin, and to eschew the extremes of sterile numbers and pointless anecdotes.[6]

A few well-known genealogical speakers and writers noticed the potential for researching and writing family history in historical context. When Val D. Greenwood revised *The Researcher's Guide to American Genealogy* in 1990, he added a chapter called "Family History: Going Beyond Genealogy." As previously indicated, Sharon Carmack (and later, I) started to include social history context as a topic in national genealogical lectures in the early 1990s. In 1996, Patricia Law Hatcher included a chapter in *Producing a Quality Family History* called "Turning Paper into People." It contained advice for the genealogist seeking historical context for a family history. In spite of these several worthy efforts, however, it has taken about thirty years of accumulated social history research and publication for a social historian to address a comprehensive guidebook to the public of genealogists and family historians.

I have always called it "putting meat on the bones": to build historical context around whatever information you have on your family. It is amazing to see how many genealogists have utilized this same phrase in recent years. A genealogy is truly skeletal in structure: charts of names, dates, and bare-bones facts. A narrative, especially with context, relays the stories, the descriptions, even the thoughts and feelings (when accessible) of the human beings whose names perch on that family tree. Social history is made up of information gleaned from the same records you use to perform your genealogical research. Your ancestors may already have been included anonymously in statistics by some social historian who then formulated generalizations based on those collective statistics. Now you can use that historian's published work to take the information back from the general to the specific. If a trend or a pattern was dominant for people like your ancestors, perhaps you will find that your ancestors participated in or at least felt the influence of that common pattern.

Reminder

Your ancestors were not unique. This sounds untrue or disappointing at first. Of course, every individual is unique. We like to think our ancestors will have been so unusual that they were famous for their rare qualities. We assume drama exists only in the unique. Our ancestors, however, were often part of group behavior. Social history documents and analyzes group behavior. Through social history research, you can discover what people like your ancestors usually, typically did every day. Social history sources about those collective experiences will provide the drama of human experience for your particular family history.

For example, if your ancestors migrated from eastern Pennsylvania to the Shenandoah Valley in the 1770s, historical sources can tell you what route they probably took, why people migrated at that time and to that place, what the trip and the new homes were usually like, and what was the likely ethnic and cultural background of those ancestors. If your mother or grandmother worked in an aircraft factory during World War II, historical sources can describe for you every aspect of that experience as it was for most of the women who shared it. Social

---

SOCIAL HISTORY SUBFIELDS AND SISTER SUBJECTS TO ASSIST FAMILY HISTORY

History of the family	Community history
Local history	Urban history
Rural and agricultural history	History of childhood
Women's history	Labor history
Immigrant history	History of education
Ethnic history	History of health and medical care
Military history	American studies
History of American character	History of science and technology
Oral history	Collective biography
Folklore studies	Material culture studies
Film history	Popular cultural history
Public policy history	Protest and reform history
Economic history	Sports history
History of aging	History of leisure
Historical sociology	Cultural or historical geography
Cultural or historical archaeology	Archival and museum studies

---

history research teaches us to be grateful that our ancestors were parts of trends, fads, and mass movements.

Social history has spawned or influenced numerous subfields and related "sister subjects" that can assist the genealogist. There are many specialties among historians that might relate to a particular family's history. The chart above indicates what some of these are. Perhaps the closest of the many sister subjects would be sociology, or historical sociology. Sociologists who study historical change in societies do almost the same work (for different reasons) as social historians. Their books and articles will tend to emphasize the statistics more than the narrative. Nevertheless, there can be valuable supporting evidence and analysis for you in sociological studies.

For example, say you are developing historical context in order to write about your family of farmers on the Great Plains. You know, from finding her keepsake pins and programs, that your great-grandmother in Nebraska, a farmer's wife, belonged to a chapter of the Women's Christian Temperance Union (WCTU), an antialcohol organization. You might refer to a social and women's history book such as Deborah Fink's *Agrarian Women: Wives and Mothers in Rural Nebraska, 1880–1940*. This book suggests that the reason many women of the region joined temperance societies was to seek a solution to the drinking problems of abusive husbands. Could this be true in your ancestor's case? If you are not sure, you might turn to a book of historical sociology, such as Scott G. McNall and Sally Allen McNall's *Plains Families: Exploring Sociology Through Social History*. From this study you would learn that typical rural plainswomen might join the WCTU, along with numerous other voluntary associations, to fill a need for socializing, public service, and a moral ideology. As you continue your research, you may determine which explanations are most appropriate to your ancestor—or you may have to speculate on all of the possibilities in your writing. Even without surety about which elements fit her most precisely, you can write narrative speculation on her motivations based on what was most common for women like her.

When genealogical sources alone do not answer a question, ask yourself whether there may be a published study of that subject area. If it is one of the

Notes

Sources

Research Tip

areas listed in the chart on page 11, there are hundreds of such resources. For example, you may not understand the cause of death as named on an old death certificate. A history of health and medicine, however, may give you a good idea of what that disease was, its causes, and its treatments. You may find that your Yankee New England ancestor farmed in the 1730s, but you wonder what he grew. The agricultural, social history *A Long, Deep Furrow: Three Centuries of Farming in New England* by Howard S. Russell would tell you that most such farmers cultivated English hay to feed stock but harvested double or triple its weight in meadow or salt hay.

When you are determining whether there are subjects around which to build your family history narrative, check the list on page 11. For example, you may not have vast detail on your immigrant ancestors, but whatever information you do possess can lead to generic information about what their lives were like. Books on immigrant history will discuss what the typical patterns were: why most people moved, what it was like for them to make the trip, how others treated them, and how they raised their children. Examine the passage on page 13, which speaks to a common set of motives for leaving the "old country." Notice that only two or three pieces of information are based specifically on genealogical research about that ancestor. The rest is a legitimate social history description of the typical experience for folks of the same background.

WHAT IS "HISTORY OF THE FAMILY"?

Definitions

Typically, when social historians refer to family history, they mean the history of the family—not yours or mine, but all families collectively. If the genealogist, then, discovers that a book or college course is about the generic history of the family as an institution, the genealogist might be put off. Wait! The history of the family is about what family life and relationships have been like throughout history. General books on the history of the family in America are excellent starting places for American genealogists seeking social history context.

One of the earliest published American works of this type was Arthur Calhoun's 1917 title, *A Social History of the American Family, From Colonial Times to the Present*. This is obviously not a modern family history monograph. It is still useful, however, for building context. When using an older analysis such as this, take care to realize that, first, the author based his generalizations on limited knowledge, scope, and research compared to more recent studies and second, the author may take a different, more judgmental, position than modern social scientists would take. Still, these volumes consider family history topics such as marriage, gender, childraising, courtship, division of labor, and ethnic and religious differences. Calhoun quoted and cited specific examples from historical records. He was doing social history and using the genealogical materials of his day. Although I would normally recommend the most recent published research, sometimes older works are the ones most available in limited libraries. Sometimes such works cover the particular items you are seeking when more recent books have not.

The history of the family took off as a popular field in historical publishing in the 1970s, as did most social history in America. Consequently, there are now many

Isaac [Zelig Meister, known as "Zaydie," Yiddish for "grandfather"] had been drafted into the Russian army, as had many of his Jewish friends. The policy . . . was to conscript all young men for a period of 25 years. Many towns and cities with a small population would lose most of the young boys to the army. In most cases, this placed a tremendous hardship on the small farmers. . . . Many of the "Jewish" towns, those that were predominately populated by Jews, were given draft quotas to meet, and many young boys, as early as age 8 or 9, were kidnapped, sent off to camps, and kept there until they reached the age of conscription. Many were never heard from or seen again. Parents would mutilate the boys by cutting off an ear [or] breaking legs [to] make them unfit for military service. One boy in a family was allowed to stay home, so families with more than one son would "give" the sons to families or relatives without any boys. The names of the boys would be changed to that of the new families, and this resulted in many brothers having different last names. Zaydie came from an area that used a lottery to determine the length of service. Although the forced conscription was for 25 years, if the town could supply enough men, some were given an opportunity to return home after a period of 5 years. After 5 years of service, names were drawn to determine who would be released. If the name was drawn, the young man could go home. Otherwise, he would stay for an additional 5 years. This would continue until his name was drawn or he completed his service. Zaydie was fortunate; his name was drawn at the end of his first five-year tour of service.

Quoted with permission from Robert P. Fineberg, "Isaac Fineberg, American," an unpublished narrative of a Lithuanian Jewish family, page 2, copies in author's possession.

books on the subject that inform the family historian of what family life was like at almost any period or place in American history. Of course, not all generalizations apply in any one instance, but many do. I have listed some of the major works for our purposes at the end of this book (see the general bibliography).

Use your own family life as a test case to train yourself. I always recommend that family historians who intend to build historical context begin with general books on the history of the family. One interesting experiment that will help you understand how to use social history is to read about what family life was like during your own childhood. This will give you a sense of

- what is worth writing about even though it seems mundane as you live it;
- the elements of family life to investigate and discuss;
- how generalizations about American families do not fit everyone's family;
- how some generalizations fit your family very well;
- how understanding the historical reasons families behaved the way they did can explain your family's behavior;
- how popular family culture explains the artifacts you have retained.

Steven Mintz and Susan Kellogg's *Domestic Revolutions: A Social History of American Family Life* will serve as a good example of how a genealogist may

Tip

Whenever you investigate or recall some aspect of your recent family history, such as your own childhood, write it down or record it on tape. No one can contribute your part of the family's history better than you can. This should take priority even over your genealogical research. When you are gone, most genealogical records will still exist for future searchers to find—but your personal memories will be lost unless you record them.

use a book on the history of the family. In the case study on page 15, I am writing about my own life and family, inspired by part of one chapter in *Domestic Revolutions*. I used the chapter to remind me of what was common for American families at that time. I had to stop myself or I might have written a complete autobiography; the descriptions were that close to my recollections. It took me fifteen minutes to write this case study. You too can do this for yourself and your ancestors, although I will grant that the further back you go the harder it gets.

Social histories of the family, such as *Domestic Revolutions*, will present for every American generation the same kind of general picture of family life that they offer for my generation. They will combine demographic information—such as birthrates, marriage ages, and life expectancies—with sociological and psychological interpretations of behavior, all based on the historical record. Social historians have used virtually every tool possible to uncover family life from the colonial period to the present, and you can reap the rewards of their efforts.

WHY SHOULD A GENEALOGIST CARE?

The same rewards many of us receive from studying history will be your rewards for using it in family history. Historian Lester D. Stephens, whose expertise was in the teaching of history, noted in his book, *Probing the Past*, that the reasons for studying history are "lessons, analogies, and prediction," "knowledge, experience, and appreciation," and "identification."[7] As you use history sources to determine the context in which your ancestors lived, you will experience some of these same rewards. The more we learn of our ancestors' realities, the more we should tolerate the diversity of people in our own times. Most of all, family history in historical context enables us to identify with our ancestors, to appreciate what they went through and its relevance to us.

Writing your family history as a narrative—a story—can be much more meaningful for you and your audiences than just charting the bare bones. Think about it realistically. If you compile genealogy for your family's sake, who reads it and which parts do they read? Most relatives would first look for themselves by name. How many do you think would read every line, word, or number of a genealogical chart, unless they were compilers themselves? If it were a family history *narrative* rather than just charts, it could contain stories, recollections, descriptions, drama, characters, and humor. It could entertain and inform. It could hold interest for even nonrelatives. It could be a historically important record with long-term value to further historical research.

Historical research can answer many questions for you even if you never intend to write a narrative. Perhaps you will understand why family members moved from one place to another, why they had so many children or so few, where on earth they got that name for that poor child, or what they did with the articles on that household inventory. Many historians who do their own family history research piece it together from historical sources, making some leaps without precise genealogical detail. Meanwhile, genealogists can become so attached to

Reminder

I was a late baby boomer, born in 1955. My father was a World War II veteran. My mother had proudly attended junior college and worked as a secretary for years, but, for us, she "had decided to forsake higher education or a career and achieve emotional fulfillment as [a wife and mother]." In 1955 her political hero, Adlai Stevenson, said that it was women's highest role to "influence" men and to "restore valid, meaningful purpose in your home." Although we did not live in the typical suburbs per se, we lived in a 1940s development of San Francisco, the Outer Sunset District. Our house was a row house, attached to the neighbors' houses, with its duplicates strung for miles up and down the city streets. Of course my father had used his GI loan but still was "preoccupied with his role as breadwinner."

I have in my possession the well-worn 1946 copy of Dr. Benjamin Spock's *Baby and Child Care* by which my parents raised me. It emphasized "a mother's love." I was their only child, unlike most baby boomers, so my mother showered all her attentions on me and I had no siblings with which to share anything, good or bad. Polio had been so frightening to parents of the postwar era that I had to take Dr. Salk's vaccine, usually by sugar cube, every year. Most other vaccines seemed to appear just after I endured the diseases that they were intended to prevent. Because of croup and pneumonia, the pediatrician—and his needles—made frequent house calls, turning my bottom black and blue.

The TV repairman made house calls, too, and we seemed just as worried waiting for him as we were waiting for my doctor. Television was essential—the set was practically our fourth family member. It stood in the "front room," half as tall as my very tall father, wider, and there all of the time. My parents bought their first TV the year before they "got" me. I watched it from my playpen for hours. Television was full of children with whom I identified. I was Kathy in *Father Knows Best*, Beaver in *Leave It to Beaver*, or Timmy in *Lassie*. And of course, once a year after I turned eight years old, I was Dorothy in *The Wizard of Oz*. Even today I recognize in myself the same conflict between trying to be both traditional wife and career woman as I saw in the show about that wily redhead, *I Love Lucy*.

Now that I am past forty, many of my childhood heroes are dead or dying. Just before I first wrote this chapter, I was saddened to hear that cowboy singer-actor Roy Rogers and actor Robert Young (Jim Anderson of *Father Knows Best*) had died. I had had a crush on Roy Rogers, but to lose Robert Young was to lose a father figure. A week or two later, friends five or ten years older than I, including my husband, mourned the death of Buffalo Bob of *Howdy Doody* fame. I remember Howdy Doody, but he meant nothing to me. My TV teachers were Captain Kangaroo (the original by Bob Keeshan), Miss Nancy of *Romper Room* (I didn't know each city had a different Miss Somebody), and Captain Satellite (played by a local TV personality named Bob March who later became a weatherman). (See Mintz and Kellogg, *Domestic Revolutions*, 181–194).

(continued on page 16)

> Addendum: During my revisions of this chapter, my father died—just eight months after we lost my mother. The whole experience of caregiving for older parents—of dealing with Medicare, Medicaid, supplemental insurance, nursing homes, Alzheimer's units, hospitals, and, finally, the wonder of hospice—is a baby boomer experience. Literature to help describe it in context abounds. Even as we deal with our own existence and accumulate information on it, we can realize that our own lives lie within a social history context. Thinking this way can help with self-realization but it also hones your family history skills.

factual detail that they miss the big-picture answers to why and how questions. You can have the best of both worlds.

Writing a family's history in historical context may actually make it commercially publishable. This is an exciting new trend in historical publishing. Rather than (or in addition to) publishing a genealogy with a specialized press, you may be able to put together a nonfiction family saga that would sell. There are many examples appealing to general audiences these days. They usually have a popular, sweeping historical theme such as slavery, westward expansion, immigration, or the family's involvement with the Civil War. Most family historians will find that their family histories also contain one or more of these themes. See chapter eight and the bibliography for more examples and guidelines.

THE ELEMENTS OF SOCIAL HISTORY: WHAT WAS LIFE LIKE?

Consider what areas of life a historian might include in a social history study of a particular place and time. **I have dubbed those areas of life the Elements of Social History.** The chart on page 18—a social historian's periodic table of the elements, if you will—can serve as an excellent guide or checklist of what to consider, what to cover, what to research, and what to ask about as you compile your information. Use this list of elements as a checklist for any portion of your family history that you are researching and writing. Ask yourself: "Have I considered each item on this list in my effort to compile this picture of what life was like?"

There are some basic concepts and attitudes that might help you as you venture into the social history of your family. Try to apply these as you utilize the Elements of Social History.

Important

- *Remind yourself to be flexible.* You can research and describe settings as interior and exterior, farm or town. You can describe the typical log cabin of that time and place even if you cannot locate a description of your family's log cabin.
- *Be open-minded.* Remember that people of other times and places may have viewed anything about life differently than the way you do. For example, in the days of preindustrial agriculture, people defined their time by seasons, weather, chores—they had a different rhythm of life than we do these days. They may

have treated a step- or adopted child as a family member or not. They may have married one another for reasons you find mercenary or unromantic.

- *Avoid anachronisms.* **An anachronism is something out of its proper historical place, such as a microwave oven in a colonial kitchen.** Do not make unsubstantiated claims that a female ancestor had no access to birth control or abortion, but likewise do not claim she did. Research it and you may be surprised at what is new and what is not so new.

- *Never assume.* Just because Puritan ancestors lost so many children and even reused the names of the dead ones does not mean they were callous about child deaths. Just because Puritan ancestors were strictly religious does not mean that a young couple would not sleep together before marriage. Research it.

- *Do not dismiss something interesting as too minor or frivolous for historical study.* If you feel curious about it, others have felt and will feel the same. What people wore, ate, and even where and how they relieved themselves is worthy of investigation if you have a reason. Social historians have probably already written about it.

- *Expect complexity.* People rarely act with one singular motive, and there is more than one side to every story. For example, when people emigrated or migrated, they usually did so because of a combination of "push" and "pull" factors. Yankee men did not usually fight in the Civil War simply to free slaves, nor did American GIs in World War II all think they were freeing Jews.

- *Think like a sociologist as well as a historian.* Sometimes you need to be clinical as well as objective in order to handle closet skeletons. If you can determine that an ancestor's behavior was typical of a social problem common in his group or his times, that gives you a context within which to understand and explain his otherwise dubious behavior. Remember, "no pride, no shame; no credit, no blame" (see chapter eight).

DIRECT HISTORICAL DETAIL VS. INFERRED HISTORICAL CONTEXT

There are two main types of historical research and sources that you might use for family history in context. One is research into the direct, precise historical details pertinent to your family's history. You will need many detailed answers to specific questions. Where in Ohio was that town they lived in? What was the exact date of that event? What battles did that regiment see? Here you are seeking direct historical detail. The sources you use might be any and every. Some answers will come from social histories, but many will come from that old county history, state history, regimental history, or a general U.S. history.

Historical inference, the second way you may use historical sources, is a kind of speculation or hypothesizing based on thorough research into a question. Inference is more liable to be an area where social histories help because they develop "conceptual frameworks" and their authors try to leave few questions unanswered. We can infer from the evidence, so long as we have gathered that

\di'fin\ *vb*

Definitions

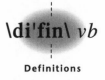

\di'fin\ *vb*

Definitions

THE ELEMENTS OF SOCIAL HISTORY

Place homeland, region, town, nearby city, countryside, neighborhood, land, property

Architecture design, usage, materials, location, landscaping, interior decor, vernacular style, outbuildings, repair, alteration, display, storage, inheritance

Time and Season ways they determined time and season, work hours, rhythm of life, climate changes, seasonal events, holiday celebrations, daily schedules

Family structure, power, division of labor, levels of cohesion, nuclear and extended, servants, adopted and step members, pets, relationships, surrogates

Marriage ceremonies, relationships, gender roles, sexuality, courtship, methods of choice, infidelity and response, widowhood, inheritance, premarital relations, customs, dress, property, divorce, nontraditional partnerships

Childraising conception, birth control, pregnancy, birth, medical care, naming practices, inheritance, nurture, discipline, religion, education, training, work, play, toys, pets, adolescence, initiations, organizations, pictures, dress, mortality, grieving

Old Age attitudes, care, power, work, ceremonies, organizations, roles, rights, inheritance, housing, hobbies, health, dress, deference, wisdom

Death life expectancy, causes, health, medical care, burial, funeral customs, grieving practices, inheritance, obituaries, tributes, naming and necronyms

Religion denominations, beliefs, practices, ceremonies, discrimination, scriptures, icons, hierarchies, group behavior, intermarriage, childraising

Education at-home, public or private, equipment, discipline, teachers, schoolroom, rural schools, advanced, apprenticeship, boarding, on-the-job, lessons, textbooks, social life, organizations, recreation, emergencies, parental roles, scholarly subjects, research, higher education, professional training

Language usage, literacy, reading material, accents, dialects, colloquialisms, proverbs, sign language, foreign, translation, technology, mass communication, oral tradition

Literature reading matter, Bibles, religious texts and tracts, books, schoolbooks, newspapers, magazines, newsletters, pamphlets, brochures, advertising, posters, documents, children's books, comic books, programs, handbills, music, ephemera, oral traditions (stories, proverbs, jokes, songs)

Arts aesthetic preferences, talents, hobbies, home decor, music, writing, painting, crafts, theatrical performance, practical design, professions, architecture, sculpture, drawing, photography

Ethnicity old culture, language, physical features, customs, religion, music, costume, arts, immigration, travel experiences, assimilation, organizations, work, housing, schools, naming, foodways, architecture, enclaves, push and pull factors, prejudice, intermarriage

Health folkways, nutrition, diet, disease, epidemics, wounds, medical care, sanitation, death, hazards, injuries, exercise, exposure, childbirth, life cycles, infant and child mortality, pregnancy, female cycles, medicines, addictions, equipment

Food foodways, crops, gardens, preservation, refrigeration, diet, nutrition, recipes, dishes, table customs, cookery, methods, tools, servants, food events

Dress fabrics, sewing, fashions, motives, styles, fads, dress events, age and class distinctions, needlework, shopping, catalogs, accessories

Work jobs, professions, types of labor, schedules, equipment, training, ethics, methods, attitudes, clothing, income, seasonality, rank, age and gender distinctions, conditions, organizations, transportation, hazards, fairness, manuals, publications, rank, structure, manufacturing

Economy business, bookkeeping, income, expenses, prices, currency, investments, losses, inflation, depression, theft, charity, taxes, inventory, property, inheritance, accounting, selling

Technology equipment, utilities, machines, tools, utensils, methods, inventions, work, household, farm, manufacturing, transportation, communication, medical, emergency, flight, space, photography

Recreation seasonal nature, timing, organizations, dress, equipment, rules, competition, popular culture, hobbies, arts, games, toys, music, awards, travel, socializing, technology, television, radio, films, oratory, festivals, traditional ethnic and regional customs

Migration mobility rates, transportation, push and pull factors, group behavior, routes, assimilation, enclaves, return migration, foodways, health, transported possessions, written accounts, work, recreation, vehicles

Rank systems, organizations, politics, work, deference, wealth, inheritance, property, influence, public office, honor and shame, publicity, display of rank, attitudes

Politics government, elections, organizations, opinions, voting, issues, political parties, interest groups, campaigning, taxes, reform, contracts, women's suffrage

War and military motives, draft, common soldier experience, costumes, equipment, health, disease, medical care, wounds, battles, chores, training, rank, civilian homefront experiences, epidemics, shortages, inflation, mobilization, transportation, alternative service, conscientious objection, veterans' experiences, property loss, death, hospitals, patriotism, opponents, organizations, pensions, widows and orphans, postwar society, wartime marriage and relationships, discipline

Social Deviance attitudes, laws, punishments, motivations, violence, crime, abuse, family secrets, suicide, theft, sexuality, group behavior, publicity, shame

evidence and made plain what we are doing. "Coherence is the aim of inference. We try to fit everything together into a plausible whole," writes Richard Marius of Harvard University in *A Short Guide to Writing About History*. If your great-grandfather was a Native American youth sent to Carlisle Indian School, but you do not have any of his recollections of the place, you can include in your family history a description of what it was like for most of the children sent there. You can surmise that his hair was cut short, that he was dressed in white man's clothes, and that he would have been punished for speaking his native tongue. You can infer that his experiences were the same or similar to all Carlisle boys', but you must make plain that the description that you are offering is generic. To claim it is *his* description or that you are *certain* of what he experienced would be to fictionalize. "When you make an inference important to your study of the sources," Richard Marius continues, "you become a questioner. You do not read your sources passively; you read them actively, trying to fill in the gaps that you always find in them."[8]

SOMETIMES YOUR ANCESTOR IS NAMED IN THE BOOK!

But When Is It Realistic to Look?

Genealogists love to search indexes hoping to find their relatives' names. It can be a fruitless search. Teachers, librarians, and old hands at family history research will warn you: do not expect to find *the* book on the library shelves that is about your family. Yet sometimes, in historical or social history sources, you may find your ancestor and the lead may take you to wonderful historical documentation. Ask yourself: "Was my ancestor or his family important enough in some sphere to be mentioned in a book?" Be realistic.

- Was your ancestor a leader during any particular event, such as an election, that might be documented in a book?
- Did your ancestor belong to an organization, such as a club or a military unit, especially serving as an officer? Could there be a book on that organization?
- Did your ancestor attend a particular institution, such as a school or a hospital, about which someone has published a history?
- Did your family live or work in a community or place for which there might be a history that mentions them as, say, farmers or property owners in that town?
- Were your ancestors among the first to do something, such as the first settlers or businessmen in an area, so that that area's history might include them?
- Did your ancestor do anything even locally "famous," such as die in or survive a disaster or commit a crime that might have placed him in a local history?
- Did your ancestor leave a diary or account during a dramatic period of history, such as the Civil War, that contemporary or historical sources might have quoted?
- Did your ancestor live in a time period or participate in an event that might lead to a social history book? For example, if your ancestor lived during the Great Depression, you may find a book or article on the Great Depression in that locality that might mention your ancestor.
- Have you found these ancestors by name in an article or book before? If so, try again.

Always remember that the historians writing such books used the same records genealogists use. Thus you may not find your ancestors in the history book, but you *may* find out from the history book what other sources are available to you. Read the footnotes and bibliography for these.

Step By Step

Example and Steps

You can strike gold in older published history sources. Many libraries will maintain copies of older books written at the time of the events in which your ancestors participated. A book written at the time is more liable to mention participants by name. Such books may give you both specific and general information about your family and their times.

We knew from family oral tradition that my great-grandfather, John Harper, was a gold miner and a mining union activist in Victor and Cripple Creek, Colorado, circa 1904. Family stories reported that he was physically threatened during a big strike and that he was "deported" from the state on a train into either the New Mexico desert or the Kansas prairie. I was conducting traditional genealogical and family history research: city directories, censuses, vital records, oral interviews, and family letters. Then one day, when we were in Colorado College's library, my husband (also a historian) picked up a book by Emma F. Langdon, *The Cripple Creek Strike: A History of Industrial Wars in Colorado*, circa 1904–1905. This was obviously written by an observer at the time. It was also that pet peeve of many researchers: a book without an index. Nevertheless, my husband flipped through the pages until the name "John Harper" leaped out at him.

When you find an ancestor in a published source, read the whole source for hidden treasure. Do not let the excitement of finding the name distract you from the opportunity to mine deeper. Watch for descriptions of anything in which your ancestor might have been involved. When you write your own narrative accounts of the family, you may use quotations—properly cited of course—from writers who were firsthand witnesses.

Never reject a book because it has no index, and never assume the index lists everything you need. Be prepared to page through patiently, even painstakingly.

From Emma Langdon's book we learned that John Harper undertook several important actions on behalf of his union, the Western Federation of Miners. He helped establish a cooperative union general store, so the men and their families did not have to shop at the dreaded company store. He was involved in a union coroner's jury, established so that the mine owners could not always blame every deadly accident on miner neglect. For these kinds of activities, he was beaten and forced to flee town along difficult roads and across long distances we can now retrace. I now knew more than I had ever dreamed I would about my great-grandfather's experiences. This source, a firsthand account of the entire strike, also gave me the explanations and descriptions I needed to write a narrative. I could quote Emma Langdon for particularly dramatic eyewitness testimony.

Finding ancestors in newer published histories can mean you have struck the mother lode. In newer, scholarly histories of the events you are researching, you may also find your ancestors by name. You will have the added advantage of the scholarly historian's research into more sources than ever and her interpretations of what happened.

Several years after we found the Emma Langdon book, we were shopping in a Barnes and Noble bookstore and my husband spotted a new book: Elizabeth Jameson's *All That Glitters: Class, Conflict, and Community in Cripple Creek*. He passed it to me, thinking I would want it for my Colorado history collection. This time *I* opened to the index and there he was: John Harper. From this source I learned that my great-grandfather was the *president* of Victor Miners' Local No. 32. He had run for public offices and attended conventions. He was the *manager* of the Victor union store. He was, indeed, deported from the state, along with hundreds of others, after being held in a barbed-wire "bull pen." On another occasion, a gang of masked men took him from his home, beat him, and drove him away to Denver. The book confirmed and augmented the family oral traditions, provided very specific, dated information, and gave me a modern historian's interpretations of the events and motives of the strike.

Look at the footnotes and bibliography to see where the author has struck gold on her claim. The scholarly historian will provide detailed foot- or endnotes and a bibliography. Read these not only for the precise sources behind the mentions of your ancestors but also for general sources and repositories on related topics you can research.

Citing Sources

Next I examined where author Jameson was getting her information. I discovered from her citations that there is an Archive of the Western Federation of Miners in the University of Colorado Western History Collections where Jameson had spent years researching. She had used union and town newspapers, union records, and the published proceedings of regular conventions, among many other sources. I had had no idea such detailed records existed on this one strike. Her lengthy bibliography also listed collections at Colorado repositories such as the Denver Public Library and the Colorado State Historical Society. There are relevant records, too, in such far-flung locations as the University of California at Berkeley and the Wisconsin State Historical Society at Madison. Now I knew where to do my research on my ancestor.

Printed Source

To find scholarly historians with university positions, as well as their areas of expertise, use *The Directory of Historical Departments and Organizations in the United States and Canada* published by the American Historical Association (AHA) every year.

Consider contacting the author, who may share the wealth. If the book is recently published and your ancestors' connection with the subject matter is close enough, it might be worthwhile to contact the author. There is usually a clue on the dust jacket to where the author lives or works. If there is not a clear enough clue, you may always write in care of the publisher.

I determined where Elizabeth Jameson worked by the jacket blurb and telephoned directory assistance for her university's phone number. I checked briefly with the university to make sure she was located there and what address to use. One clue that perhaps the author would respond to a letter was that she had used oral interviews with descendants of the striking miners as resources. Therefore, she might be particularly receptive to a letter from another such descendant. I wrote Elizabeth Jameson a three-page letter and she wrote a three-page letter back. She told me exactly where she thought I could find more on John Harper. Being a well-organized researcher herself, she had files of data cards on her named subjects. In her letter she recited the offices he held, the conventions he attended, the events that affected him, even information from newspaper announcements about his children. She shared her expertise, speculating on what he did after the strike and why his family soon moved out of state. She even called to my attention some quotes from telegrams—my great-grandfather's own words about the strike.

Remember that serendipity—by definition—just happens, but sometimes you can help it along. The above events may seem fortuitous rather than something you can *make* happen in your own research. *Think like a historian.* If you know the subjects relevant to your family history, and are constantly on the lookout for them in libraries and bookstores, you will make such discoveries too. Not every author or expert will be as responsive to your inquiries as Jameson was to mine, but common-sense guidelines to letter writing (as discussed in chapter six) will encourage folks to respond to you.

CONCLUSION: DO IT! YOU DON'T KNOW WHAT YOU'RE MISSING!

As I hope that you can see, social history offers a new world of opportunities for research and writing in family history. Let it excite you. Do not let it intimidate you. If you are a seasoned genealogist, you already have done more primary research in records than most undergraduate history students do. If you follow professional genealogical standards for recording information and citing sources, you are already meticulous. If you enjoy history and discovery, you can advance to a new level of satisfaction in your family history research and writing. As said by so many history professors I have known: "If you're going to do it anyway, why not make it a publishable book?"

CHAPTER BIBLIOGRAPHY: WORKS CITED IN EXAMPLES

1. Fineberg, Robert P. "Isaac Fineberg, American." Unpublished narrative of a Lithuanian Jewish family, copy in author's possession.
2. Jameson, Elizabeth. *All That Glitters: Class, Conflict, and Community in Cripple Creek.* Urbana: University of Illinois Press, 1998.
3. Langdon, Emma F. *The Cripple Creek Strike: A History of Industrial Wars in Colorado.* Denver: Great Western Publishing, Co. 1904–1905. New York: Arno Press, 1969.
4. Spock, Benjamin. *The Common Sense Book of Baby and Child Care.* New York: Duell, Sloan, and Pearce, Inc., 1946.
5. Weber, Mary A., "Women of the Western Slope of Colorado, 1930–1960." Unpublished bachelor's thesis, History Department, University of Colorado at Colorado Springs, 1994. Copy in author's possession.

For More Info

Henry Z Jones, a well-known genealogical author and speaker, has written about such serendipitous moments in his *Psychic Roots* and *More Psychic Roots* (see the general bibliography).

TWO

A Historian's Approach to Home Sources: Artifacts

And then there are things, the clutter left by the past, which are keys to it when
properly understood.

—Louis C. Jones[1]

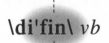

Definitions

WHAT ARE HOME SOURCES?

Home sources are the materials already owned by family members from which you might extract family history information. These would include heirlooms and memorabilia, photographs, interviews, and stories told by relatives. Genealogists are more inclined to use the general term *home sources* than are historians. When historians consider these sources, they usually see them in other professional categories. Knowing these categories—"speaking the language"—may help you when addressing historians, librarians, archivists, and others.

HOME SOURCES AS HISTORIANS AND HISTORICAL
INSTITUTIONS OFTEN CATEGORIZE THEM

heirlooms and collectibles artifacts, material culture, archaeology (in museums)
letters, scrapbooks, certificates documents (manuscript collections in libraries and archives)
family pictures photographs (photograph archives in libraries and museums)
taped interviews with relatives oral history interview collections (in libraries and museums)
family stories handed down oral tradition, folklore (in oral history collections)

Historians use different categories for these items than genealogists for three main reasons:

Notes

Endnotes for this chapter begin on page 220.

1. Historians usually use home sources to reveal or illustrate general social history, not one family's history.
2. Historians, particularly social, public, and American Studies historians, regularly use the language and methods of related professional fields (such as archives, museum studies, and folklore) in order to be professional, scholarly, and to show interdisciplinary expertise.
3. When historians look for home sources to use in general history research, writing, and teaching, they usually look in museums and libraries at collections rather than knocking on residential doors, searching from one family to another.

"So what does this have to do with my grandmother's crazy quilt or my dad's stories about the war?" you may say. "How does knowing this help me with my own family history?" Again, the methods and sources of historians and related professions can assist you with your home sources in ways that expand beyond traditional genealogical practices. If you think like a historian when you approach your home sources, these treasured items will become gold mines of information for researching and writing your family history. **If you think like a social historian, then home sources can reveal not only the character of your ancestors but also how your ancestors fit into their own society.**

GRANDPA KNEW WHAT HE WAS DOING AFTER ALL
Historical Use of Home Sources

Many historians and genealogists see credibility issues in home sources that make the sources seem frivolous, less important, or entirely unreliable. Grandpa may have been certain that he was saving the most valuable part of his family's history in that cigar box. Grandpa or Grandma may also have told you why these items were so important to the family's history. More than likely, however, they did not or could not—or you heard it but did not record it and now your memory for the details is fading. Often the scrupulous genealogist examines such treasures, extracts what factual information they contain, then leaves them behind in the search for censuses, vital records, and other documents outside of the home. The *family historian* would come back to the artifacts again and again for the additional information available when one analyzes them.

The Source: A Guidebook of American Genealogy, edited by Loretto Szucs and Sandra Luebking, is one of the most highly regarded genealogy guides. As its title suggests, it has an almost scriptural authority in the field. It contains superb advice about home sources in its "Foundations" chapter, addressing most of the same sources that historians would. Even so, *The Source* directs the family historian to extract mostly names and dates from home sources, then to carefully crosscheck that information in the customary public records. The advice about respectful handling of home sources is some of the best and most descriptive in *The Source*, but the reasons for preserving home sources (listed below) are incomplete.

1. Preserve home sources for the genealogical names, dates, and other "evidence" they contain.
2. Preserve home sources for their inherent family and historical value.

I would add a third, equally important reason.

3. **Preserve home sources for the stories, descriptions, and social history connections they offer for writing narrative family history.**

Think of how you best learned and liked history as a child. Few of us revel in rote memorization of names and dates. How special it was, though, to handle a historical object, share it through show-and-tell, or learn what living in another time was like from firsthand accounts. As a teacher, I hear from the majority of every semester's new crop of college freshmen that history had been a less than favorite class. It too often consisted of just the memorization of names and dates. The same students love history when it is taught through stories, analysis of issues, and portrayals of what daily life was really like.

Using the methods of social historians and other professionals will imbue your home sources with this kind of value and meaning. You will extract more usable information than you ever dreamed you could from treasures and stories. A description of an artifact is text for your narrative. Analyzing a photograph also creates text and adds depth; reproducing it illustrates the narrative. Quoting a firsthand account from a letter or interview supplements your own narrative passages. Researching the social history behind the ordinary use of an artifact allows you to place your ancestors in the context of their times. **You are writing history into your family and your family into history.**

Reminder

As you become aware of libraries and museums that preserve other families' home sources, you can use that information from other families the way a historian would: to show in your writing how a family like yours lived. You will also become more aware of the proper treatment of such sources, and of the fact that yours are just as worthy of preservation as another family's.

MATERIAL CULTURE: ARTIFACTS IN FAMILY HISTORY

Definitions

Material culture studies is another "new" field of history (historians tend to think thirty years old is new), borrowed like many others from social science fields—in this case, anthropology, archaeology, folklore, and archiving. **Material culture, according to a leading proponent historian, Thomas Schlereth in *Artifacts and the American Past*, "encompasses the entire natural and man-made environment with which researchers can interpret the past."** It particularly involves analyzing artifacts (objects), be they tools, clothes, toys, buildings, or anything tangible, in order to understand the culture that made and used them. "The historian's primary purpose in using artifacts," Schlereth continues, "is always to interpret them in their cultural history context."[2] We can borrow the methods of material culture historians (methods that the historians already borrowed from someone else) and transform our family heirlooms into artifacts. We can extract new information from home sources that we thought we had already exhausted.

What Is an Artifact?

Definitions

Every thing made or modified by humans is an artifact. Size—large or small—does not disqualify an item from being an artifact. Buildings and landscapes are artifacts. Documents are also artifacts. The term *artifact* carries with it an implication that one may study it for information. Using the term *artifact* is simply a reminder that we can and should analyze an object for what it reveals about the culture that produced and used it. Your "stuff" is made up of artifacts. Rummage through it. Look in older homes, closets, basements, attics, sheds and outbuildings, boxes, trunks, and anywhere dusty for family artifacts. Anything and everything can be a family history artifact. They surround you right now if you are sitting in a family home or your workspace.

WHAT YOU CAN DO WITH YOUR HOME SOURCES, PROFESSIONAL STYLE
(Or, Serious Stuff to Do With Your Stuff
So That You Can Have More Fun With It!)

Locate and collect home sources in your own family.

Organize and catalog them for their best use and care.

Analyze and interpret the information the sources hold.

Identify and find more information by comparing the sources to books about them.

Care and conserve sources by archival standards to preserve them.

Describe and quote from the sources in your family history narratives.

Illustrate your narratives with pictures of your home sources.

Cite sources with proper footnotes or endnotes to enable professionals to respect your sources.

Donate home sources to proper repositories if the family cannot best keep the sources.

Locate and use other families' home sources for information in your narratives.

Identifying and Analyzing Artifacts

After locating artifacts, use every available source to make sure that you correctly and thoroughly identify them. *Thoroughly* identifying an artifact goes beyond just determining what it is. Be as thorough as you possibly can in your mental deductions and documentation. If a small artifact grows into a frustrating brick wall, set it aside in a safe place, with its documentation up to that point, and come back to it later. If it stumps you, take it to a museum curator or a material culture specialist for identification.

Consider and record where you found the artifact. What was next to it? What type of container was it in and in what part of the house? Obviously, if it was in the kitchen as opposed to the barn you have strong clues as to its use. If it was in Great-Aunt Eunice's keepsake box it was probably hers. You must record such information before you move the item or you may destroy its significance. You must either label the artifact (safely) or work up some kind of inventory code for future investigators. In this case, *think like an archaeologist.*

Look through the other items that exist in the "sphere" of the artifact for more clues to its identity. For example, perhaps Grandma was the sort of woman who kept instructions, labels, packaging, unused parts, broken pieces, receipts, and anything else that went along with almost any artifact she had. She did not necessarily keep all of that together, but probably within the same general location. We might not know at first what that kitchen utensil was for, but eventually

Sources

A good service is Replacements, Ltd.; 1089 Knox Rd., P.O. Box 26029, Greensboro, NC 27420; (800) REPLACE; fax (336) 697-3100; http://www.replacements.com. It deals with china, crystal, some stoneware dishes, and silverware.

One way to identify the patterns of heirloom silver and dishes is through replacement services. These businesses specialize in buying up old, discontinued patterns for resale to collectors. They will help you identify, date, price, replace, and augment your collection. Knowing the years of manufacture and availability and the name and design of a pattern can help determine original ownership of the item and perhaps even who gave it to your ancestor. Replacement services will provide help with identifying patterns. For example, say a replacement service helps you identify one group of six silver spoons in your great-grandmother's silver as a pattern called Lancaster, circa 1898. You know she was married in 1904. These are the only spoons of that design. (Guests did not as often attempt to match a chosen pattern in the past as they do now with bridal registries.) You have Great-Grandma's wedding book containing a gift list that shows "Mr. and Mrs. Lancaster, six silver spoons." Even if there are other gifts of six silver spoons in other patterns, one can speculate that the Lancasters thought a pattern in their name was special. Be sure to study engraved monograms on silver as well; they are usually the couple's surname initial, sometimes the bride's first initial and more rarely the groom's. Children's silver might be specially marked with their first or all three initials. People tended to give silver cups and spoons to babies soon after birth.

we would find an instruction book that identified it by picture, serial number, manufacturer's name and year, and how to use it. A receipt would tell us when she bought it at the hardware store, as well as what she paid for it.

Check to see whether historical owners of a particular artifact kept their own records of its identity and meaning. For instance, many newlyweds cataloged their wedding gifts. In a wedding guest book, in news articles about the wedding (especially in small-town newspapers), or in thank-you notes and letters there might be a list of who offered what gifts to the happy couple. Wedding gifts (before electrical appliances were common) often included silverware, crystal, china, and table linens. For most of middle America, one can surmise that Grandma's surviving Victorian silver, cut crystal, Haviland china, or damask tablecloths were wedding gifts. Grandma probably used them in her everyday life—which is why the edges of the tablespoons are so worn down (from stirring in metal pans), the crystal is cracked, the china is chipped, and the tablecloth is stained. What else was she supposed to do with them? She never knew that someday they would be your antiques, and she probably could not afford to set everything aside, unused, just for you, even had it occurred to her to do so.

Other common ways for ancestors to leave us records of artifacts are through baby books (again, a gift list), correspondence (especially good for the stories behind the gifts loved ones mailed to each other), business inventories, thank-you notes, wills, probate inventories, bills of lading (cargo inventories), photographs displaying the items, and oral tradition. If you have none of these, show the artifact to family members or old friends who might remember it. When you discover clues, remember to attach them to the artifact or store them with it, but only if that is possible without harming the artifact.

Artifacts are tied to oral history and oral tradition—and if they're not, you should tie them. Take relevant artifacts with you when you go to interview family members. (See the oral history guidelines in chapter five.) This is a good way to identify the artifacts and elicit relevant stories. When generations of a family have treasured a particular artifact, they usually have passed along an oral tradition about it and its meaning to the family. When you hear a story like this, record it (including any variations) so that it will remain with the artifact from then on. That the teapot belonged to the Civil War ancestor or the candlesticks were the sole possession of the Swedish immigrant woman—these are precious stories that make good family narrative. Of course you must also investigate their accuracy, but in narrative, even inaccurate stories can be interesting to analyze— as long as you do not misrepresent their accuracy. Here is an example of how you can incorporate dubious information into your narrative:

Important

> Great-Grandma always claimed these were the candlesticks that she held pro-tectively to her breast as she sailed the Atlantic. These very candlesticks, she insisted, were her most prized heirlooms from her Swedish ancestors, which she guarded carefully as she passed through the stations of Ellis Island. We never had the heart to ask her, then, why the stamp on the bottom reads "Made in Taiwan."

Historical research can help you identify and analyze artifacts and what they reveal about the family. Perhaps you have no relatives to interview. Other folks may help. Showing an artifact to someone of a generation older than yours can be a quick way to get started. For example, I teach about how Ellis Island staff medically examined immigrants' eyes with shoe buttonhooks. I carry an old but-tonhook in my purse just to have it for that lecture. When I show it to the students without identifying it, usually someone older than age forty can tell us the instru-ment's intended use, but the younger students have no clue. No one of any age knows that the buttonhook was perfect for turning the eyelid to check for con-junctivitis or trachoma. Older people, however, have a historical literacy that younger ones do not. Suppose your artifact is military. Try showing it to a mili-tary historian, a soldier of some vintage, or a history teacher. I will never forget the student who wanted to show me her great-grandfather's medal because she thought it might be something important. She handed me a Civil War Congres-sional Medal of Honor. She got an earful of history in short order, and I took her straight out to my waiting husband after class so he could see the medal, too. We then proceeded to research its specific origins for her and finally found an article and a new history book about her ancestor's unit and its medals.

Research Tip

A next step might be to visit antique stores to spot similar items and ask storekeepers about them. This will also help you assess the monetary value of your artifacts for insurance purposes. (Please do not sell your family history.) Antique dealers often have libraries of collector's guides that they might allow you to peruse. It is very likely that you will find duplicates of your ancestors' household and everyday possessions in antique stores because, remember, your

Printed Source

Reminder

Remember to analyze your ancestors' tastes. In most cases tastes will be representative of and typical for their day. Tastes were very sentimental and ornate in the Victorian period (1830–1900) and still elaborate but less so in the Edwardian period (1900–1910). Styles were plain and austere or modern and streamlined during the decades before and after, respectively.

ancestors were not unique. Next, search guides to collectibles in bookstores or libraries or magazines about antiques that have object identification columns and articles. **A handy reference to buy and keep at home is a reproduction turn-of-the-century mail order catalog, such as Sears Roebuck or Montgomery Ward.** You will be amazed how many of your ancestors' artifacts you see pictured and described there—and what they used to cost.

Most importantly, look for history books in public, museum, historical society, and college libraries and in bookstores to help you with your artifacts. In some instances these will be books about a particular kind of artifact, such as collector's guides or an actual history of one item. There are history books on items ranging from the pencil and the paper clip to railroad locomotives and barns. Even better, look for social history books about the larger themes that relate to this type of artifact in order to learn more about its use and meaning.

PRACTICE WITH YOUR OWN POSSESSIONS

Look around your own house first. It is full of artifacts from your life. The house and its surroundings are also artifacts of your life. To hone your curatorial skills (you are the curator of your own life's museum), identify at least ten artifacts that represent your own life—ones that you can see around you without moving from where you sit. Here is a list of ten modern kitchen artifacts that I might make for myself.

- the computer on the kitchen table (we know it shouldn't be there, but it is)
- the microwave oven
- the coffeemaker
- the bread machine that I never use
- the side-by-side refrigerator
- the antique china plates on the wall
- the vacuum cleaner
- the dishwasher
- the stove
- the small kitchen television

Imagine an archaeologist or a family historian finding these in the year 2075 and extrapolating history and culture from them. Obviously technology and how you used it would be important. A historian would date the types of machines and speculate on the late-twentieth-century woman trying to write books, cook meals, wash dishes, clean house, and watch TV all at once. By investigating additional social history sources, such as Ruth Schwartz Cowan's *More Work for Mother*, one could question whether "labor-saving" devices really lessened women's work, or just changed it.

Do the same analysis with *your* stuff. Practice turning your artifacts this way and that to see them from different angles. Think like a historian. Look for the collective meaning, not just the singular. Research creatively. Let's try this with an artifact that many American families, particularly their female members, save from one generation to the next: the recipe collection.

ANALYZING AND RESEARCHING ARTIFACTS: THE RECIPE COLLECTION

Hidden Treasures

Very commonly a family, or often a female member, will have saved a collection of recipes from her ancestors. The recipes may be in a box, a coffee can, or an album of some kind. Often there will be recipes in the collection identified as coming from other ancestors and friends. Usually there are recipes that are tried and pronounced true by repeated generations. Characteristically, the oldest, most used ones are torn, yellow, fading, stained, and crumbling. Knowing what heavy use they received causes true aficionados of these treasures to love the disintegrating ones best. Even though descendants may treasure these collections, many are unappreciative of their family history significance. They are just old recipes—not artifacts, not something one can analyze. They do not offer genealogical facts.

Think like a social historian. There is much social history in a vintage recipe collection. One way to analyze the collection is to pose questions to yourself about each aspect that seems unusual in your modern world. Test yourself on the following questions. (Yes, folks, I know some of the following are familiar to many of you. Do you think the answers will be so obvious to Generation X, Y, or Z?)

1. Why did Great-Grandma have so many large-scale recipes, such as fried chicken to serve fifty people?
2. Why did she make out menus with multiple courses?
3. Why did she keep lists of people's birthdays, curtain measurements, and home remedies in the same book as her recipes?
4. Where did she get the large quantities of cucumbers, green beans, beets, peaches, pears, plums, corn, tomatoes, green tomatoes, apples, crabapples, black raspberries, gooseberries, mulberries, chokecherries, and elderberries that were needed for the canning, pickling, and preserving recipes in the collection?
5. Each canning recipe could make as many as twenty quarts. What did she do with all of those full canning jars?
6. Why did she have so many recipes that called for rare and expensive nuts such as black walnuts, hickory nuts, and butternuts?
7. Why did she keep a list of women's names and addresses with her recipes?
8. Why did she keep little notes from her children in the recipe book?
9. Why are there two different copies of the same recipe for suet pudding, and who wrote them?

    Recipe A is written on a worn, yellow, crumbling scrap of paper in shaky handwriting that you do not recognize.

    Recipe B is on one of Great-Grandma's regular pages, in better condition. You recognize that it is in Great-Grandma's handwriting. She gave the recipe a title that it did not have on copy A: "Mother's Suet Pudding."

    So who wrote copy A?
10. What is suet pudding anyway?
11. Why did she use so much graham flour?
12. Why are there almost no meat recipes? Did they eat meat, and if so, what kinds?

Citing Sources

A non-footnote: To cite my sources, I should admit that these examples were inspired by the collections of Maybelle Lavina Chandler Sturdevant (1895–1986), my husband's grandmother, and Kate Dickey Harper (1881–1942), my grandmother. They were women of similar middle-American backgrounds, and each detail is authentic to one or the other.

13. Where did she get her dairy products and eggs?
14. What can you say about Great-Grandma's cooking based on her vague measurements, curt instructions, and strange terms?

boil until it cracks	bologna cookies
drop	chow chow
bake in a slow oven	milk to fill freezer
flour to roll	handful nuts
ice box cookies	pinch sugar
brine	boil until thick
sour milk	enough flour to make a soft dough
oleo	dates, nuts, raisins
salt pork	1 pail tomatoes
war-time cake	

a list of ingredients with no instructions at all, whether the recipe is for cake, pie, bread, cookies, "do-nuts," ice cream, salad, salad dressing, or soup
15. Who are all of the people, such as "Mrs. Hans Hansen" and "Aunt Mabel Dickey," whose names are written in the corners of some of the recipes?

Answer your own questions. Questioning an artifact is as close as you may get to interviewing the ancestor who owned it. Try to answer the questions yourself. Try studying the context contained in the recipe or other parts of the collection for your answers. Try interviewing relatives and friends with longer memories. Try researching both the direct historical detail (perhaps in comprehensive or thematic cookbooks) and the social history (in historical books about foodways, kitchen culture, women's work, or everyday life). I will give answers from my personal and historical knowledge based on research, oral history, and observation.

1. *Why did Great-Grandma have so many large-scale recipes, such as fried chicken to serve fifty people?* In her day, she served threshing crews on the farm at wheat harvest time. She provided food for the church suppers that were so common for rural and small-town communities.

2. *Why did she make out menus with multiple courses?* She entertained, but she always took serving her family seriously as well.

3. *Why did she keep lists of people's birthdays, curtain measurements, and home remedies in the same book as her recipes?* Try putting yourself in her historical place. Her recipe book was, to her, what a planner or calendar is to many of us. In addition to her Bible, it was the main book that was always where she could lay her hands on it. It was her "hot file." Aren't we glad she did write such information as birthdays in here? Of course, her notes also indicate that she made her own curtains, how big her windows were, that she treated her family's ailments, what those were, and whose birthdays she celebrated.

4. *Where did she get the large quantities of cucumbers, green beans, beets, peaches, pears, plums, corn, tomatoes, green tomatoes, apples, crabapples, black raspberries, gooseberries, mulberries, chokecherries, and elderberries that were needed for canning, pickling, and preserving recipes in the collection?* She had a garden for the cucumbers, green beans, beets, corn, and tomatoes.

She also grew her own salad greens. There were fruit trees nearby, including pear, plum, apple, crabapple, and mulberry. She bought flats, crates, or bushels of things she especially liked from sunnier climes, such as peaches from Colorado, California, or Florida. She (probably with her children and grandchildren) went into the woods and thickets for buckets of berries. Think how scratched and stained they were when they returned. (But some of the stains, no doubt, would be encircling their smiling mouths.) Later, as the towns grew, she bought fresh produce from the Italian-American truck farmers nearby.

5. *Each canning recipe could make as many as twenty quarts. What did she do with all of those full canning jars?* She had a root cellar with rustic shelves lined with Ball brand jars. The pantry off the kitchen was full, too. She gave some food away but did most of her canning so that her family could continue to eat fruit and vegetables through the winter, spring, and early summer.

6. *Why did she have so many recipes that called for rare and expensive nuts such as black walnuts, hickory nuts, and butternuts?* Those nuts were not rare or expensive in old middle America. She taught the children to "go nutting" every fall. The hardest part was washing and cracking the black walnuts, with their black stain and nearly impenetrable shells.

7. *Why did she keep a list of women's names and addresses with her recipes?* These women were her fellow club members—typically from the Order of the Eastern Star (the women's auxiliary to the Masonic Lodge) or a literary society—or church ladies. Sometimes they were the group for which she cooked fried chicken for fifty people or developed a menu.

8. *Why did she keep little notes from her children in the recipe book?* Where else would she keep her most precious treasures?

9. *So who wrote copy A?* Recipe A was the original one, written in the hand of Great-Great-Grandma, and later copied by her daughter in recipe B. We would not know who wrote recipe A without also finding recipe B. Both become precious.

10. *What is suet pudding anyway?* Like the plum pudding of old, suet pudding is a dense, heavy ancestor of fruitcake, with finely chopped nuts and fruits. Folks served it with "hard sauce" flavored with lemon or brandy, sometimes flaming. Suet is the fat from around the internal organs of animals like sheep or cattle. It was the fatty shortening for the rich cake.

11. *Why did she use so much graham flour?* Graham flour is whole wheat flour, and its use was a fad at first. Dr. Sylvester Graham recommended the use of whole wheat flour and other "natural" or "health" foods starting in the 1830s. He was the inspiration for Kellogg's and Post cereals. We are not used to seeing recipes call for it anymore: they use the term "whole wheat" instead. Great-Grandma was trying to be a healthy cook.

12. *Why are there almost no meat recipes? Did they eat meat, and if so, what kinds?* Few middle Americans were vegetarians. She cooked many meats by roasting, frying, baking, and stewing. There was no need to write the instructions down as recipes because the procedure was simple. The recipes that she did write down were usually for foods with lists of ingredients to measure and remember. Great-Grandma knew how to kill chickens, skin

or pluck game, and butcher or carve. There were beef or pork roasts, pork chops, hams, river fish, rabbits, holiday turkeys and goose, and a singularly memorable experience with a raccoon. Other folks also ate squirrel, venison, and wildfowl. Without recipes, though, this information comes from oral history and historical research.

13. *Where did she get her dairy products and eggs?* We mentioned she had chickens. For years they were in a coop on her property and foxes would raid the hen house. Later, as the town grew and she grew older, she bought her eggs from others nearby. Some folks still had cows. Women would sell their butter and eggs for extra pocket money. Later, Great-Grandma's family would drive to the creamery to get their dairy products. Still later, in town, milkmen delivered bottles to the door.

14. *What can you say about Great-Grandma's cooking based on her vague measurements, curt instructions, and strange terms?* Great-Grandma assumed anyone using her recipes was as familiar with how to cook as she was; it was considered almost a genetic or instinctive talent. Certainly, her girls and their girls would know. You measure ingredients by "feel." Anyone knows that. You do not need instructions very often. If you had the list of ingredients, you already knew what to do with them.

    You boil candy until it *cracks*, or reaches the hard crack stage.

    You *drop* biscuits onto a cookie sheet.

    A "slow oven" is set at a low temperature such as 325°.

    Flour helps you roll dough without its sticking to the rolling pin.

    Ice box (a.k.a. refrigerator) cookies came from a roll of dough that you sliced and baked.

    Brine was the boiling salt water for pickling.

    Sour milk got that way by spoiling. Why waste it?

    Oleo was an early form of margarine.

    Salt pork was used to flavor a pot of beans or as shortening similar to suet. It is the fat of bacon preserved in salt.

    War-time cake was from the world wars, when sugar and flour were scarce or rationed, thus scant in the recipe.

    Bologna cookies were thin slices from a dough log.

    Chow chow was a pickled vegetable chutney, canned in multiple quarts.

    Milk to fill freezer meant you added enough milk to the other ingredients to fill the inner cylinder of the ice cream freezer.

15. *Who are all of the people, such as "Mrs. Hans Hansen" and "Aunt Mabel Dickey," whose names are written in the corners of some of the recipes?* Great-Grandma cited her sources. A name on a recipe card meant it was that lady's recipe. It also provides the family historian with clues about relatives, friends, and neighbors.

Researching the Recipe Collection

I answered my own questions from off the top of my head (from previous research and from oral history), but there are sources that can help you. Remember that you want to be able to professionally cite all of your sources. For the recipe collection, what you have already learned from oral tradition and what you can gain from oral history may be the best sources. **There are also many books on women's history, the history of housework, and food history, and there are even cookbooks that are comprehensive or historically oriented.**

WRITING FROM ARTIFACTS: THE RECIPE COLLECTION

Now, after examining artifacts, social history, family tradition, oral history, antique stores, and collectors' guides, I can write my artifacts into my family history narrative to make it more detailed, interesting, and meaningful.

Maybelle put what her mother had taught her to good use in the kitchen. In the summer and fall she rounded up the children to help her harvest her garden and to gather wild foods from the Big Woods. From her garden, she put up quarts of cucumber pickles, green beans, beets, corn, tomatoes, green tomatoes, and spiced crabapples. She bought flats of Florida peaches to can from the grocer and she received pears and apples from her neighbors. From the Big Woods and the Dry Run she and the children gathered raspberries, gooseberries, chokecherries, elderberries, mulberries, butternuts, and hickory nuts. From the spreading tree in her own yard she gathered black walnuts and had the children wash them, then crack them with hammers. She also harvested her root vegetables and rhubarb and traded for some squash with neighbors. All of this went down the steep stairs into the cellar. There, one overhead light bulb revealed rustic wooden shelves loaded with blue Ball jars. Assorted crocks and bushel baskets lay here and there on the floor.[1] Maybelle was typical of most Midwestern women of her generation. As one Indiana homemaker recalled

> We raised what we ate, and ate what we raised. You didn't go into town and buy it, so it really was important to put your garden out and really take care of it when it was ready to harvest.[2]

[1] Maybelle Sturdevant, recipe card collection, circa 1918–1960, in brown-stained wooden "Recipes" box, in the author's possession; Rick Sturdevant, oral history interview with author, Colorado Springs, Colorado, September 3, 1999; personal recollections of author from 1984–1985 visits to Maybelle's home and cellar.

[2] Beulah Rawlings quoted in Eleanor Arnold, ed., *Voices of American Homemakers* (Bloomington: Indiana University Press, 1985), 133.

RECORDING YOUR FAMILY HISTORY ARTIFACTS

We all need a system to keep track of our artifacts. If you do not write down the information as you discover it you may forget it. If you do not find a way to either attach it to the right artifact, keep the information and artifact together, or set up a numbered inventory system, the information will become separated from the artifact, probably forever. On page 37 is a sample form to help you. Feel free to devise your own. There is nothing so helpful as a specific place to write the information. Consider attaching a photograph of the artifact to the form for identification and preservation.

RESEARCHING SOCIAL HISTORY THEMES FROM ARTIFACTS

Social historians have already researched and written about many types of artifacts that you may find. In many instances, they have written the social history of a group, place, or time by studying such artifacts. For most artifacts that you might find in the typical American family, there are collector's guides, museum exhibit catalogs, histories that build text around the artifacts, and histories that use the artifacts to illustrate the text. There are some areas of the past in which social historians have done much publishing. Here are summaries of areas in which you can do library or bookstore research. Do not limit your expectations to these, however, as there is probably some kind of social history source addressing any common artifact. These books will identify many relevant artifacts, answer questions, and offer you more to write in a family history narrative than you ever expected.

BOOKS THAT TELL SOCIAL HISTORY THROUGH ARTIFACTS

Everyday Life in America by Time Period

There are several series and individual volumes that address everyday life from a social history perspective. Some are scholarly and some are not. Yet both kinds tend to use artifacts and pictures of them as a way to illustrate everyday life. These are all books that can help you identify artifacts and write narrative about your family; you can quote the books or base your descriptions on what you learn from them.

Older books on artifacts and architecture are essentially early social history—before it became a field of intense scholarly analysis. One example is William Chauncy Langdon's *Everyday Things in American Life, 1607–1776*. If you want to research and write about your colonial ancestors, Langdon described and sometimes pictured artifacts including furniture, silver, glass, clothing, architecture, ships, and schoolbooks for almost every colonial culture. A notable exception is slave artifacts, but many historians did not treat slaves as a culture with artifacts in 1937, when Langdon wrote. This is a good example of the shortcomings or prejudices of older books but does not mean that the rest of the information is less valuable. Cross-checking in more recent and scholarly sources is always worthwhile.

Ivor Noël Hume, a historical archaeologist who published interesting books about life in early colonial Virginia, also wrote *A Guide to Artifacts of Colonial America*. This book is an unusual and happy combination of well-illustrated guidebook and scholarly historical analysis. Most books are either one or the other, and you will need both. A pathbreaking little book for many historians in this area was James Deetz's *In Small Things Forgotten: The Archeology of Early American Life*. Deetz especially addressed gravestones, pottery, and architecture

**A USEFUL FORM
YOU CAN REPRODUCE**

For a full-size, blank copy of the Artifact Identification, Analysis, and Cataloging Form, see page 232. You are free to photocopy this form for personal use.

Printed Source

ARTIFACT IDENTIFICATION, ANALYSIS, AND CATALOGING FORM

Cataloger's Name and Address ____ *Katherine Scott Sturdevant* _____

street address, Colorado Springs, Colorado, zip code _____

Date ____ *January 28, 2000* _____

Name(s) of Artifact (family, popular, or generic) ____ *Grandma Sturdevant's recipe box* ____

_____

Description and Identifying Features (material, construction, measurements, color, function)

Wooden, hinged-lid box, size 5¹/₂" wide by 3¹/₄" deep by 4¹/₄" tall to hold 3" by 5" cards, labeled "Recipes"

with black decal (wearing off), stain of yellow paint down front of box

Contents: set of yellowing cardboard divider cards with tabs marked for food categories; brown instruction card for

how to use "Weis Recipe Outfit"; handwritten recipes on ruled cards (see separate list); printed recipe brochures

from Robin Hood Flour and Kellogg's Corn Flakes

Inventory Number ____ *243* _____

Estimated Year of Origin ____ *circa 1920–1950s* _____

Original Location and Date Found ____ *Maybelle Sturdevant home, Waverly, Iowa, address, 1984* ____

Current Location and Ownership ____ *R. Sturdevant, address above* _____

History of Ownership ____ *Maybelle Sturdevant from purchase until 1984* _____

Identifying Source Citations, Cultural Analysis, and Interpretive Information

For dating, see commercially produced cards and box instructions.

For sources, see records for grocery store and family credits on recipes.

Checklist for Future Investigation

Research Robin Hood Flour, Kellogg's products, and Weis Recipe Outfit.

Identify handwriting by comparisons.

Develop instructions to go with recipes that are just lists of ingredients.

Acquire archival plastic sleeves for recipe cards.

Research names on recipes: Mrs. Hans Hansen; Aunt Sarah Harris; Esther Chandler; Etta Royer;

Aunt Mae Sturdevant

from sites such as Plymouth and Jamestown. He then combined archaeological information with historical documentation such as probate inventories. Deetz's deceptively simple little book can introduce you to an archaeologist's approach to artifacts of our early American ancestors.

Recent scholarly, yet popularly written, everyday life books include The Everyday Life in America series, edited by Richard Balkin for HarperCollins. The series is now in reprint and distributed in paperback by the University of Arkansas Press. The volumes in the series include, in order of the chronological periods they cover,

David Freeman Hawke, *Everyday Life in Early America*

Stephanie Grauman Wolf, *As Various As Their Land: The Everyday Lives of Eighteenth-Century Americans*

Jack Larkin, *The Reshaping of Everyday Life, 1790–1840*

Daniel E. Sutherland, *The Expansion of Everyday Life, 1860–1876*

Thomas J. Schlereth, *Victorian America: Transformations in Everyday Life, 1876–1915*

Harvey Green, *The Uncertainty of Everyday Life, 1915–1945*

These social histories often rely on artifacts. They contain many of the elements of social history that I discussed in chapter one. They are well-researched books by highly respected scholars but are also pleasantly written, making much descriptive information available to you for your family history writing. These books take the form of social history narratives, therefore serving as good examples for how *you* might write.

The Henry Francis du Pont Winterthur Museum published a series of anthologies that tie museum artifacts to everyday life and changing American tastes. If you have an interest in American cultural tastes, or if you own finer and earlier American family artifacts, particularly furniture, art, silver, or ceramics, these books both identify and analyze such artifacts for you. Also, if your ancestor was one of the craftsmen say, creating colonial furniture, carving tombstones, or painting as a folk artist, these books document their working lives. These I have listed alphabetically by author.

Alan Axelrod, ed., *The Colonial Revival in America*

Simon Bronner, ed., *Consuming Visions: Accumulation and Display of Goods in America, 1880–1920*

Catherine E. Hutchins, ed., *Everyday Life in the Early Republic*

Catherine E. Hutchins, ed., *Shaping a National Culture: The Philadelphia Experience, 1750–1800*

Ian M.G. Quimby, ed., *Arts of the Anglo-American Community in the Seventeenth Century*

Ian M.G. Quimby, ed., *Ceramics in America*

Ian M.G. Quimby, ed., *The Craftsman in Early America*

Ian M.G. Quimby, *Material Culture and the Study of American Life*

Ian M.G. Quimby and Polly Anne Earl, eds., *Technological Innovation and the Decorative Arts*

Ian M. G. Quimby and Scott T. Swank, eds., *Perspectives on American Folk Art*

Gerald W. R. Ward, ed., *Perspectives on American Furniture*

Writer's Digest Books also presents a series of everyday life books for various historical periods. The first five American titles, in chronological order of their publication, were

Dale Taylor, *The Writer's Guide to Everyday Life in Colonial America, From 1607–1783*

Marc McCutcheon, *The Writer's Guide to Everyday Life in the 1800s*

Candy Moulton, *The Writer's Guide to Everyday Life in the Wild West, From 1840–1900*

Marc McCutcheon, *The Writer's Guide to Everyday Life From Prohibition Through World War II*

Michael J. Varhola, *Everyday Life During the Civil War: A Guide for Writers, Students and Historians*

Although the authors of this series are not academic historians, they are experts on popular historical interpretation. They rely on artifacts and good historical sources. Taylor's and Moulton's books are divided into social history subtopics. McCutcheon organizes his books in dictionary or encyclopedia style. These books aim to inform writers and would-be writers of historical fiction. The publisher has been surprised to see their popularity extend from writers to genealogists, who obviously crave social history information for family history. Although I recommend cross-checking any historical information from these books in some more traditional scholarly sources, such as those discussed in chapter seven, these are readily accessible guides that may offer detail about your ancestors' lives.

Popular "Good Ol' Days" and "Vanishing Americana" Books

Nostalgia waves have affected publishing trends. Decades ago, numerous books came out commemorating the "good old days" and supporting the collection of Americana. Today there are still more, although they may have a different appearance. All are helpful to family historians and all are heavily oriented toward material culture—"vanishing Americana." In these books, artifacts inspire and illustrate stories. The older books tended to be cheaply produced, with black-and-white woodcuts, sketches, and cartoons. Libraries discard them as too dated, but book dealers price them highly for the value of the illustrations. The newer nostalgia books tend to be glossy, coffee-table affairs with plenty of photographs, some color, and sometimes an outrageous cover. Look for and use both the old and the new. Question the scholarship behind them, checking reliable sources before including a piece of information in your family history. These books may, however, be the handiest guides to the artifacts and customs of the very times and places you seek. They are a legitimate starting place, and perhaps using them will prime you to seek and use more scholarly sources.

Older Books

David L. Cohn, *The Good Old Days: A History of American Morals and Manners As Seen Through the Sears, Roebuck Catalogs, 1905 to the Present*

Eric Sloane, *Eric Sloane's America*

For More Info

Eric Sloane was a particularly fine expert on early Americana who wrote books placing the artifacts and architecture in context. He also drew his own accurate sketches. In *Eric Sloane's America*, for example, he drew, described, and explained the distinctive characteristics of the following, as well as the tools and methods used to create and make use of them.

barns	hammocks
barrels	hex signs
bathtubs	milestones and road signs
canals	mills
carpenter's tools	outbuildings
carriages	roads
churches	sleds and sleighs
covered bridges	taverns
cradles	weather vanes
fences	wooden tools and utensils

Everett B. Wilson offered photographs with explanatory text for artifacts such as the following. You can identify family items by picture and begin to develop a social history context.

bootscraper	foot warmer	stereoscope
carpet beater	hand-crank telephone	tea caddy
coal bin	hand pump	thundermug
corn sheller	lard kettle	umbrella stand
dry sink	shaving stand	washstand

You can use these sources to identify artifacts that you have or recall, to learn what kinds of artifacts your ancestors used, to understand the materials, make, and use of the artifacts, and to obtain illustrations of the artifacts.

Everett B. Wilson, *America's Vanishing Folkways*
Everett B. Wilson, *Early America at Work*
Everett B. Wilson, *Vanishing Americana*

Newer Books

Ronald S. Barlow, *The Vanishing American Barber Shop: An Illustrated History of Tonsorial Art, 1860–1960*

Ronald S. Barlow, *The Vanishing American Outhouse: Privy Plans, Photographs, Poems and Lore*

Susan Jonas and Marilyn Nissenson, *Going Going Gone: Vanishing Americana*

Bettina Miller, ed., *From Flappers to Flivvers—We Helped Make the '20s Roar!*

Deb Mulvey, ed., *We Had Everything but Money: Priceless Memories of the Great Depression*

Derek Nelson, *Moonshiners, Bootleggers, and Rumrunners*

In *Going Going Gone*, items of vanishing Americana include

carbon paper	men's garters
card catalogs	paper dolls
fan magazines	telegrams
girdles	typewriters
handkerchiefs	vinyl records
marbles	white gloves

In this case, consider the possibility that you need to document the artifacts and relevant social history of your own times, as I did earlier with television and on page 45 with Dick and Jane. Use recent nostalgia books to remind yourself of what you might need to write down before it is too late.

Facsimile Mail Order Catalogs

I cannot say enough about how handy reproduction catalogs are for a quick reference. **I use them to identify artifacts and to determine whether a certain invention was available at a particular time.** When I use them in reference to my family, I can even speculate that my ancestors bought the item I am researching from the same catalog in its original form. Some middle Americans, especially out on the farming frontier around the turn of the century, ordered almost everything that they needed from these catalogs. These were the "wish books" that families kept for daydreaming and Christmas shopping.

Montgomery Ward Co. catalog No. 57, 1895
Sears, Roebuck and Co. catalog, 1897
Sears, Roebuck and Co. catalog, 1905
See also David L. Cohn, *The Good Old Days*

Women's Private and Very Private Lives

Women's history and material culture are closely tied. Thus you can find many books that will help you identify the artifacts that women ancestors used, how they used them, and what deeper significance this information might have for how women lived, thought, and were viewed by others. See the case study on page 42.

Women's Work and Home Life

The artifacts of home life and women's work are good examples of items of material culture that have received much attention from historians. Collectors' guides will help you identify an item, but social histories will explain how it was used and what it meant.

STEP 1: You find Grandma's cast-iron pan.

STEP 2: You turn to *300 Years of Kitchen Collectibles* by Linda Campbell Franklin to identify, date, and value the pan.

STEP 3: You turn to a social history, Susan Strasser's *Never Done: A History*

Case Study

It may seem rather startling how far into the area of women's private lives social historians have journeyed. For example, Rachel P. Maines's recent book, *The Technology of Orgasm: "Hysteria," the Vibrator, and Women's Sexual Satisfaction*, might sound obscure, esoteric, or potentially offensive to some. Yet it is an excellent example of how one might discover the history behind a family artifact and its possible use.

Suppose you find an odd, old electrical appliance in a carrying case. It was made by Hamilton Beach, is handheld, and looks a bit like an old-fashioned electric hair dryer. An identical artifact is on the cover of Maines's book, photographed from a collection at the Schenectady Museum. Inside the book are illustrations of similar mechanisms, of how medical doctors applied them, and of catalog advertisements selling them. What you have found is a vibrator. The author explains that doctors recommended these for problems with the back, scalp, and elsewhere. The doctors also recommended them as a self-applied version of what doctors had been providing in their offices for years: massage of women's private parts in order to cure "hysteria." Of course, women privately purchased the devices, often by mail order. They were available in the favorite "wish books"—the Sears Roebuck and Montgomery Ward catalogs.

You may well hesitate to write this artifact into your family history. When I saw an identical vibrator at an antique mall and asked the vendor about it, she was very reticent about the identity and uses of the device herself. Think like a social historian. Social historians such as Maines take a professional stand on discussing any and every part of everyday life in the past. This is the kind of authoritative and objective voice I am recommending to you for writing your own family history as narrative.

Finding a vibrator in its box is not that different from finding the magnetic machine that ancestors used in an attempt to cure rheumatism, gout, headache, paralysis, epilepsy, and all nervous disorders. Perhaps your family stashed dozens of patent medicine bottles from which they had sipped elixirs that were sometimes 35 proof. Perhaps they burned a Cresoline lamp for a sick child, unknowingly exposing him to toxic fumes. In my own childhood, I had croup so often that my parents accumulated several large "steamers" to create a mist and ease my breathing, yet they did not realize that they should stop smoking cigarettes around me. I found the steamers in my parents' closet a few years ago—artifacts of my childhood that tell many stories.

All of these artifacts tell stories that build family history narrative. You may choose not to write about your ancestors' most private possessions, but at least if you wish to research what they are, social historians have written many of the books to help you do so. They have also demonstrated the tone and language that you could use to analyze the artifacts professionally.

of American Housework to learn that "Most cooking pots were designed to fit in the stove holes (Sears advised its customers to 'be sure and buy the same size as your stove')" and that, before convenience metals and steel wool, pans rusted. "The extra minutes required for caring for the pots added to the burdensome housekeeping routine."[3]

Perhaps you are investigating how the family lived in its home and rooms. You know from your own observations or from oral history that they set aside a parlor just for guests. Social history will tell you whether this was common, whether it varied regionally, and why families did it. *Our Own Snug Fireside: Images of the New England Home, 1760–1860* by Jane Nylander; *American Home Life, 1880–1930: A Social History of Spaces and Services*, edited by Jessica H. Foy and Thomas J. Schlereth; and *At Home: The American Family, 1750–1870* by Elisabeth Donaghy Garrett all contain many entries about parlors, their furnishings, and use.

Women's arts and crafts, such as quilts, have been the subject of much attention. If you have quilts in your family, you may not only identify them but, given the right books, you may find there is much social history to write about them. A good example is *Hearts and Hands: The Influences of Women and Quilts on American Society* by Pat Ferraro et al. From this book, you might be able to use the information that, "Far from being a creature of leisure and lace, gauze and crinoline, [the Southern plantation mistress] was often driven, harried and over-worked." Or, you might discover that "Friendship and other precious quilts were taken on the [overland] journey even when space in the heavily packed wagons had to be measured carefully."[4]

Clothing

Perhaps you have some heirloom clothing to identify and weave into the family history. Or you wish to know what styles were like for people such as your ancestors at a certain time, place, and economic status. **There are books to help you identify, describe, and analyze historical clothing.** Older classics, such as Elisabeth McClellan's *Historic Dress in America, 1607–1870* and Alice Morse Earle's *Two Centuries of Costume in America, 1620–1820* detail the clothing variations all over the country. Modern works, such as Ruth P. Rubenstein's *Dress Codes: Meanings and Messages in American Culture*, can reveal whether certain styles represented self-restraint, authority, vulnerability, or rebellion. Our standards of what is attractive change so much over time that you may well find that your ancestor, who looked tubby or disheveled to you in old photographs, was stylish for his or her day. There are also books specific to the clothing of one region, group, or line of work, such as Tom Lindmier and Steve Mount's *I See By Your Outfit: Historic Cowboy Gear of the Northern Plains*.

Sources

Child's Play

It is often difficult, especially without oral history or personal recollection, to reconstruct an ancestor's childhood for a family history narrative. **One way to do it is to use childhood artifacts as the basis for social history research and**

Tip

descriptive writing. Let us say that you have Grandpa's childhood building blocks, or even that you know from a reliable source that he played with wooden building blocks. *A Century of Childhood, 1820–1920* by Mary Lynn Stevens Heininger et al., will tell you why adults encouraged boys to play with blocks. You may discover that Grandma had a "Campbell's Kid" doll based on the characters who advertised the canned soup. You figure that this just means that Grandma's family ate lots of Campbell's Soup. Miriam Formanek-Brunell's book, *Made to Play House: Dolls and the Commercialization of American Girlhood, 1830–1930,* will tell you it meant more. You will see pictures of the dolls, advertisements, and analysis of what these dolls symbolized about American culture and its views of childraising.

Another childhood artifact is children's *literature*. Knowing what a person read as a child or youth can reveal much worth writing about them. When you know an ancestor read a particular book or magazine, you can read the book yourself. You may approach the material from a different standpoint, but you will still learn more about your ancestor's background. You can investigate books of literary criticism or biographies of the authors to grasp the popularity of that writer or story and thus, perhaps, why your ancestor read the material. Again, your ancestor was not unique. Many everyday life and social history books discuss what adults and children were reading. Sometimes, what a child read directed his life. Imagine, for instance, how many men and women who later entered careers in air and space flight took their first inspiration from H.G. Wells, Jules Verne, or from stories of the Wright Brothers, Charles Lindbergh, or Amelia Earhart. If you make such a discovery or hypothesis, you have something more to write into your interesting family narrative—something that can give it a theme. **Remember that I always recommend that you do not fictionalize. If you believe a connection is there but you can't prove it, you may still write about it speculatively in a "thinking out loud" manner, as long as readers know what you are doing.**

Important

Military Americana

There are many collectors of military memorabilia and, so, many guidebooks. The Civil War in particular occasions so much interest that every uniform button is well documented and priced. Some books are more helpful than others with artifacts and for helping to build context for family history writing. The large-format, colorfully pictorial volumes by William C. Davis are excellent for identifying the material culture of your Civil War ancestor:

Sources

Rebels and Yankees: The Battlefields of the Civil War
Rebels and Yankees: The Commanders of the Civil War
Rebels and Yankees: The Fighting Men of the Civil War

Each volume is filled with impressive and detailed illustrations of the uniforms and all of the paraphernalia that a typical soldier or officer would have and use. This includes uniforms illustrated for many specific units and photographs of currency, belt buckles, buttons, hat brasses, badges, weapons, ammunition, flags, games, books and letters, prison chains, medical instruments, and medals. Each site where your ancestor might have served, whether a battlefield, on board a

Case Study

In school, I read the Dick and Jane books for several years. I can remember that I even had a vague notion that all schoolbooks written anywhere, ever, were about Dick, Jane, and their dog, Spot. I know that reading about Dick and Jane was one long, cultural lesson for me, but as with many childhood experiences, I cannot recall many specifics. Social history came to the rescue again. I found the book *Growing Up With Dick and Jane: Learning and Living the American Dream* by Carole Kismaric and Marvin Heiferman. Bob Keeshan (Captain Kangaroo) wrote the preface—could this book be more appropriate to *my* social history context?

At the time I was reading them, Dick and Jane books taught us how to define a perfect American family (just as my favorite television shows did). Two mainstays of little Jane's life that I always wanted were a big brother and a dog. Just glancing through the book's illustrations reminds me of other features of my early childhood that are artifacts and could provide social history context: air raid drills, Mr. Potato Head, Silly Putty, plaid dresses with full skirts, comic books, watching nationally televised events on a television brought into the classroom (the World Series, John Glenn's earth orbit, and the John Kennedy assassination for me). My parents gave me the dog but it was too late to have a big brother. I have often said I finally found one and married him. Someday I will have to analyze Dick of the Dick and Jane books to see if his qualities were those I sought and got in a husband!

ship, in a trench, or in a prison, is well mapped, charted, and even illustrated in three-dimensional cross section to give you a better picture of exactly what the experience would have been like. Even if you do not have your military ancestor's artifacts, you can discover what was typical for men like him to wear, carry, or use, and you can describe these things in your narrative family history.

Land Use, Vernacular Architecture, Folk Architecture, and Building Ways

Historians, geographers, anthropologists, and folklorists often treat architecture and even patterns of land use—the "built environment"—as artifacts. Specialists writing about this can be very helpful for family historians. *Vernacular architecture* **means local architecture, designed and constructed by locals with local materials.** From a book about vernacular architecture you can discover what buildings were typical, why, what they looked like, and what it was like to live in them. Vernacular architecture usually evokes a distinctive, recognizable local style and flavor. It changes over time, primarily from the influences of culture and social history.[5] *Folk architecture* **more specifically refers to the traditional, original building methods of a culture that largely passes on its construction and design knowledge through oral tradition and imitation.** David Hackett Fischer, whose book *Albion's Seed* seems to be the most heavily cited social/cultural history in the presentations of professional genealogists, prefers the term *building ways* to describe a culture's determination of a group's architectural patterns. **As you research and**

\di'fin\ *vb*

Definitions

Tip

write about your ancestors, use their vernacular architecture, folk architecture, or their cultural building ways as a theme to help you describe the *setting* in which your ancestors lived.

Most Americans with long American heritage have farmers in their backgrounds. This may seem ordinary, uneventful, and thus uninteresting for family history research and writing. However, books on rural life can help you construct a picture of that pastoral lifestyle that is fascinating. For rural architecture, you might use historian Sally McMurry's *Families and Farmhouses in 19th Century America* to help you understand and describe why your ancestors designed their room arrangements in their farmhouses the way they did and how and why they changed those arrangements over time. Perhaps you would turn to *Back of the Big House: The Architecture of Plantation Slavery* by John Michael Vlach to figure out and write about your ancestors' lives in the plantation slave quarters, outbuildings, and yard.

Historical and cultural geographer Terry Jordan has published material culture studies of our ancestors' interactions with architecture and landscape, specializing in the backwoods, western frontiers and Texas, and particularly in log buildings. Even barns, windmills, fences, and corncribs have received book-length cultural analysis. My great-grandfather built a sod house in Kansas where the family lived for several years. Thus a book such as *True Sod* by Barbara Oringderff appealed to me for its photographs and descriptions of sod-house building and living in Kansas. With its help I can augment the family sources that I have for narrative writing.

House Histories and Architectural History

Printed Source

Some professional genealogists have ventured into researching and writing house histories for clients. In *House Histories: A Guide to Tracing the Genealogy of Your Home* (note the G-word in the title) Sally Light uses many of the same sources that both genealogists and historians would use to compile the history of a house. Public historians have also done this kind of research, usually in order to help a historic property qualify for the National Register of Historic Places. The forms and standards used by the National Trust for Historic Preservation require information similar to that on our Artifact Identification, Analysis, and Cataloging Form on page 37 and in the appendix. Try using the same form and asking the same questions about a house that is important to your family history—particularly one that originated with an earlier generation such as the old homestead or the original cabin. The National Trust expects documentation to prove ownership history, architectural changes, historical value, and the like—not that different from what genealogy expects of us.

Analyze the interiors of the houses in your family history as well. Even if they no longer exist, piece together their histories with photographs, oral history, research into similar architecture, and personal recollection. Emily Croom, in *Unpuzzling Your Past: A Basic Guide to Genealogy*, recommends sketching the floorplan of any of the family homes you are researching.[6] Take these to other relatives, both to spark recollection and to more accurately fill in the sketch.

It will fascinate family members to recall room arrangements, furnishings, and lifestyles of grandparents, great-grandparents, aunts, and uncles. Then you have created a useful document and artifact. **Again, treating a house as an artifact pushes you to examine it and all its parts in order to extract information for family history.**

If it seems as though you have no clues to the kinds of houses in which your family lived, consider general research into architectural history for that time and place. If the family lived in colonial Massachusetts or Delaware, in early French Louisiana, or in a Gothic Revival gingerbread house, you can find books that describe the likely architecture for that time and place. (See this chapter's bibliography on pages 51–55 for books by McAlester, Morrison, and Roth, for example.) Also consider researching architectural histories when you write about your ancestors' activities in and around other buildings: churches, schools, libraries, workplaces, entertainment spots, and government buildings. If these were influential in your ancestors' lives, then describing them and how their architecture represented their times might be appropriate in your family history narrative. For example, there are several good histories of early colonial taverns, such as the older ones by Edward Field and Elise Lathrop (see pages 52 and 53). Perhaps your ancestor left a record of attending a tavern. These books will describe that general experience for you.

Cemeteries and Funeral Practices

Remember that tombstones are artifacts, too, even though most of us would not literally make them home sources. Genealogist Sharon DeBartolo Carmack recommends ways to "bring a tombstone home legally": photograph tombstone inscriptions or make rubbings or plaster casts of them. Any of these would be artifact replicas of an artifact. Carmack's practical advice on this topic is available in *The Genealogy Sourcebook*. The National Trust for Historic Preservation now discourages gravestone rubbings, but there is plentiful advice for photographing inscriptions successfully.

Now, think like a historian! Apply analytical methods to tombstones just as you would to any artifact. Consider the cemetery itself as an artifact in the same sense that vernacular architecture and land use are artifacts. In a small town or rural area, on family property, or even in an urban or public cemetery where the cemetery is divided into group plots, the whole site is important to your family history. Most genealogical authors describe the value of meticulously examining tombstones, their neighbors, and their surroundings for either more genealogical information or as a general principle. Family historians could also look for the social history context surrounding death and burial that will yield more material for a narrative.

Take notes or talk into a microphone as you step gently through a family cemetery. Oh, you think someone might wonder about you if they hear you talking to yourself in a cemetery? It is better that you take along a companion anyway. As a historian, one should record the appearance and layout of the cemetery. What do the groupings of headstones tell you about ethnicity, membership in organizations, economic status, and who was related to whom? Do the

For good advice on visiting cemeteries and photographing tombstones, see Sharon Carmack's *The Genealogy Sourcebook* (pages 102–108), Loretto Szucs and Sandra Luebking's *The Source: A Guidebook of American Genealogy* (pages 80–82), Christine Rose and Kay Ingalls's *The Complete Idiot's Guide to Genealogy* (pages 166–174) and Val Greenwood's *The Researcher's Guide to American Genealogy*, 3rd ed. (pages 611–621). The American Association for State and Local History has two excellent technical leaflets: "Photographing Tombstones: Equipment and Techniques" by Mary-Ellen Jones and "Cemetery Transcribing: Preparations and Procedures" by John J. Newman.

Case Study

I must confess that I had never visited a cemetery before. What a deprived existence! My immediate family preferred memorial services to funerals and cremation to burial. So, when my husband first took me back to his hometown, I did not realize that we would visit the cemeteries.

Perhaps no one could be more sentimental about someone else's family history than I was about Rick's. After all, we were both history graduate students and our families' historians, so how else should he woo me than with family history? Rick had told me much of the oral tradition of the Sturdevants. I knew about old Ira, the 1812 veteran and patriarch. I knew his son, John George Lafayette, was a Civil War veteran who met his wife Sarah at a picnic. I knew that Sarah had deeply mourned the loss of two of her small children, little Johnny and Sarah, to epidemic disease. I especially knew Frank, Rick's grandfather, who had been the family historian before Rick and who had served in World War I.

We climbed a grassy slope and all of a sudden, there they were—all of them, dead! As I read the inscriptions and thought of each character whom Rick had brought to life for me, I began to mourn their loss. It was as if I had not realized they were all dead. There was the oldest stone, teetering, for Ira. There were the two little children under one combined headstone with two arches. There was Frank with his veteran's marker. I sobbed as though their deaths were recent because, to me, they were.

family graves offer clues to the stability of the family in this one place? Record this information on a form like the one on page 49.

Feel comfortable to experience the cemetery as you were meant to do. Mourn the dead, respect their resting places, and read their life clues. Their graves, their artifacts, and their descendants are what is left of them. This is the material you want to bring back to life in your family history. Doing family history is living a story while researching and writing that story.

Look beyond the dates and names. Examine and record the nature and materials of the epitaphs and the tombstone art that your ancestors chose. Are there quotations or sentimental adjectives that speak of the individual? Even where these are suppressed by military regimentation, feel what it means to see row upon row of soldiers' graves at a military or battlefield cemetery. In Appalachia, are there evergreen trees around the small, family plot to symbolize eternal life? In the Dakotas, are there the iron crosses and hearts on stake markers that the Germans and Czechs so liked? Do you see carved tree stumps as tombstones? In Indiana these represented an artistic trend, while elsewhere they often represented membership in the Modern Woodmen, a fraternal organization that sold burial plots. Do the death dates of neighbors—especially children—fall close together, bespeaking an epidemic? Were there distinctions of class and rank for burials or did a disaster cause folks to ignore them? Are people with different surnames probably related to your family because they were buried side-by-side? Clues abound for family history.

Reminder

CEMETERY ANALYSIS FORM FOR FAMILY HISTORY

Name of Cemetery _Pumpkin Center Cemetery_

Date Cemetery Opened _October 31, 1913_

Date of Visit _October 31, 1999_

Location (Quarter Section, Town or Township, Nearest Roads, County, State)

From the town of Pumpkin Center take Highway 50 west, turn right at County Road 7, go about 2 miles.

Cemetery is on left across from All Saints' Church.

Family Graves Sought _Mehitable Hobson_

Family Graves Found _yes_

Transcribe Tombstone Inscriptions Exactly on Separate Sheet _____

Location of Tombstone in Cemetery (Section, Lot, and Block Numbers) _section 4, lot 2, block 3_

Material, Construction, Design of Tombstone _red granite_

Relevant Nearby Graves _Hortense Hobson, Dorcas Hobson_

Relevant Nearby Foliage or Decoration _Weeping willow behind all three graves_

Clues in Nearby Graves to Common Cause of Deaths _Common death dates 1919 for these three women and_

numerous other citizens, especially children and older people

Unmarked Vacancies Nearby That May Have Been Graves _none_

Surnames of Cemetery Neighbors Who May Be Relevant _Laughton, Mills, Lancaster_

Other Historical Clues (Fraternal Symbols, Metal Markers) _On all three headstones appears the star emblem_

of the Order of the Eastern Star

Condition of Tombstone _good_

Condition of Grounds _grass trimmed, plastic flowers on graves_

Photograph Taken? _yes_   Rubbing or Cast Taken? _no_

CEMETERY ANALYSIS FORM FOR FAMILY HISTORY

Name of Cemetery

Date Cemetery Opened

Date of Visit

Location (Quarter Section, Town or Township, Nearest Roads, County, State)

Family Graves Sought

Family Graves Found

Transcribe Tombstone Inscriptions Exactly on Separate Sheet

Location of Tombstone in Cemetery (Section, Lot and Block Numbers)

Material, Construction, Design of Tombstone

Relevant Nearby Graves

Relevant Nearby Foliage or Decoration

Clues in Nearby Graves to Common Cause of Deaths

Unmarked Vacancies Nearby That May Have Been Graves

Surnames of Cemetery Neighbors Who May Be Relevant

Other Historical Clues (Funereal Symbols, Metal Markers)

Condition of Tombstone

Condition of Grounds

Photograph Taken? _____ Rubbing or Cast Taken?

**A USEFUL FORM
YOU CAN REPRODUCE**

For a full-size blank copy of the Cemetery Analysis Form for Family History, see page 233. You are free to photocopy this form for personal use.

Important

Consider what historians can offer for deeper, narrative explanations of what you see in the cemetery. For example, in *The Sacred Remains: American Attitudes Toward Death, 1799–1883*, Gary Laderman analyzes the general impact of death and reactions to it. In your ancestors' day, "death was an integrated element of everyday life."[7] What Laderman calls the "signs of death" were everywhere, many of them artifacts: church bells, mourning dress, jewelry, decor, funeral processions, language and vocabulary in anything printed, and local graveyards. What survives in the cemetery is the stony artifacts at the end of a long series of artifacts used to lay out and pay tribute to the dead. Imagine what the burial was like. Did family members weep and cast handfuls of dirt into the grave as a farewell? Perhaps a source such as a newspaper obituary will offer clues.

Ethnic and Regional Americana

Artifacts can give you themes within themes when they represent the special character of an ethnic group or a region. Your artifact could help you determine ethnicity or regional character when you did not already know these things. Knowing that the artifact represents something about the family's ethnic group or region means that you can research and write about all of those elements, building themes in the family history. Social history resources can interpret those elements into interesting narrative information. For example, you find that stone walls are present around your family's ancestral home in upstate New York. Susan Allport's *Sermons in Stone: The Stone Walls of New England and New York* could help you determine when they were built, how, and by what sort of person. Knowing when could make the difference as to whether your wall builders were Yankee, Irish, or Italian. Say you had ancestors in western mining towns. *The Mining Camps Speak* by Beth and Bill Sagstetter describes and illustrates mining structures, equipment, town buildings, the labor itself, and daily life through artifacts and architecture. It can identify your heirlooms and also clue you into the special lifestyles of mining families.

If you have Native American ancestry, you probably are finding that to say so is almost as vague as it would be for someone with Irish ancestors to say their ancestors were European. You will need to learn the names of specific tribes, cultures, and bands. If you have artifacts or simply wish to know what kind of material culture your ancestors had, there are books—mostly anthropological—to help. Another book by the publisher of William C. Davis's Civil War guides, *The Native Americans: The Indigenous People of North America* by Colin Taylor and William Sturtevant, offers vivid photographs of artifacts from many tribes. The most authoritative and detailed series, which is very artifact oriented, is *The Handbook of North American Indians*, edited by William C. Sturtevant. Its twenty heavy volumes are divided by region and theme. Each volume pictures artifacts and provides both analysis and extreme detail about each group. **Remember that artifacts can be sacred within cultures.** Indian people have been subject to so much investigation and artifact collection by outsiders that, ultimately, the most authentic answers about your heritage and its artifacts may come through respectfully contacting Indian people themselves.

Often the interpreters of vernacular architecture explain it in terms of the particular ethnic group(s) that lived in that spot and introduced those styles. With a book such as *To Build in a New Land: Ethnic Landscapes in North America*, edited by geographer Allen G. Noble, you can learn about Native Americans, English, Scotch-Irish, Germans, Creoles, African Americans, Cajuns, Belgians, Danes, Norwegians, Finns, German-Russians, Czechs, Basques, and the Spanish-speaking peoples of the American Southwest. You will find what building ways and agricultural practices immigrants brought to their new world, how certain groups changed in response to others, and how they used architecture, land, and artifacts to put their particular stamp on their territory.

CHAPTER BIBLIOGRAPHY

1. Allport, Susan. *Sermons in Stone: The Stone Walls of New England and New York*. New York: W.W. Norton and Co., 1990.

2. Axelrod, Alan, ed. *The Colonial Revival in America*. Winterthur, Del.: Henry Francis du Pont Winterthur Museum, 1985.

3. Baker, T. Lindsay. *A Field Guide to American Windmills*. Norman: University of Oklahoma Press, 1985.

4. Barlow, Ronald S. *The Vanishing American Barber Shop: An Illustrated History of Tonsorial Art, 1860-1960*. El Cajon, Calif.: Windmill Publishing Co., 1993.

5. ———. *The Vanishing American Outhouse: Privy Plans, Photographs, Poems and Lore*. El Cajon, Calif.: Windmill Publishing Co., 1992.

6. Blumenson, John J. G. *Identifying American Architecture*. Nashville: American Association for State and Local History, 1977.

7. Bronner, Simon, ed. *Consuming Visions: Accumulation and Display of Goods in America, 1880–1920*. New York: W.W. Norton, 1989.

8. Cohn, David L. *The Good Old Days: A History of American Morals and Manners as Seen Through the Sears, Roebuck Catalogs 1905 to the Present*. New York: Simon and Schuster, 1940. New York: Arno Press, 1976.

9. Crown Publishers. *1902 Edition of the Sears, Roebuck Catalogue*. Facsimile printing. New York: Crown Publishers, 1969. New York: Bounty Books, 1986.

10. Davis, William C. *The American Frontier: Pioneers, Settlers and Cowboys, 1800–1899*. New York: Smithmark Books, 1992.

11. ———. *Rebels and Yankees: The Battlefields of the Civil War*. New York: Smithmark Books, 1991.

12. ———. *Rebels and Yankees: The Commanders of the Civil War*. London: Salamander Books Ltd., 1990.

13. ———. *Rebels and Yankees: The Fighting Men of the Civil War*. London: Salamander Books, Ltd., 1989.

14. Deetz, James. *In Small Things Forgotten: The Archeology of Early American Life*. Garden City, N.Y.: Anchor Books, 1977.

15. Dover Publications. *Montgomery Ward and Co. Catalogue and Buyers' Guide, No. 57 Spring and Summer 1895*. New York: Dover Publications, 1969.

16. Earle, Alice Morse. *Two Centuries of Costume in America, 1620–1820*. 2 vols. New York: Dover Publications, 1903, 1970.

17. Ferraro, Pat, et al. *Hearts and Hands: The Influences of Women and Quilts on American Society.* San Francisco: Quilt Digest Press, 1987.

18. Field, Edward. *The Colonial Tavern: A Glimpse of New England Town Life in the Seventeenth and Eighteenth Centuries.* Facsimile reprint. Bowie, Md.: Heritage Books, 1897, 1989.

19. Fischer, Roger A. *Tippecanoe and Trinkets Too: The Material Culture of American Presidential Campaigns, 1828–1984.* Urbana: University of Illinois Press, 1988.

20. Fleming, E. McClung, "Artifact Study: A Proposed Model" *Winterthur Portfolio 9* (1974): 153–173.

21. Formanek-Brunell, Miriam. *Made to Play House: Dolls and the Commercialization of American Girlhood, 1830–1930.* New Haven: Yale University Press, 1993.

22. Foy, Jessica H., and Thomas J. Schlereth, eds. *American Home Life, 1880-1930: A Social History of Spaces and Services.* Knoxville: University of Tennessee Press, 1992.

23. Franklin, Linda Campbell. *300 Years of Kitchen Collectibles.* Florence, Ala.: Books Americana, 1984.

24. Garrett, Elisabeth Donaghy. *At Home: The American Family, 1750–1870.* New York: Harry N. Abrams Inc., Publishers, 1990.

25. Green, Harvey. *The Light of the Home: An Intimate View of the Lives of Women in Victorian America.* New York: Pantheon Books, 1983.

26. Heininger, Mary Lynn, et al. *A Century of Childhood, 1820–1920.* Rochester, N.Y.: Margaret Woodbury Strong Museum, 1984.

27. Horridge, Patricia, et al. *Dating Costumes: A Checklist Method.* Nashville: American Association For State and Local History, 1977.

28. Howard, Hugh. *How Old Is This House? A Skeleton Key to Dating and Identifying Three Centuries of American Houses.* New York: Farrar, Straus, and Giroux, 1989.

29. Hubka, Thomas C. *Big House, Little House, Back House, Barn: The Connected Farm Buildings of New England.* Hanover, N.H.: University Press of New England, 1984.

30. Hume, Ivor Noël. *A Guide to Artifacts of Colonial America.* New York: Vintage Books, 1969, 1991.

31. Hutchins, Catherine E. *Everyday Life in the Early Republic.* Winterthur, Del.: Henry Francis du Pont Winterthur Museum, 1994.

32. ———, ed. *Shaping a National Culture: The Philadelphia Experience, 1750–1800.* Winterthur, Del.: Henry Francis du Pont Winterthur Museum, 1994.

33. Israel, Fred L. *1897 Sears, Roebuck Catalogue.* Facsimile Printing. New York: Chelsea House Publishers, 1968.

34. Jonas, Susan and Marilyn Nissenson. *Going Going Gone: Vanishing Americana.* San Francisco: Chronicle Books, 1994.

35. Jones, Mary-Ellen. "Photographing Tombstones: Equipment and Techniques." Technical leaflet no. 92. Nashville: American Association for State and Local History, 1977.

36. Jordan, Terry G. *American Log Buildings: An Old World Heritage*. Chapel Hill: University of North Carolina Press, 1985.

37. Jordan, Terry G., and Matti Kaups. *The American Backwoods Frontier: An Ethnic and Ecological Interpretation*. Baltimore: Johns Hopkins University Press, 1989.

38. Jordan, Terry G., et al. *The Mountain West: Interpreting the Folk Landscape*. Baltimore: Johns Hopkins University Press, 1997.

39. Kismaric, Carole and Marvin Heiferman. *Growing Up With Dick and Jane: Learning and Living the American Dream*. San Francisco: Collins Publishers, 1996.

40. Laderman, Gary. *The Sacred Remains: American Attitudes Toward Death, 1799–1883*. New Haven: Yale University Press, 1996.

41. Langdon, William Chauncy. *Everyday Things in American Life, 1607–1776*. New York: Charles Scribner's Sons, 1937.

42. Lathrop, Elise. *Early American Inns and Taverns*. New York: Arno Press, 1926, 1977.

43. Light, Sally. *House Histories: A Guide to Tracing the Genealogy of Your Home*. Spencertown, N.Y.: Golden Hill Press, Inc., 1989, 1995.

44. Lindmier, Tom, and Steve Mount. *I See By Your Outfit: Historic Cowboy Gear of the Northern Plains*. Glendo, Wyo.: High Plains Press, 1996.

45. Maines, Rachel P. *The Technology of Orgasm: "Hysteria," the Vibrator, and Women's Sexual Satisfaction*. Baltimore: Johns Hopkins University Press, 1999.

46. McAlester, Virginia, and Lee McAlester. *A Field Guide to American Houses*. New York: Alfred A. Knopf, 1993.

47. McClellan, Elisabeth. *Historic Dress in America, 1607–1870*. New York: Arno Press, 1904–1910, 1969.

48. McCutcheon, Marc. *The Writer's Guide to Everyday Life From Prohibition Through World War II*. Cincinnati: Writer's Digest Books, 1995.

49. ———. *The Writer's Guide to Everyday Life in the 1800s*, Cincinnati: Writer's Digest Books, 1993.

50. McMurry, Sally. *Families and Farmhouses in Nineteenth-Century America: Vernacular Design and Social Change*. New York: Oxford University Press, 1988.

51. Miller, Bettina, ed. *From Flappers to Flivvers—We Helped Make the '20s Roar!* Greendale, Wis.: Reminisce Books, 1995.

52. Miller, Gary and K. M. Scotty Mitchell. *Price Guide to Collectible Kitchen Appliances, From Aerators to Waffle Irons, 1900–1950*. Radnor, Pa.: Wallace-Homestead Book Company, 1991.

53. Morrison, Hugh. *Early American Architecture: From the First Colonial Settlements to the National Period*. New York: Dover Publications, Inc., 1952, 1987.

54. Moulton, Candy. *The Writer's Guide to Everyday Life in the Wild West, From 1840–1900*. Cincinnati: Writer's Digest Books, 1999.

55. Mulvey, Deb, ed. *We Had Everything but Money: Priceless Memories of the Great Depression*. New York: Crescent Books, 1992, 1995.

56. Nelson, Derek. *Moonshiners, Bootleggers, and Rumrunners.* Osceola, Wis.: Motorbooks International, 1995.

57. Newman, John J., "Cemetery Transcribing: Preparations and Procedures." Technical leaflet no. 9. Nashville: American Association for State and Local History, 1971.

58. Noble, Allen G. *Wood, Brick, and Stone: The North American Settlement Landscape, Volume 2: Barns and Farm Structures.* Amherst: University of Massachusetts Press, 1995.

59. ———., ed. *To Build in a New Land: Ethnic Landscapes in North America.* Baltimore: Johns Hopkins University Press, 1992.

60. Nylander, Jane. *Our Own Snug Fireside: Images of the New England Home, 1760–1860.* New York: Alfred A. Knopf, 1993.

61. Oringderff, Barbara. *True Sod: Sod Houses of Kansas.* North Newton, Kans.: Mennonite Press, Inc., 1976.

62. Petroski, Henry. *The Evolution of Useful Things: How Everyday Artifacts—From Forks and Pins to Paper Clips and Zippers—Came to Be as They Are.* New York: Alfred A. Knopf, 1992.

63. Quimby, Ian M. G., *Arts of the Anglo-American Community in the Seventeenth Century.* Charlottesville: University Press of Virginia, 1975.

64. ———. *Ceramics in America.* Charlottesville: University Press of Virginia, 1973.

65. ———. *Material Culture and the Study of American Life.* New York: W.W. Norton and Co., 1978.

66. ———, ed. *The Craftsman in Early America.* Winterthur, Del.: Henry Francis du Pont Winterthur Museum, 1984.

67. Quimby, Ian M.G., and Polly Anne Earls, eds. *Technological Innovation and the Decorative Arts.* Charlottesville: University Press of Virginia, 1974.

68. Quimby, Ian M.G., and Scott T. Swank, eds. *Perspectives on American Folk Art.* New York: W.W. Norton, 1980.

69. Roe, Keith E. *Corncribs: In History, Folklife, and Architecture.* Ames: Iowa State University Press, 1988.

70. Roth, Leland M. *A Concise History of American Architecture.* Boulder: Westview Press, 1989, 1990.

71. Rubinstein, Ruth P. *Dress Codes: Meanings and Messages in American Culture.* Boulder: Westview Press, 1995.

72. Sagstetter, Beth, and Bill Sagstetter. *The Mining Camps Speak: A New Way to Explore the Ghost Towns of the American West.* Denver: BenchMark Publishing of Colorado, 1998.

73. Schlereth, Thomas. *Artifacts and the American Past.* Walnut Creek, Calif.: Alta Mira Press, 1996.

74. Schroeder, Fred. "Designing Your Exhibits: Seven Ways to Look at an Artifact." Technical leaflet no. 91. Nashville: American Association for State and Local History, 1976.

75. Sloane, Eric. *Eric Sloane's America.* New York: Promontory Press, 1954, 1955, 1956.

76. Soike, Lowell. *Without Right Angles: The Round Barns of Iowa*. Des Moines: Iowa State Historical Department, 1983.

77. Strasser, Susan. *Never Done: A History of American Housework*. New York: Pantheon Books, 1982.

78. Sturtevant, William C., ed. *The Handbook of the North American Indian*. 20 vols. Washington, D.C.: Smithsonian Institution, 1970s–present.

79. Taylor, Colin F., and William Sturtevant. *The Native Americans: The Indigenous People of North America*. New York: Smithmark Books, 1991, 1992.

80. Taylor, Dale. *The Writer's Guide to Everyday Life in Colonial America From 1607–1783*. Cincinnati: Writer's Digest Books, 1997.

81. Varhola, Michael J. *Everyday Life During the Civil War: A Guide for Writers, Students and Historians*. Cincinnati: Writer's Digest Books, 1999.

82. Vlach, John Michael. *Back of the Big House: The Architecture of Plantation Slavery*. Chapel Hill: University of North Carolina Press, 1993.

83. Ward, Gerald W.R., ed. *Perspectives on American Furniture*. New York: W.W. Norton, 1989.

84. Wilson, Everett B. *America's Vanishing Folkways*. New York: A.S. Barnes and Co., 1965.

85. ———. *Early America at Work: A Pictorial Guide to Our Vanishing Occupations*. New York: A.S. Barnes and Co., 1963.

86. ———. *Vanishing Americana*. New York: A.S. Barnes and Co., 1961.

THREE

Artifacts II: Culture, Citing, and Caring

"If you want expert advice, the best place to get it is from an expert."

—Ralph and Terry Kovel[1]

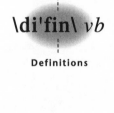

\di'fin\ *vb*

Definitions

Notes

Endnotes for this chapter begin on page 220.

\di'fin\ *vb*

Definitions

MATERIAL FOLK CULTURE: HOW FOLKLORISTS HELP US ANALYZE ARTIFACTS

Folklorists and historians who specialize in the study of material culture identify two fundamentally different categories of artifacts: popular material culture and material folk culture. Knowing the difference, and especially knowing how to define *folk* will clarify your artifacts for you and open research doors.

Material folk culture consists of the handmade artifacts that reflect traditional ways of life. The skills to make these artifacts pass from person to person in a local community rather than through mass media or formal (academic) instruction. The folk crafter has learned how to make the artifact through oral tradition and imitation, and the artifact represents the shared values of the crafter's group. Although we sometimes see faddish interest in folk items develop, the items are *traditionally* made and sold or traded at a local level, usually within the group. Many folk items were made by individuals for their own use and not necessarily sold at all. Folk items are one of a kind. In modern America, when a mass market develops for original and old folk art, each piece may achieve an extraordinarily high price because it is *folk*, as in the case of old quilts or Navajo rugs. Designs may change over time in folk culture, even because of inspiration from popular culture, but the basic form and construction of the item remains folk, or traditional.[2]

Popular material culture is, on the other hand, the artifacts of mass popularity, mass production, and mass advertising. The TV dinner, Elvis Presley memorabilia, Barbie Dolls, and Beanie Baby stuffed animals are items of popular material culture. Popular culture tends to dominate and overcome folk culture to varying degrees, as even the traditional crafter realizes that it is quicker and easier for him to buy the popular item than to make his own. Popular culture catches on and fads develop through mass communication. In modern America, when masses nostalgically want folk designs but cannot afford one-of-a-kind, genuine folk art, they create a market for mass-produced imitation folk artifacts or crafts modeled on mass-distributed imitation folk designs.

FOLK CULTURE IN YOUR FAMILY HISTORY

There are many sources to help you interpret the material folk culture in your family history. Folklorists identify five categories of material folk artifacts: folk architecture, folk art, folk crafts, folk foodways, and folk costume. Together, these make up folk life.[3] Generally, the difference between folk art and folk craft is that the folk artist clearly intended an aesthetic function for the art—the crafter's primary purpose, however, was utilitarian. Many artifacts cross this line. It is important that you understand what the sources are saying, and perhaps how to speak the language yourself, in order to find and use the information.

Perhaps the single most available effort at having amateurs collect folklife has been the *Foxfire* **series.** B. Eliot Wigginton established a program at Rabun County High School in Georgia in which his students used oral history and other collecting techniques to gather folklore from Appalachian practitioners. *Foxfire Magazine*, the ten paperback volumes of *Foxfire*, and other related books are treasure troves of material folk culture. Although these are compilations by high school students rather than professionals, they are readily available and respected in the historical community. If your family ever lived in Appalachia and its surrounds, or if you need to know the pre-industrial method of making something in backwoods America, these books may provide not only the information you need but the lore surrounding it. *Foxfire* books frequently offer photographs and instructions for making folk articles along with oral history from the makers. You will find instructions for

Printed Source

banjo making	fiddle making	shoe making
berry bucket making	flintlock making	snake cane making
blacksmithing	gourd art	toy making
butter churn making	iron making	wagon making
chair making	log cagin building	whirligig making
cloth weaving	pottery making	wooden lock making
dulcimer making	quilting	yarn spinning

Here is a small example of how you could use information from a *Foxfire* book.

Grandpa fashioned rustic chairs of the ivy wood that he found in the woods. Knowing him, he might have agreed with a chairmaker in those parts today who said "I don't try to make two that match . . . I just make 'em however they turn out."

Clyde Runion quoted in George P. Reynolds, et al., eds., *Foxfire 10* (New York: Anchor Books, 1993), 408.

Case Study

Lesser known and harder to come by is the Maine version of *Foxfire***, called** *Salt***.** Kennebunk High School in southern Maine produced *Salt Magazine* and a book *Salt* modeled on Wigginton's efforts and edited by teacher Pamela Wood. *Salt* did for New England what *Foxfire* did for the Appalachians. The book

Printed Source

includes artifacts such as lobster traps, stone walls, maple syrup, snowshoes, lighthouses, and flintlocks. The magazines included articles on

apple squeezing	lighthouse keeping
barn raising	lobstering
bee keeping	logging and papermaking
blueberry and cranberry harvesting	making ships in bottles
butter churning	maple sugaring
chair caning	model shipmaking
charcoal making	potato barrelmaking
clam digging	pottery making
commercial fishing	rum running
designing with shells	sail making
dowsing	sheep shearing
duck hunting	ship building
fly fishing	snowshoe making
fur trapping	soap making
horse pulling	stone wall building
ice fishing	wooden whistle making
Indian basketmaking	Yankee gadget making

As in the case of *Foxfire,* these articles always described the technology that went with the artifact and included plenty of folklore, vocabulary, and personality.[4] Note how much just a list of skills reveals the environmental differences that created regional character! This is what makes the folklore and artifacts of our ancestors' lives very worthy of description in our family histories.

If you have original, one-of-a-kind, antique material folk culture pieces in your family, you may want to consult museum specialists for identification and care instructions. Do not be surprised if they suggest donation. You can hold your artifacts in your family as long as you want, but if you fear for their survival there, donation might be the best you can do in your ancestors' memory. When you write about these artifacts in your family history, sources such as *Foxfire* and *Salt* can help you build story, description, and social history context around the artifact.

POP CULTURE IN YOUR FAMILY HISTORY

We all have popular material culture in our families and lives. Several of the examples that I earlier provided about myself, such as television shows I watched or the Dick and Jane books, fall within what historians often call *pop culture.* Examine your nuclear family's popular material culture. See how many artifacts you can list. There are many nonacademic books about pop culture these days. One example is Jane and Michael Stern's *Encyclopedia of Culture.* The Sterns identify a list of pop culture artifacts that I am sure will contain something familiar to you. Here are just a few.

answering machines	baseball caps
Avon products	Cabbage Patch dolls
"baby on board" signs	CB radios

Cheese Whiz	miniskirts
Cuisinart	pantyhose
deodorant	pet rocks
disposable diapers	Pez candies
fanny packs	pickup trucks
frisbees	refrigerator magnets
hula hoops	remote controls
lunch boxes	Tang
microwave ovens	toilet bowl cleaner

Whether or not your pop culture artifacts are someone else's idea of bad taste, there are many books available that place them in a social history context so that you can write them into your recent family history.

CROSSOVER ARTIFACTS WORK HISTORICALLY, TOO

There are types of material folk culture that have slipped into pop culture. These can become problematic in family history research and writing if you do not do

Case Study

Imagine that your grandfather, Ethan Greene, tapped maple trees in New Hampshire. You know this from genealogical sources such as land records. Among his things are numerous old contraptions you have never seen before. *Salt Magazine* might show you a picture of the contraption, tell you what it is, how it was used, the whole process of maple sugaring, and the folklore that went with it. Or, perhaps you do not have his artifacts but you want to know what they were and how he used them. Even if you are not absolutely certain that he did his work the way most men did, some tools and methods were so standardized that historical research can help you come as close as possible to knowing what he had and did. When you find the information in a source such as *Salt*, you can quote the source. It is not necessary to fictionalize and, in a family history, you absolutely should not. Here is what I mean.

Ethan Greene had forty acres of maple trees in New Hampshire. The seasonal labor involved in tapping those trees and processing the maple syrup was hard and yet provided a satisfying routine and sense of accomplishment for many. According to local custom, " 'in the springtime . . . we wash the spiles. (Spiles are cone-shaped funnels with a lip at one end measuring about 3½″ to 4″. They have a hook attached to hold a bucket and are inserted into the tree to funnel sap into the buckets.) Go out to a tree using a brace and bit to drill a hole . . . just long enough to stick the spile in, drive the spile . . . tap 'em with a hammer, and then we hang the buckets on.' "[1]

[1] Donald "Woody" Wood quoted in Louie Burns, "Making Maple Syrup," *Salt Magazine* 3:1-2 (June 1976), 133–134.

careful research. I have found that many students who set out to write family history narrative will mistakenly assume that a pop version of something historical is authentic enough to rely upon for family history information. Here is what I mean.

Country Stores

"Country life," including its artifacts, is a fad. One recent manifestation and vehicle for this fad has been the restaurant and gift shop that re-creates a stereotype of the country store. The food, although mass-produced, is probably closer to the original than the knickknacks in the gift shop or the "antiques" on the walls. Visiting such places is like getting a tiny taste of a nostalgic amusement park. I enjoy them, too. If you want to know about the *authentic* country store and its goods for your family history writing, however, there are books such as Thomas D. Clark's *Pills, Petticoats, and Plows: The Southern Country Store* and Gerald Carson's *The Old Country Store*. What you see in the nostalgia shop is not worthless. It may inspire you to recall something from your family history and to research further. It also reminds you of your heritage, and that makes it grist for the family history mill. It is important to remember, though, that the pop nostalgia version and use of an item is not necessarily identical to the earlier artifact and how people originally used or viewed it.

Cowboy Culture

Western history is another subject where material folk culture and pop culture cross over. Suppose you are trying to separate the real boots and spurs that your ranching ancestors wore from the styles influenced by television and movies. You will find historical representations in a book that seeks authenticity, such as William C. Davis's *The American Frontier: Pioneers, Settlers, and Cowboys, 1800–1899* or Ernest L. Reedstrom's *Scrapbook of the American West*. You can also locate books that discuss cowboy movies and pop culture, such as *Box Office Buckaroos: The Cowboy Hero From the Wild West Show to the Silver Screen* by Robert Heide and John Gilman. On the other hand, if you collected pop culture items yourself, such as Hopalong Cassidy or Roy Rogers lunch boxes, that is part of your family history too. If members of your present family like to dress "western" and line dance at a Texas-style chain steak house, we family historians can put them in social history context—right pardner?

Negative Pop Culture Artifacts

Reminder

Popular culture is not always attractive and sometimes its ugliness is more than just bad taste. You can use this to worthy effect in family history. You may have the experience of locating a family artifact that displays a racist stereotype of African Americans. Perhaps it is Aunt Jemima, Uncle Ben, Little Black Sambo, Buckwheat, or similar images on kitchen artifacts or children's books. There are books that can help you identify and analyze these artifacts, too. See Marilyn Kern-Foxworth's *Aunt Jemima, Uncle Ben, and Rastus: Blacks in Advertising: Yesterday, Today, and Tomorrow* or M.M. Manring's *Slave in a Box: The Strange Career of Aunt Jemima*. There are also antique dealers and collectors' guides now specializing in such artifacts because some African Americans collect them as symbols of the treatment that their ancestors received. Combined with books on the roles and relationships of southern white women and their servants, such as *Telling Memories Among Southern Women*, by Susan Tucker, one could make an interesting analysis of why a family hung onto any image of the beloved "Mammy" character.

A similar gallery of racist stereotypes exists for Native Americans. Suppose that you find chiefs, princesses, and cigar-store Indians represented in your family history artifacts. Or perhaps your family retained souvenirs of wartime enemies represented as evil races. Consider in each case what the artifact may reveal about its owners, their society, and their times. Social history sources will help.

Tourist Souvenirs and Fads

Remember, too, that your family may have accumulated artifacts from other folk cultures as souvenirs from their travels or as fads. For example, if a relative picked up a folk artifact in his travels, it will tell us something about where he went, when, and what interested him. Even mass-produced souvenirs, such as embroidered pillows, glass paperweights, and molded ashtrays, give us information. Many people have Southwest decor in their homes outside that area. There are certainly books on this fad to help you analyze what it says about the person practicing it and the times in which they live(d).

CITING ARTIFACTS: HOW TO FOOTNOTE A "THING"

Citing Sources

Citing artifacts in as serious and professional a style as possible is essential when using them as sources of information in our written family histories. The first reason to cite carefully is to enable future researchers to locate your sources or judge the reliability of your information. Genealogists may want to find the same sources for their own research. When we are citing a more creative source, such as an artifact, however, our scholarly and professional colleagues will watch us with extra-critical eyes. Most importantly, the readers who need to know exactly what something is, where it is, or how we are using it can only know if we tell them clearly.

To Cite or Not to Cite

While reading genealogical publications and team-teaching genealogy and family history with a professional genealogist, I came to the conclusion that meticulous genealogists cite their sources in a more detailed fashion and with higher frequency than do most historians. I had been editing scholarly historical publications for about ten years when I made this discovery. The trend in historical publishing has been to reduce footnotes or endnotes to save printing costs and because many footnotes were redundant or unnecessary.

Some historians and many college students (recently drilled by their English teachers) religiously cite a source for every piece of information. Meanwhile, a historical publication might have one footnote for each paragraph to encompass the sources for all of the information in that paragraph. If a historian were writing a narrative of a family's history, the historian might take bits of information from many documents and then cite, say, "The Townsend Family Papers" rather than each document for each piece of information. The historian or historical editor would cite a precise source for a *quotation*, to credit someone else's words, but not for an ordinary piece of information such as a *birthdate*. A professional genealogist would cite a source for every date, name, or small piece of information. Obviously, the difference is partly whether one is writing about people and the details of their lives collectively or as individual subjects of intense interest. The genealogist must consider the possibility that other genealogists will want the same precise source to check their own family information.

Elizabeth Shown Mills, longtime editor of the *National Genealogical Society Quarterly*, in her book *Evidence! Citation & Analysis for the Family Historian*, lists as the first "guideline for documentation" in genealogy that "any statement of fact that is not common knowledge must carry its own individual statement of source."[5] Perhaps the difference in frequency of citation is: whose common knowledge? The historian or the sparse footnoter would say **the gauge is not common knowledge of the general public but common knowledge among the sources.** So, for example, if every history book that mentions the Homestead Act says that it was passed in 1862 and offered 160-acre homesteads, I would tell my history students they need not attribute that information to a particular source because it is common to all of the sources. (I can assure you, though, that the date or number of acres of the Homestead Act is no longer common knowledge for the general public.) Why footnote a source for information common to most sources? If you did that, by rights you should list in that footnote every source you found containing that same piece of information—a prohibitive prospect. If, on the other hand, a source provided radically different information or an opinion that most other reliable sources did not, such as the preposterous idea that the Nazi-perpetrated Holocaust never happened, that information would be so shocking and unusual that we historians would need a source citation. **Quoted passages, of course, always require citations.**

Important

Using artifacts as sources creates an interesting new wrinkle in the rules of citation. It is extremely rare to find a footnote or endnote citation of an artifact, or to find instructions on how to do one in the citation guides that family historians use. *The Chicago Manual of Style* (14th edition) is the ultimate authority for scholarly publishing in history and genealogy. (Some organizations, publishers, periodicals, and editors create a "house style" that varies in some ways from the *The Chicago Manual*.) *The Chicago Manual* gives instruction in citing, among other things, the following untraditional materials:

Reminder

- captions and legends for illustrations in your text, sections 11.1–11.49, pages 385–404
- references to photographs and illustrations in another book or source, section 15.200, page 567
- manuscript collections (these may sometimes contain artifacts), sections 15.277–15.292 and 16.135–16.138, pages 589–594 and 679–680
- musical scores, sections 15.412–15.413 and 16.199–16.200, pages 628–629 and 695–696
- nonbook materials, including sound and video recordings, slides and films, sections 15.414–15.420 and 16.201–16.206, pages 629–632 and 696–697

In *Evidence!*, Elizabeth Shown Mills suggests how to cite a

- cemetery marker, differentiating between "published," "rural, small," and "urban, large," page 73
- photograph, portrait, or illustration, differentiating between "archival," "digital," and "private possession," pages 94–95

Mills observes that her recommendations deviate from *The Chicago Manual* partly because the manual does not adequately address certain sources that genealogists use, "notably the records of local governments, churches, cemeteries, and family archives."[6]

The most common way to incorporate artifacts individually in a narrative is to picture them as illustrations, assign captions and credit lines, and attach figure numbers so that one can refer to them in the text. If, however, we are going to extrapolate specific historical information about our families from specific artifacts, we need to develop conventional forms for footnotes and endnotes. Just as amateur genealogists (or history students) need to err toward overscrupulous citations, people using a previously underappreciated source such as artifacts need to take citation standards very seriously.

It is probably not necessary to place an artifact in a source citation, if the artifact itself is not providing evidence. Follow the same common-sense rules for artifacts as you do when deciding whether to give credit to any source. **If the artifact provided the who, where, or when of genealogy (names and dates), then the genealogical community would want a citation of that artifact as a source. If the artifact provided the what, why, or how of family history narrative (explanation and description), then the historian would want a citation. If the artifact offered only *clues*, but other sources brought the answers, then citing the artifact is less important.** For example, if you asked me what book you might use as a source and I gave you a book title, and the information you needed came from that book, you would not footnote me for suggesting the source. It is sometimes easier to acknowledge artifacts within the narrative itself. Artifacts as illustrations would have captions and credit lines. Artifacts could appear as descriptions and as part of stories within the text. You might even reproduce your artifact inventory at the back of your working family history book—the version for you and family rather than the public—as a sort of artifact bibliography.

Citing Sources

Language Is Key

One of the reasons that I have introduced you to the terminology of several professional fields is to encourage serious, scholarly language when referring to artifacts. "Things" are liable to seem frivolous next to documents and records. They suffer under the skepticism that has been generated by the misuse or indiscriminate use of oral history. See how language helps in the following hypothetical references to artifact sources. In each group of three potential footnotes, which is best? Why?

1. Grandma's box of recipe cards.
2. I found this information in the recipe cards in Grandma's box that my mother had and gave to me.

3. Maybelle Sturdevant, recipe collection, c. 1918–1960, in brown-stained wooden "Recipes" box, in the author's possession.

1. French silk handkerchief, from Frank Sturdevant to Maybelle Sturdevant, upon return from World War I in 1919.
2. Frank Sturdevant, silk handkerchief embroidered "Pax 1919," found in Frank Sturdevant's World War I trunk, now in author's possession.
3. I found this square of pink fabric that I thought was probably silk, embroidered "Pax 1919," in trunk with Frank Sturdevant's World War I memorabilia.

Obviously (I hope), the professional-sounding number three in the first group is best. It also tells the current location of the artifact. The same is true for number two in the second group. It is best not to assume ownership or other information in a footnote, as number one does about the hanky. You could only state ownership with some certainty if you had that information from another source, such as oral history or family tradition.

Step By Step

How to Cite

Based on the conventions for similar kinds of footnotes, here are some models to follow with artifacts. When we know who made the artifact, we can treat the maker as author and the artifact as title.

> Eunice Boudreaux, "Crazy Quilt," 4′ × 6′ bed quilt, multicolored fabric pieces of varying shapes and sizes, embroidered edges, some wear, red backing. Made in New Orleans, Louisiana, c. 1940, in possession of author.

In the above example, I am assuming that I have not already described the quilt in the text. If I have done so, the footnote would be

> Eunice Boudreaux, "Crazy Quilt." Made in New Orleans, Louisiana, c. 1940, in author's possession.

One inconvenience in citing artifacts as sources is that they do not often carry the names of their creators. For example, people today who make quilts and other needlecrafts often sew on preprinted labels: "Handcrafted for you by _____." In the past, those labels were not available. Many handmade artifacts bear no name, whereas a letter or diary probably would. Nevertheless, you may be convinced that you *know* who made the item from information passed down through oral tradition. If you are relying heavily on artifacts in your family history, then you should explain what policy of attributing ownership you have followed and why, either in the footnotes, endnotes, or introduction.

Example of a Statement in an Introduction

I have used numerous artifacts as resources in this work, relying on them for some family history information. In every case, unless otherwise noted, the identity of the creator or owner of the artifact is based on my firsthand personal knowledge from witnessing its creation or ownership and/or hearing the information directly from the creator or owner.

If you are not sure of the creator of the artifact, but suspect it is a family member, it is good to note this in the citation.

> Unknown maker (possibly Eunice Boudreaux), "Crazy Quilt," found in Boudreaux home in New Orleans, Louisiana, 1965, estimated 25 years old, in author's possession.

If the artifact was mass-produced or not made by a family member, either list the maker as author or, if you do not have that information, list the family member who owned the item as though that person is in the position of author. In these instances you would write:

> Sears, Roebuck, and Co., Hoosier cabinet, made c. 1890, from the home of Joseph Johnson, c. 1900–1980, currently in author's possession.
>
> Joseph Johnson (maker), violin, c. 1880, in the possession of Virginia Johnson Bates, c. 1920–1950, currently in author's possession.
>
> Virginia Johnson Bates (original known owner), unidentified jewelry box, c. 1945, still in her possession.

The use and thus the citation of artifact sources in scholarly family history writing is still so new that there will certainly be many refinements of how best to do this. In the meantime, it would be better to err on the side of citing more often, including more information, and modeling on scholarly citations rather than being too brief or casual.

CARING FOR ARTIFACTS: WHAT THE EXPERTS SAY

I am not claiming to be an expert on archival or artifact conservation. I have learned from some good conservators, books, and articles. I provide some basic advice here, but I encourage you to look through the bibliography for more resources. I have tried to state the most immediate concerns and solutions that I have ever learned in each instance. Think like a historian about caring for artifacts. You have adopted them in a role of surrogate archivist and curator. They are your fragile charges.

General Care Advice for Most Family History Artifacts

Conservators, curators, and archivists agree on some main points of artifact care. Wherever you store artifacts

Tip

1. *Regulate temperature.* If the temperature is too high or too low, it can facilitate deterioration. The ideal temperature range for storage is 65–71° Fahrenheit, with 68° being ideal. This usually excludes basements, attics, and other favorite places to store old stuff.

2. *Regulate humidity levels.* It is best to keep humidity between 45 and 50 percent. High humidity can warp items and cause mildew to spread. Extreme dryness can cause disintegration, shrinkage, and loss of the glue that once held things together. Basements—where most family historians are

most likely to store things—are the worst places to store in terms of humidity. Do not store near windows that you keep open. Keeping a window constantly open in our San Francisco home near the ocean caused black mildew to form on the walls behind stored boxes. The moisture damaged numerous items. Packets of silica gel (like the ones you sometimes find in new shoeboxes) will reduce humidity if you place them inside containers. Silica gel is available in hobby shops. See the discussion of books and paper on page 74 for a trick to kill mildew.

3. *Avoid water.* It damages, ruins, stains, and causes mildew. Avoid storing heirlooms where pipes, windows, an air conditioner, or a ceiling might leak. If you live in an area that floods, avoid storing in the lowest levels of the house.

4. *Avoid sunlight.* It can speed disintegration and fade some items beyond recognition. Try blinds, curtains, ultraviolet filters, and incandescent (rather than fluorescent) bulbs to minimize damage.

5. *Encourage air circulation around the storage area* by setting shelves so that they are some distance from the walls on several sides. You can also introduce a fan or air conditioner to the area. Winter furnace heat will dry the air, so monitor to maintain correct humidity. Archival supply catalogs offer several gadgets and supplies to check humidity.

6. *Avoid pollutants,* such as tobacco smoke, which can discolor artifacts from white to yellow to brown.

7. *Handle fragile original heirlooms infrequently.* When you do handle them, wear white cotton gloves to keep your skin's oils and dirt away. White gloves are less liable to contain chemical dyes than colored gloves. Archival and photographic supply stores and catalogs sell cheap gloves for this purpose.

8. *Clean only when certain of safe methods and equipment.* Clean only if the dirt is more of a threat to the artifact than the cleaning is. For cleaning things that need wiping, use clean, soft cotton cloths, such as the fabric of an all-cotton undershirt. To dust for fragile items, such as the surface of a photograph or document, try a soft camel-hair brush.

9. *Consider carefully before doing any repairs or restoration.* Generally, keeping an original as is maintains its historical integrity and value better than trying to fix it. Investigate professional restorers. If you repair something, study first the best methods. The repairs must be archivally sound, and must duplicate the original without looking artificial or devaluing the piece.

10. *When copying, interleaving, or wrapping, use acid-free paper.* Use 100 percent rag content paper. Do not use newspaper. Acid-free and buffered papers have pH levels of 7.0–7.5 and 8.5, respectively. (Remember pH balance? It makes me think of shampoo commercials.) Buffered paper has an alkaline content that actually counteracts some of the acid in your artifact, while acid-free paper is pH neutral. (See the discussion of photograph care in the next chapter for some exceptions to this.)

11. *When covering, displaying, or storing in plastic, use Mylar type D, polyethylene, or polypropylene. Do not use polyvinyl chloride (PVC) or polyvinyl acetate (PVA).* These unwanted plastics chemically degrade and can take

your materials with them. The proper materials are available in archival supply catalogs.

12. *Use acid-free, archival materials for containers: boxes, binders, envelopes, and albums.*

13. *When framing family or antique documents, pictures, or memorabilia, use archivally safe materials such as acid-free mats and archival glass.*

14. *For drawers, boxes, or shelves, use steel cabinets with a baked-on enamel finish.* Avoid wooden or painted cabinets or non-archival cardboard. Wood cabinets have chemicals that could damage artifacts. Make sure that your metal cabinets have no sharp edges. If you live in earthquake country, consider the stability of your shelves and cabinets. Is there a way to bolt them to the wall? If you live on a floodplain, perhaps you should leave bottom shelves empty.

15. *Use only archival tapes and glues,* such as 3M Scotch Brand no. 415. Never use any on a chemically fragile surface. Of familiar, everyday glues, the only one that is relatively safe is a Gluestick, the white rather than the clear. For adhesive labels, see an archival supply catalog. Do not attach these directly to artifacts.

16. *Avoid and remove staples, paper clips, string, and rubber bands.* The first two can rust, and all can pinch. Rubber bands disintegrate quickly, leaving a residue.

17. *Do not laminate. Use encapsulation instead.* Lamination involves heat and a chemical reaction that immediately destroys the integrity of the document; it can never be reversed. If you must enclose a fragile item in plastic, encase it in polyethylene or polypropylene sheets that have acid-free adhesive around the edges. Once encapsulated, the document floats securely inside, away from the edges, held there partly by static electricity. Now you may handle it safely. If necessary, you could remove the document by carefully cutting the plastic edges. Do not encapsulate chalk or charcoal drawings because the static electricity of the plastic sheets could remove the substance from the paper.

18. *Use soft pencil or archival pens* when writing to identify an heirloom on any label that will be next to it. Do not write on the item's surface.

19. *Handle artifacts on a safe surface* where they will not catch, tear, bend, or sustain other damage.

20. *Do not roll or fold items, especially documents.* If a precious document is already rolled or folded, gently flatten it and store it that way. A bone knife may be helpful in flattening creases, but be gentle with those that are already tearing.

21. *Discourage rodents and insects.* Silverfish nibble lacey holes in documents. Moths chew holes in woolens. If you use pest controls, avoid any chemical contact with the artifacts.

22. *Copy originals and store the copies in separate facilities* to avoid loss to theft, fire, or natural disasters. This is a good reason to consider donation of your artifacts.

Here are some additional tips pertinent to particular kinds of artifacts. See the bibliography for more.

Tip

Warning

FAMILY HISTORY PESTS (THE FOUR-LEGGED VARIETY)

I believe that cute little field mice have a special affinity for family history. Grandma Sturdevant had a kitchen drawer full of recipe clippings. Perfect for the mice! When I opened the drawer, the shreds of paper were more fine, delicate, and uniform than any modern office shredder could have accomplished. Then there was the field mouse that visited my parents' house. It came in under the kitchen sink and made its way through the living room and hallway, stopped rudely at the bathroom to leave its trail of little black mouse droppings, then traveled into the bedroom bureau. There it found my mother's manila envelope of old family photographs and letters. The mouse must have recognized the oldest and most important family documents in the house, for it nibbled those edges only. (Actually, mice like the adhesives in old envelopes.)

Fortunately, the damage was not severe before we caught the culprit. At one point, I had seen the mouse hide behind a bookcase. Rick stood in front with a broom, jabbing the straw end behind the bookcase on this side, then that. Peering behind with a flashlight, Rick spotted the mouse clinging to the back of the bookcase, cleverly positioned to avoid the broom. Then, suddenly, the mouse scurried out from under, boldly passing right between Rick's feet! Of all the items in that entire house, the only damage the mouse had done was to family history documents—of course.

Textiles: Table Linens, Quilts, Lace, Needlework, and Clothing

Reminder

Clothing and other textiles are keys to our families' past. Think of how clothing styles have changed and how those changes reflect social changes. Perhaps only artifacts of technology show more starkly how radically we have changed. Textiles, then, are useful in capturing the whole picture of past family life. **As with all artifacts, be sure to note the identifying and historically relevant information about clothing or textiles before you move them.** Writing a description into an inventory and/or photographing the item before you store it away will enable you to use it for family history information and writing without frequently handling the artifact itself.

Experts recommend rolling textiles, rather than folding them. If you do fold an item, at least pad in between folds to prevent creasing. Archival boxes and cloth bags are safer from mildew than plastic bags. Archival supply catalogs offer acid-free storage boxes in a variety of sizes, shapes, and designs. Some boxes, such as those for wedding dresses, are made to be very pretty. The suppliers also offer acid-free tissue paper for light wrapping, safe cotton tape to label garments, and large storage tubes with inner spools to roll, store, and seal rugs or fabrics.

You may choose to make minor repairs to a fabric artifact and, if so, should use the best quality thread that matches, as well as stitches that match. It may be especially important to mend a tear at a seam or replace missing stitches in a needlepoint. Do not darn holes in antiques. Repair books and experts usually suggest attaching fine netting or lining to support the artifact where holes exist.

Clean dirty textiles, if they were meant to be washed, just before storing. Test for colorfastness first by wetting an unobtrusive corner and dabbing it on white paper towel. Cotton, synthetics, and some woolens may be washable. Use the gentlest of soaps, such as Woolite. Live with older stains because the chemicals to remove stains can damage older fabrics. See Albert Jackson and David Day's *The Antiques Care and Repair Handbook* for advice on removing specific stains. **Never agitate heirlooms in a washer or subject them to the harshness of a dryer.** Take silk, satin, or anything you doubt to professional cleaners who specialize in cleaning antique fabrics by hand—do not trust ordinary dry cleaners who use harsh chemicals. If the artifact does not appear to carry destructive dirt, don't wash it. Sometimes it seems as though the dust and dirt have been holding the item together. The gentlest treatment may be to soak rather than wash. You can lay the item on a flat piece of netting and dunk it gently. Lay items such as lace and sweaters flat to dry so that they regain their shape.

Warning

Take extra care with heirloom quilts. The mix of fabrics and colors can make cleaning too much of a challenge to be worth the risk. You may gently air them out, very lightly vacuum dust from them, or, best of all, ask your nearest museum to recommend a professional cleaner. Many museums have been collecting and displaying quilts for at least a couple of decades now. Heirloom needlework such as tatting, crochet, or embroidery may require professional care as well. Professionals can also help with blocking such items.

For displaying or wearing heirloom fabric artifacts, consider treating them as a rotating collection in a museum. Susan Langley, in *Vintage Hats and Bonnets, 1770–1970, Identification and Values*, suggests you "display rather than wear any hat over fifty years old" and "display rather than wear hats in original, pristine condition. Instead," she continues, "wear those you know have had repairs and/or modifications."[7] This is good general advice for textile artifacts. Ilene (Chandler) Miller, in *Preserving Family Keepsakes*, says you should "display quilts for no more than three months at a time. Then, rest them for four months. . . ."[8] If you wear an antique article of clothing, avoid contact with either heavy perspiration or modern deodorants.

As a historian, I encourage you to enjoy surrounding yourself with those textile artifacts that you can. Living with them and looking at them may help inspire you to relate them to descriptions for family history narrative. If you do not have them in your family, there are vicarious ways to find and analyze textile artifacts as a help to family history research and writing.

1. What clothing styles and materials are ancestors wearing in photographs?
2. What textiles appear in interior photographs, such as framed needlework on the wall or tablecloths, runners, and doilies on the furniture?
3. What were the styles typical of their day, as seen in books, magazines, catalogs, museums, and living history sites?

Jewelry

Think of how often jewelry marks a special event in people's lives. Babies may receive baby-sized jewelry. Jewelry is sometimes symbolic of rites of passage—

Case Study

EXAMPLES OF FAMILY HISTORY FROM JEWELRY ARTIFACTS

Will had three daughters in quick succession. As they grew into attractive women, he recalled what he had been like as a young man. So he made a bargain with each daughter. If she could reach her eighteenth birthday without becoming pregnant, he would give her a ruby ring. He dispensed three ruby rings.

When Archie and Kate married, their ring bearer was Kate's little niece, Frances. Frances had become Archie's pet and he made her feel special. Frances formed the idea that someday Uncle Arch would marry her. Archie encouraged what he thought was an innocent idea. At the wedding, Frances came down the aisle, proudly bearing Archie's ring. During the ceremony, when he asked her to give it to him, Frances was shocked and refused. She cried and called out "Mine!" She parted with the ring so that the ceremony could continue only when Archie promised to get her a ring of her own. He did. Little Frances died a few years later during an epidemic. This makes the story of her ring from Uncle Arch all the more poignant.

Reminder

Grandpa's pocket watch for the young man, engagement and wedding rings, graduation and fraternal pins, and mourning jewelry. Sometimes jewelry carries photographs or engraved monograms and messages. Jewelry styles and materials also change with social trends. These are all clues to family history information. **Again, before you remove a piece of jewelry from where you found it, document the clues that you found with it.** Take it to oral history interviews. Search photographs of family members to see whether you might locate that brooch or necklace on an ancestor. Old photographic portraits show jewelry remarkably well. Use magnifiers to see it better. Research the styles in collector's guides and historical sources. Even if you do not own the jewelry or have never seen it, you may find family traditions and oral history surrounding the jewelry.

Warning

The first step to caring for jewelry is to check the settings, links, pins, and clasps of an item to make sure you will not lose a stone or the piece itself along the way. You may check the settings yourself with a loupe or magnifying glass, but consider taking valuable stone pieces to a reputable, trustworthy jeweler to check the settings. **Never clean jewelry over a sink.** Use only the finest quality cleaners or, better yet, ask a jeweler who specializes in antique jewelry to clean it if necessary. Ask a museum to recommend a jeweler. There are horror stories of jewelers replacing valuable stones with imitations. Not just any jeweler will recognize the value of older cuts and settings.

Wear the jewelry only after you have checked its safety and only in circumstances that protect that safety. Again, make history come alive for yourself by using your ancestors' treasures. Write it into your family history.

Silverware

Silverware, silver serving pieces, and commemorative spoons were popular gifts to mark important events and places that are part of family history—weddings, births,

One type of jewelry that you may find among family collections is fraternal, organizational, or institutional insignia. These may include pins, charms, buttons, tie clips, rings, cuff links, hat brasses, and belt buckles. This is another occasion when the facsimile Sears Roebuck or Montgomery Ward catalogs may come in handy. You will find pages that illustrate the pins, charms, and buttons that the stores kept in stock. Pages 180–181 in the Montgomery Ward Catalog No. 57, for example, depict emblems of the Masonic Lodge, Order of the Eastern Star, International Order of Odd Fellows, Knights of Pythias, Good Templars, Red Men, Modern Woodmen, Grand Army of the Republic, American Railroad Union, Epworth League, Christian Endeavor, and more. I have used these pages to help someone identify an emblem—they were then able to research the organization. Just think what you have learned about an ancestor when you find such jewelry and how much more research you can do!

If the commemorative jewelry has unknown initials or dates on it, analyze carefully what it might have represented in the owner's life. An acronym ending in "HS" on a pin is probably the name of a high school, making the " '01" next to it a likely year of graduation. A pin with the caduceus on it probably belonged to someone in a medical line of service. A locomotive design may mean a railroad employee. Keep looking.

anniversaries, historic events, places, or personalities. (See page 28 in chapter two for an example of judging wedding silver.) Many people purchased silver spoons as souvenirs, so study old family silver carefully for family history clues. Try spreading the pieces of silver out on a large, flat surface. As with a jigsaw puzzle, you will start to see patterns, designs, and engravings that match (this method also works with photographs—see chapter four). If you have an inventory or other source of information, get them out and start matching pieces to that. Make notes about all of the family history information so inspired. Take samples to oral history interviews for identification and to inspire stories. Encourage relatives to reunite matching pieces that have strayed and to care for them as heirlooms.

Protect old silverware from further damage. **Do not ever let silverware come into contact with rubber.** Those who have held groups of knives, forks, and spoons together with rubber bands have found that a chemical reaction leaves a mark where the rubber band contacted the silver, a mark that may last forever. It is good to use silverware in everyday dining because use, washing, and gentle rubbing increases the patina, a desirable sheen. You should, however, avoid contact with certain corrosive foods and wash the silver as soon as possible after contact with such foods. These include vinegar, salt, egg, fruit juice, and foods containing these such as tomatoes or salad dressings.

Every time you use silver, or when it has gathered dust, wash it gently with gentle dish soap and a soft sponge. Never put good silver (or any antiques or heirlooms) in a dishwasher. Dry it with soft, cotton cloths. Wear latex (not rubber) gloves. If it has tarnished, use the finest polishes—they are gentle and leave a shield against future tarnish. Hagerty is one of the best polishes. Follow the manufacturer's directions. If you are looking for cheap and easy protection, store silver in acid-free tissue paper within closed polypropylene bags to cut out air exposure. Pacific Silvercloth is famous as a wrap or bag to prevent tarnish. Archival supply catalogs such as University Products offer it all.

Replacement and replating services will send you pattern identification guides as well as guides that identify the uses of mysterious pieces. In flatware there were so many pieces that seem unfamiliar to many folks now: tomato servers, tea caddies, seafood forks, demitasse spoons, and pickle forks. In hollowware, such as a tea service, you might find extra pieces that seem purposeless, such as a waste bowl or spoon holder. Identifying the pieces and doing historical research can give you family history information such as habits of dining, entertaining, collecting, and gift-giving.

To replate or not to replate silver is a controversial issue. Services offered by companies like the Senti-Metal Company will repair, smooth, and resolder bent, dented, and broken pieces, then replate the whole with silver. **Here are the best tips.**

1. First, make sure the item is not sterling or nickel silver. These do not need or take replating.

2. Is the piece very old silverplate, such as rare eighteenth-century Sheffield silver? In addition to the marks, you can tell by the style of these old pieces—they are recognizably simple, the edges of obvious copper show through, and the silver was applied in a sheet, the edges of which you can sometimes find. You would destroy the value of this vintage silver by replating.

3. The pieces you would most likely have in your family would date from the late Victorian era (post-Civil War) and beyond. They were originally triple or quadruple plated with silver over some base metal by an electrical process. The process of replating is almost the same process, so you are only recreating what was done in the first place.

4. How damaged is the piece? If it is in good condition, without dents or breaks, and has retained most of its silverplate, there is no reason to replate. To test spoons, look at the underside of their bowls. Wear occurs there from setting them on surfaces. If the silver is intact or nearly so there, they are fine.

5. If the piece has lost most or all of its silver, but you like the look of it and do not intend to use it for food, you may wish to keep it as is.

6. If the piece has lost silver and is badly dented or broken, you may want it fixed. A good repair job necessitates replating afterward or you will simply have exchanged the ugly dents for the ugly marks of a hammer or solder.

7. If the piece has lost much or all of its silver and you want to use it as readily as you do other tableware, replating will bring it back to life and protect it from further severe loss of silver.

8. Replated pieces may look starkly new at first, but tarnish, washings, and use will improve the patina. Most replating adds value to damaged Victorian pieces. It will not obscure a monogram unless the monogram area is very worn.

Tip

For More Info

The Senti-Metal Company is even cuter in its address pun than its name. For information about repairs, rates, and discounts, you may reach them at 1919 Memory Lane, Columbus, Ohio, 43209-2761 or (800) 323-9718. Their homepage is http://www.abcbronze.com and their E-mail address is bronzeinfo@bronshoe.com. In case it is not obvious, they also will bronze your baby shoes for you.

Paper Artifacts

Of course, genealogists and historians use documents regularly. We do not, how-ever, always remember to think of them as artifacts. An old, original document such as a certificate, scrapbook, or autograph album is loaded with family history information, yet it is also fragile, often beautiful, and full of sentimental value. **Photocopy your precious original documents onto good-quality, high-rag-content, acid-free bond paper.** Use a photocopying machine that uses powdered, carbon-based toner for permanence. The goal is to create copies to use for re-search or display that are fine documents in and of themselves, so you don't have to expose the original documents to the elements. Even the light of the photocop-ier is harsh, so you should try to avoid copying documents repeatedly. You may also want to scan documents into your computer as a way to preserve them. This makes it possible to send them to family members electronically. Encapsulation, discussed on page 67, is a good way to keep fragile documents safe when you expect to be handling and viewing the originals frequently.

Tip

Newsprint (such as your newspaper clippings) is so acidic that you may want to "wash" it before encapsulation. Washing means rinsing in distilled water and then allowing to thoroughly dry flat. There are also deacidifying sprays in archi-val supply catalogs. If your clippings seem too fragile to wash, you may wish to encapsulate them with a sheet of buffered paper to back them. Flatten documents such as rolled diplomas or folded letters. You may need a special press and you will need acid-free folders for storage. Archival supply catalogs have a wide variety of containers for almost every shape and size of document. I have incorpo-rated much of my best advice for document care in the twenty-two general points about artifact care starting on page 65, so please revisit those. For hints on framing and displaying documents, see page 77.

Books

There are two types of books that you will collect as a family historian.

First, there are the books that you buy because you are now thinking like a historian and building a library of resources. Even these deserve special care so that they will last and retain value. Archival supply catalogs offer Mylar covers for dust jackets just like the ones libraries use. A bibliophile such as my husband will lecture you if you mishandle your books. Evidence of mishandling lowers the value of used books. **Here are the don'ts.**

Warning

1. Do not bend or break the spine of a book by trying to open it too far, by leaving it open on its back, by leaving it open face down, or by photocopying across its breadth on a flat screen.
2. Do not turn down its page corners. Use thin bookmarks.
3. Do not pull a book off the shelf by the top of its spine.
4. Do not line up books so tightly on a shelf that you pull them harshly trying to get them out.
5. Do not use bookplates or a book embossing stamp to identify your ownership.

6. Do not pack or stack a book so that it loses its shape.
7. Do not mark in a book with anything.
8. Do not ask to borrow a book from a book owner who believes in these rules.

Writing in books arouses controversy somewhat similar to that over replating silver. Some people feel strongly that their own marginal comments add value to a book. Certainly, when those comments are in the handwriting of an ancient ancestor or historical figure and reveal his or her thoughts, we might agree. I guess whether you feel comfortable writing in your books depends on your vision of how important you will be someday, historically or ancestrally. I have only done it in a few modern pocketbooks, myself, when I bought the copy for use that way in a special project.

The second type of book is the old books such as schoolbooks or favorite fiction, that you collect from the family. These are artifacts. If you find books in the family, examine and record where you found them, what was with them, and any other clues. Often books became containers themselves. Their owners pressed flowers, stored clippings, and hid money in them. On page 75 is a quiz about the book for which most genealogists would give their eyeteeth and even suffer a root canal.

Mildew can be extremely damaging to a book collection. It stains covers and pages. If your books have a sour smell, they may be developing mildew whether or not you can see it. **If you find mildew in books, you need to kill it. Isolate the book(s) with either visible signs or the smell of mildew.** An excellent professional conservator taught me this trick. Her employer had just spent a fortune on a large decontamination chamber, but she said this technique would work just as well for those who cannot afford one!

Technique

The general idea is to spray Lysol *about or toward* the book—not in it or on it directly, but about it and toward it while fanning the pages. Stand the book on end outdoors in sunlight. Spray the Lysol at the fanned pages from several feet away, misting but never making wet spots on the pages. Let the book stand in the sun for one to three hours. Then put the book in a mock decontamination chamber made of a thirty-gallon plastic trash bag and a wire tie. Put the book in the bag, spray another mist into the bag without wetting the book, and seal it with a twist tie for one to two weeks. When you take it out, the mildew is gone and the book smells of Lysol, if anything. Use the spray lightly—better to have to do it again than accidentally wet or warp the pages. It works, but don't overdo it.

Archival supply houses have special acid-free boxes for books whose covers and bindings are failing. A good conservator can restore the cover of a fine book for you, but be sure you are dealing with a qualified person.

Cemeteries and Headstones

Sometimes a hurried genealogist runs into a cemetery, rushes through snapshots or rubbings, and runs out again—especially on an out-of-town trip. All of the major genealogical guides, however, encourage a more patient and holistic approach to cemeteries. Think like a historian. As discussed in chapter two, each tombstone is an artifact for your family history. As with textiles, books, jewelry,

THE FAMILY BIBLE QUIZ

You find a fragile, crumbling, family Bible stuffed full of memorabilia in your great-grandmother's attic. You take it home with you.

1. What should you have done when and where you found it?

2. How would you store it in your home?

3. Would you remove the memorabilia from between the pages? Why or why not?

4. How might you determine the Bible's age?

5. In the middle are some pages that list the names and birthdates of people with your family name. They go back as far as 1800, and the most recent date is 1925. Is this reliable genealogical information? How could you tell?

6. Here is a list of the memorabilia that were between the pages. What might you learn from these scraps?

   the ABCs written on a piece   locks of hair
   of paper in a childish hand   obituaries
   calling cards   photographs
   church service programs   a poem about "A Boy and His Dad"
   funeral cards   a poem about a dead baby
   greeting cards   pressed flowers
   letters   wedding invitations

7. Would you pay any attention to the marginal marks calling attention to particular passages?

8. How did the owner use the Bible from day to day?

9. How would you rank this book as a source of family history information in terms of usefulness?

(see page 78 for the answers.)

or any other family artifacts, it is best to study and document where you find it, what is around it, and what clues the whole cemetery gives you. Perhaps no one (except veterans' organizations) has done more to recognize, record, and preserve the value of cemeteries than genealogists. Yet perhaps no one (except vandals) runs a greater risk of underappreciating and even harming cemeteries than genealogists.

If you discover a family graveyard, or one that is neglected, you may consider starting or joining an effort to preserve it. The local genealogical or historical society might already be undertaking a preservation project or might be interested in starting one. The American Association for State and Local History (AASLH) primer by Lynette Strangstad, *A Graveyard Preservation Primer*, is a good, overall guide to the problems and solutions of cemetery care. It was cosponsored by

For More Info

For information on gravestones and their preservation, contact Association of Gravestone Studies, 278 Main St., Ste. 207, Greenfield, MA 01301. E-mail: AGS @javanet.com; Web site: http://www.gravestonestudies.org.

the Association for Gravestone Studies. Perhaps the most fundamental argument of this book is that preservation needs to be undertaken by an organized and methodical group of people who are highly motivated, like you, using informed, professional standards and methods.

Historians and graveyard preservationists have guidelines for cemetery research that may seem more cautious than the usual instructions that genealogists give one another. **Individual family historians should follow the cemetery care guidelines below.**

Tip

1. Research in advance whether there are cemetery records. Often local genealogical societies and individuals have compiled inventories of the headstones in local cemeteries. If you do not know where the records or authorities connected with the cemetery might be, start by contacting the nearest historical society.

2. Contact the managers of the cemetery before your visit to determine what is allowed and whether there is a fee that goes to maintenance.

3. Control children that you may bring with you, or do not bring them. Do not bring pets.

4. Make rubbings of inscriptions only if the rules allow. Rub only sound stones. If a stone is weak, only photograph it.

5. When preparing to rub or photograph, do not clean stones with chemicals or anything but a soft nylon (not wire) bristle brush and water. Live with lichen or moss if it does not brush off lightly.

6. Whatever paper or fabric you use for a rubbing, cover the edges of the stone and make sure no ink or crayon is going through to the stone. If you have used masking tape to hold the material at the back, leave no tape stuck to the stone.

7. Avoid rubbing either deeply carved stones or coarse stones such as marble because both are more susceptible to damage. Do not press hard when rubbing.

8. Transcribe inscriptions exactly. See John J. Newman's AASLH technical leaflet, "Cemetery Transcribing: Preparations and Procedures." Your transcription could survive the tombstone itself.

9. Do not attempt to reset a fallen, broken, or vandalized stone. Contact the cemetery authorities about what should be done. Then consider sponsoring an effort if the stone is important to you.

10. Carry away your trash and someone else's, but do not take souvenirs such as broken stone pieces or grave decorations.

11. If rules allow, picnic (respectfully) in the cemetery. As a historian, I believe in re-creating this historical event of Memorial Days gone by. As your ancestors did, think of the family time in the cemetery as a way of visiting and paying tribute to those who came before.

PURCHASING ARCHIVAL SUPPLIES

There are several sources for archival supply catalogs. I recommend Archival Quality Materials. **You can qualify for the best prices by purchasing in large volumes—even if it is more than you need.** If necessary, go in with friends, buying

Money Saver

the highest number to get the lowest price, then splitting the supplies among yourselves. Check with your local museum or historical society to see if they sell archival supplies to the public. Those will be in smaller quantities.

Sources to Help You With Your Artifacts

There are relatively few sources advising a family historian how to care for artifacts. The scholarly conservators and archivists seem to write mostly for institutional use. See the bibliographies at the end of this chapter and book, contact the organizations, and watch for more attention to this topic in the future. Meanwhile, if you have many family artifacts to preserve, I would most recommend Deidre M. Paulsen and Jeanne S. English's *Preserving the Precious*, Ilene (Chandler) Miller's *Preserving Family Keepsakes*, and Craig A. Tuttle's *An Ounce of Preservation: A Guide to the Care of Papers and Photographs*. All of these books are written by and for family heirloom collectors. Thus they are comprehensive in their discussions of assorted family artifacts, and the language and instructions are written in an appealing, down-to-earth style.

Supplies

To request the catalog "Archival Quality Materials," call University Products, Inc. at (800) 628-1912, or write to 517 Main Street, P.O. Box 101, Holyoke, MA 01041-0101. Fax: (800) 532-9281, E-mail: info@universityproducts.com, Web site: http://www.universityproducts.com.

DISPLAYING FRAMED ARTIFACTS

Archivists and curators hang the world's valuable treasures for display. That means that there are supplies and methods available to you so that you can display your family artifacts safely. Displaying family artifacts keeps them visible and accessible in your life. This helps research, encourages analysis, and promotes the feeling of identification that inspires writing. *Proper* archival framing is also a way to protect an artifact.

Archival supply catalogs carry substantial amounts of framing supplies: acid-free mounting board and foam board, precut archival mats, ultraviolet glass or Plexiglas, safe aluminum and wood frames, and archival backing, adhesive, and hanging materials. You can frame your artifacts yourself if you wish. This will save some money, although the archival supplies are substantially more expensive than ordinary picture frames. **You want acid-free, 100 percent rag mounting board for both the backing and the matting. Nothing else is safe.** Attaching the artifact requires archivally sound adhesives because all others will stain or damage the original. The glass or Plexiglas should be "UV," resistant to ultraviolet light, if the artifact will be seriously exposed. UV glass may not be archivally safe, however. You can use it if the window mat is sufficiently thick to prevent the artifact from touching the glass. Experts argue about whether to seal the back, but if, like me, you have imperfect air and dust levels in your home and hometown, sealing is advisable. Hang your artifacts away from either direct or indirect sunlight. Do not expose them to fluorescent light either. Avoid heat and cold. Control humidity.

Warning

We always thought we would frame our things ourselves, but we never had time. So I finally took them to a reputable framer at a gallery. As always, if you

ANSWERS TO THE FAMILY BIBLE QUIZ

1. *What should you have done when and where you found it?* Of course, you should have documented where it was, what was near it, and other clues before moving it.

2. *How would you store it in your home?* You might store it in an archival box.

3. *Would you remove the memorabilia from between the pages? Why or why not?* This is debatable. Old Bibles themselves are not that valuable as books because they were common and cheaply made. The family history information inside is more valuable. The memorabilia is tied to where it is. If you must move it for safety, document what was where. I have recommended leaving such items in the Bibles that I have observed. It seemed disrespectful to disturb them unless their presence in the Bible was causing damage.

4. *How might you determine the Bible's age?* There may be publishing dates in the front of the book. The family history information is the best clue to the Bible's age if publishing dates are missing. One clever trick for some Bibles: there may be a second title page introducing the New Testament. Thus if the front matter is missing or damaged, a pristine second title page near the middle of the book may give you publishing information.

5. *In the middle are some pages that list the names and birthdates of people with your family name. They go back as far as 1800, and the most recent date is 1925. Is this reliable genealogical information? How could you tell?* No one person could have written entries from 1800 to 1925. The tests of relative reliability are
   a. the inks and handwriting styles should change over time;
   b. none of the entries should predate the publication date of the Bible.

6. *Here is a list of the memorabilia that were between the pages. What might you learn from these scraps?* There is room for much interpretation in these artifacts. Extract information from the documents. Analyze beyond the obvious. If it is in this Bible, it had value to the keeper, who perhaps read it repeatedly. Calling cards suggest visitors. Poems and clippings suggest personal meaning for the owner.

7. *Would you pay any attention to the marginal marks calling attention to particular passages?* The marginal comments (writing in books—horrors!) suggest important passages to the owner. With repeated analysis, these may relate to the other artifacts or a family event such as a death. They make it clearer how carefully the ancestor read this book. Imagine how regularly your ancestor held this book in hand or on lap, ritualistically turning its pages each day.

8. *How did the owner use the Bible from day to day?* Like Great-Grandma's recipe collection, the Bible was a keepsake album and planner. Possibly the owner read devotionally each day. Possibly he or she quoted scripture during life's great moments. One Sturdevant family Bible (not in our possession) was published in 1826. A page in one of the flyleaves contained the following, handwritten litany:

> This bible bought September 5th 1827 and i give it to my dafter Lucy
> May 10th 1829
> i have red it twice threw . . .
> January 31st 1830   i have red it three times through
> July 25th 1830   i have red this bible fore times threw
> January 20th 1831   i have red this five times
> June 5th 1831   i have red this bible six times threw
> January 3 1832   i have red this seven times threw
> October 24th 1832   i have red this bible eight times threw
> June 9th 1833   i have red this bible nine times threw
> April 6th 1834   i have red this book ten times threw
> December 13th 1835   i have red this book eleven times threw
> June 2 1836   I have red this bible twelve times threw
> I have red this holy book thirteen times threw
> martins burgh   July 10th 1837 Caleb Sturdevant
> finis

The handwriting deteriorates with each entry, probably a reflection of age. At first this was just endearing. Combined with other evidence, however, interesting corrections emerged. Caleb Sturdevant signed his Revolutionary War pension application with an X several years before this, suggesting that perhaps his Bible notations reflected exercises in gaining literacy late in life. Perhaps his daughter Lucy was his teacher. He died in October 1837, and so had been reading at regular intervals all of that time. He was seventy-eight when he died. He seemed to know that the thirteenth reading was his last. Also, the Bible was published in Cooperstown, New York. During the whole period of the readings, Caleb lived in Martinsburg, New York, in the vicinity of the "Burned-Over District" during the Second Great Awakening. Thus it makes even better sense that he was so dedicated to reading his Bible and that this particular copy was just the New Testament. Thanks to a family Bible, these connections form the stuff of narrative family history in social history context.[9]

9. *How would you rank this book as a source of family history information in terms of usefulness?* This artifact, the family Bible, containing these treasures, is a miraculous family history source. Some genealogists have doubted this because the genealogical information is not necessarily reliable and the other materials are scattered and sentimental. But viewed from the social and family historian's perspective, an old Bible may be the best key to ancestral character and daily life for the purposes of descriptive narrative.

want it done expertly or just want expert advice you know what to do. **Ask a museum curator what framers or conservators to use.** This is especially important if your artifacts need restoration of some kind. I found that a test of a reliable framer is to telephone and ask questions about whether they could handle the particular job. They will speak the archival language, or they will not. Good ones will not turn down any framing challenge. They are patient with decision-making processes. They may state emphatically that they do not do restoration, but they know who does. They will get you what you know is needed without recommending expensive archival materials for ordinary prints or slipping in lower-quality goods when you need archival-quality.[10]

If you do not have old photographs or artifacts suitable for framing, you may create your own. Some folks copy the more interesting documents that they have found in their research such as an ancestor's diploma, war record, or signature, and frame those. Others hang tombstone rubbings as works of art. Remember, too, that it is a service to future generations to create such would-be heirlooms from the present. Frame your immediate family's memorabilia so that it will stay together, last, and provide enjoyment for you and future generations.

Military Shadowboxes

Rick, my husband, told my father to close his eyes. He put the shadowbox in Daddy's hands. When my father opened his eyes and recognized a display case neatly arranged with new or nearly new specimens of all of his missing World War II medals, badges, ribbons, and insignia, my father literally leapt from his seat with joy. "Oh, Boy!" he shouted, laughing and smiling. Rick repeated the moment with his maternal grandfather, Grandpa Gates, and Rick's own father, Wendell. For Grandpa, on his ninety-fifth birthday, it was a solitary World War I medal that he had earned yet never seen. Grandpa, feebly facing his last days, said quietly, "I didn't know I got that!" Then there was my father-in-law, who had been a prisoner of war in Nazi Germany and, for many years, could not discuss the experience comfortably. He cried at the sight of his shadowbox. To complete the shadowbox family as much as the availability of medals would allow, Rick also made a shadowbox for his father's father, Frank Sturdevant, who served in World War I. Although Frank had been dead since 1950, the box was another special gift from Rick to his father, Frank's son.

Military shadowboxes are one example of a meaningful way to display artifacts. They are frames with hinged openings that are deep enough for you to pin flat artifacts to the felt or cork backing inside. The display cases themselves are readily available in catalogs and hobby shops. Most have glass doors and hangers on the backs. Rick used map pins (from office supply houses) to hold the artifacts in place. This is preferable to attaching adhesive Velcro patches that come with some cases. The same kinds of shadowboxes are suitable for any family history theme: wedding souvenirs, baby memorabilia, etc.

It is possible to apply to the government for new medals in order to replace old or missing medals. You need some of the same information that you send and receive when requesting military records. New medals will arrive in handsome cases and you will also have created some new government files on your veteran. For instructions, see William B. Thayer's "Getting Those Well-Deserved Medals" in the November and December 1990 issues of *Veterans of Foreign Wars Magazine*. Local Department of Veterans Affairs agents or veterans' organizations such as the Veterans of Foreign Wars or the American Legion may also be able to help. Older, rarer medals, such as those from World War I, are available through dealers in *militariana*. See your Yellow Pages, or ask local antique dealers for someone who specializes in antique military collectibles.

To finish the shadowboxes, Rick went to a local trophy and plaque-engraving shop to have brass plates made commemorating the veterans by name with their units and years of service. He attached the brass plates underneath the rows of medals. The well-labeled cases will survive better as family heirlooms than scattered, dusty medals would have done. The best result of my husband's efforts was three veterans who had never seen their medals so complete or looking so good. I know how much it meant to them that he recognized their patriotic contributions. Therefore, an important tip: **Complete this type of project while the person being honored is still alive and able to appreciate what you have done.** If you are a surviving direct heir, you can apply for a late veteran's medals and frameable funeral flags and, of course, you can collect antique or replica militariana to represent your ancestors' accomplishments.

Tip

ARTIFACT COLLECTIONS IN MUSEUMS AND LIBRARIES

"That is all well and good, Kathy," some folks have said, "but we just do not have any such family artifacts. I would love to have things to write about in my family history, but I don't have anything like that from my grandparents or their parents."

Remember that the same books, museums, libraries, and archives that can help someone identify and analyze their family artifacts can also help you see and analyze our public collections. I could live in the Smithsonian Institution's Museum of American History and still not see everything that I want to see. Many of its exhibits contain social history artifacts that relate very directly to the experiences of your ancestors. Suppose you cannot go, or I cannot live there. In that case, there are books that encompass such exhibits and with which you can probably extract more information at your own pace than when visiting. A good example is Barbara Clark Smith's *After the Revolution: The Smithsonian History of Everyday Life in the Eighteenth Century*. This volume uses the artifacts of four families in Massachusetts, Delaware, Virginia, and Pennsylvania to illustrate American social history of the period. The pictures tend to be Smithsonian artifacts.

Museums sometimes bring to us in books the social history that we need for family history writing. *The Light of the Home*, *A Century of Childhood*, and the Winterthur everyday life series (see chapter two) are all museum-produced. Museum exhibit catalogs often become published books that offer many illustrations of artifacts in the historical context of time and place. For example, *Agreeable Situations: Society, Commerce, and Art in Southern Maine, 1780–1830*, edited by Laura Sprague, was a catalog for the Brick Store Museum in Kennebunk. If your family lived in that region, or even generally in New England, at that time, this would be a small gold mine of social history for you.

Investigate historical museums and sites in your own area or the areas where ancestors lived. Cities have museums that record and display urban life throughout their history. Smaller towns have pioneer museums. These museums along with the name "pioneers' museum," have come under fire for allegedly propounding only the point of view of white settlers. Nonetheless, these collections will teach you about your ancestors if they were the "pioneers" of that area. Most museums have been featuring exhibits on previously neglected groups such as women, African Americans, and other minorities. Now you have a better chance of finding relevant information and artifacts regardless of cultural heritage.

Idea Generator

Living history museums are popular and very appropriate to family history research. In an area where your ancestors lived, you may find a living-history farm, ranch, plantation, fort, or village. If the directors are professionals, you will learn useful information about daily life that applies to your ancestor. One must keep in mind, however, that some scholars believe that living history museums, with their pleasant appeal to family audiences, have a tendency to limit themselves to pioneers' culture and to romanticizing the "good old days." There may also be historic houses in your town or nearby. These houses capture the way people lived in them during certain periods—again, helpful to family history research. Any local or social history museums may house artifacts like those your ancestors used and, therefore, can help answer questions such as, "What did my ancestors use to accomplish that task?"

If the steps that I have suggested for your own artifact care seem to be too much work, if you just do not have the space or the time and money to properly archive your artifacts, or if the collection has true historical value, consider donating it to a museum, library, or local historical society. You would still have access to it there, but so would others. You would be giving more people access to your artifacts longer than if you just kept them stashed around your house. Whatever you do, I hope that you will enjoy your artifacts as family history sources.

CHAPTER BIBLIOGRAPHY

1. Brunvand, Jan Harold. *The Study of American Folklore: An Introduction.* 2nd ed. New York: W.W. Norton and Co., 1968, 1978.

2. Butler, Joseph T. *Field Guide to American Antique Furniture.* New York: Henry Holt and Co., 1985.

3. Carson, Gerald. *The Old Country Store.* New York: Oxford University Press, 1954.

4. Clark, Thomas D. *Pills, Petticoats, and Plows: The Southern Country Store.* Norman: University of Oklahoma Press, 1944, 1989.

5. Davis, William C. *The American Frontier: Pioneers, Settlers, and Cowboys, 1800–1899.* New York: Smithmark Books, 1992.

6. Dorson, Richard M. *Folklore and Folklife: An Introduction.* Chicago: University of Chicago Press, 1972.

7. Gillespie, Paul F. *Foxfire 7*. Vol. 7 of 10. Garden City, N.Y.: Anchor Books, 1982.

8. Glaser, Mary Todd. "Framing and Preservation of Works of Art on Paper." Pamphlet distributed by Bernard Ewell Art Appraisals, Colorado Springs, Colo., c. 1999.

9. Glassie, Henry. *Folk Housing in Middle Virginia*. Knoxville: University of Tennessee Press, 1975.

10. ———. *Pattern in the Material Folk Culture of the Eastern United States*. Philadelphia: University of Pennsylvania Press, 1968, 1978.

11. Heide, Robert, and John Gilman. *Box-Office Buckaroos: The Cowboy Hero From the Wild West Show to the Silver Screen*. New York: Abbeville Press, 1989.

12. Jackson, Albert and David Day. *The Antiques Care and Repair Handbook*. New York: Alfred A. Knopf, 1984.

13. Kern-Foxworth, Marilyn. *Aunt Jemima, Uncle Ben, and Rastus: Blacks in Advertising, Yesterday, Today, and Tomorrow*. Westport, Conn.: Praeger Publishers, 1994.

14. Kovel, Ralph, and Terry Kovel. *Kovels' Know Your Antiques*. Revised and updated. New York: Crown Publishers, 1967, 1981.

15. Langley, Susan. *Vintage Hats & Bonnets, 1770–1970: Identification & Values*. Paducah, Ky.: Collector Books, 1998.

16. Leon, Warren, and Roy Rozenzweig, eds. *History Museums in the United States: A Critical Assessment*. Urbana: University of Illinois Press, 1989.

17. Manring, M.M. *Slave in a Box: The Strange Career of Aunt Jemima*. Charlottesville: University Press of Virginia, 1998.

18. Mibach, Lisa. "Collections Care: What to Do When You Can't Afford to Do Anything." Technical leaflet no. 198. Nashville: American Association for State and Local History, 1997.

19. Miller, Ilene (Chandler). *Preserving Family Keepsakes*. Yorba Linda, Calif.: Shumway Family History Services, 1995.

20. Mills, Elizabeth Shown. *Evidence! Citation & Analysis for the Family Historian*. Baltimore: Genealogical Publishing Co., 1997.

21. Newman, John J. "Cemetery Transcribing: Preparations and Procedures." Technical leaflet no. 9. Nashville: American Association for State and Local History, 1971.

22. Northeast Document Conservation Center. "Encapsulation." NDCC leaflet. Andover, Mass., 1987.

23. Paulsen, Deidre M., and Jeanne S. English. *Preserving the Precious*. Revised edition. Sale Lake City: Restoration Source, 1989.

24. Reedstrom, Ernest L. *Scrapbook of the American West*. Caldwell, Idaho: Caxton Printers, Ltd., 1991.

25. Reynolds, George P., ed. *Foxfire 10*. Vol. 10 of 10. Garden City, N.Y.: Anchor Books, 1993.

26. Ritzenthaler, Mary Lynn. *Archives and Manuscripts: Conservation*. Chicago: Society of American Archivists, 1983.

27. Schoemaker, George H., ed. *The Emergence of Folklore in Everyday Life: A Fieldguide and Sourcebook*. Bloomington: Trickster Press, 1990.

28. Smith, Barbara Clark. *After the Revolution: The Smithsonian History of Everyday Life in the Eighteenth Century*. New York: Pantheon Books, 1985.

29. Sprague, Laura Fecych. *Agreeable Situations: Society, Commerce, and Art in Southern Maine, 1780–1830*. Kennebunk: The Brick Store Museum, 1987.

30. Stern, Jane and Michael Stern. *Encyclopedia of Culture*. New York: Harper-Collins Publishers, 1992.

31. Strangstad, Lynette. *A Graveyard Preservation Primer*. Nashville: American Association for State and Local History, 1988.

32. Thayer, William B. "Getting Those Well-Deserved Medals." *Veterans of Foreign Wars Magazine*, November and December 1990. For assistance, contact your nearest veterans' organization or Veteran's Administration office.

33. Tuttle, Craig A. *An Ounce of Preservation: A Guide to the Care of Papers and Photographs*. Highland City, Fla.: Rainbow Books, Inc., 1995.

34. University of Chicago Press. *The Chicago Manual of Style: The Essential Guide for Writers, Editors, and Publishers*. 14th ed. Chicago: University of Chicago Press, 1993.

35. Wigginton, Eliot, ed. *Foxfire* and *Foxfire 2–6*. Vols. 1–6 of 10. New York: Anchor Books, 1972–1980.

36. Wigginton, Eliot, and Margie Bennett, eds. *Foxfire 8* and *Foxfire 9*. Vols. 8 and 9 of 10. Garden City, N.Y.: Anchor Books, 1983, 1986 respectively.

37. Wood, Pamela, ed. *The Salt Book*. Garden City, N.Y.: Anchor Books, 1977.

FOUR

A Historian's Approach to Family Photographs

We are poor passing facts, warned by that to give each figure in the photograph his living name.

—Robert Lowell[1]

F amily photographs are among those heirlooms most liable to have survived the hazards of time and mobility. They are relatively small and thus easy to pack or carry. Ancestors often seem to have understood that throwing them away would be akin to throwing their own ancestors away. Only today do we see families actually selling their ancestors' images to antique stores. It is sad to see those lonely, abandoned faces sell for little better than a few dollars a piece. These are, after all, literally representations of ancestors, one of their few means of immortality. We owe them proper appreciation, just as we would hope descendants would appreciate us.

Certainly many families have lost their old photographs over the years. A highly mobile family, especially if it gained and lost property often, might lose its photographs. People in oppressed conditions, such as African Americans in the post-Civil War South or Native Americans, may not have had the wherewithal, access to or desire for much photography. Natural disasters, such as fire, flood, or severe storms, may have destroyed the photographs. My experience suggests, however, that **if a branch of your family has been in the United States since the 1880s, there may still be a cache of photographs somewhere.** Yours may simply not be the branch that has them—yet.

Very often you can deduce which branch might have the most photographs and other heirlooms. The branch that stayed in the same place the longest might have them. In the Sturdevant family, an aging father and his grown sons settled in Iowa's Cedar River Valley in the 1850s. Several branches and generations stayed in that one town, Waverly. The last members left in the 1970s. Meanwhile, the last collateral branch in town, the Lovejoys, are still there. These are the two branches that have the most photographs. Others, who in the 1890s traveled west to the Dakotas or to Washington and Oregon, tend to have photographs and heirlooms that document their mobile family histories but not so many heirlooms of the stationary, earlier generations. You can also deduce that photographs are located with the VIPs of family history: the acknowledged family

Notes

Endnotes for this chapter begin on page 221.

Hidden Treasures

historians, the sons of sons, the daughters of daughters, and the Keepers of Everything. If one relative's name comes up most often in your contact with relatives, he or she may be the Keeper. I have the accidental honor of being the only daughter of an only daughter of an only daughter. Fate has bestowed upon me the role of Keeper, especially of supposedly female things. Sometimes photographs have been included in these female things. Try to discern who the photograph keepers may be in your family, although any relative may have some.

Reminder

You need to find, copy, study, and analyze your family photographs thoroughly and often. If you order archival supplies for no other reason, order them for this one: you will need to examine your old family photographs again and again, seeking new clues and new identities. There are ways to make good copies but, in the meantime, you will probably be handling the originals for a while. Handling them is essential to discovering their clues. Placing them in archival sleeves will enable you to handle them with less fear.

IDENTIFYING AND ANALYZING FAMILY PHOTOGRAPHS

Historians and photograph archivists examine the content of photographs carefully. An older photograph deserves repeated study. Most folks have no idea how much information they can extract from a collection of one family's photographs. There is genealogical and historical information galore to glean from them: your ancestors in social history context.

Step By Step

Steps for Historical Analysis of Family Photographs

1. Record where and when you found the photograph, in terms of precise container, room, building, town, and owner. If you are taking it away from that location, or if someone did so in the past, note what you can discern about who kept it where and when. Ask relatives these questions.

2. If the photograph is or was in a container with other heirlooms or memorabilia, note whose other things were in the box, album, drawer, or chest. What items were keeping it company for years? Each item may help identify the others.

3. If possible, keep the photograph with its companion heirlooms in their original container as long as you can. If someone tucked the photograph in a letter, Bible, album, or box of souvenirs, that person probably connected them all. Moving any item prematurely could mean you lose its significance to others. If you are worried about preservation, you can probably make photographic copies, photocopies, and/or place the originals in archival sleeves. If you remove the original photograph to preserve it archivally, place a copy in its original nesting spot to remind you of what items you found together.

4. Examine each photograph for immediate identifying features such as the name, date, and other information written in the margins or on the back.

Copy this information onto the Family Photograph Inventory and Analysis form that appears in this chapter and in the back of the book (see pages 99 and 234).

5. If some of the information is handwritten, try now or later to identify who wrote it. You will want to look repeatedly at the information during your ensuing research. If it is extensive, you may wish to photocopy it. Later you may find letters that reveal the same handwriting, or you might learn enough about the people in the picture that you can understand an otherwise mysterious comment they wrote. Remember that parents and their grown children often had similar handwriting, especially in the days when schoolteachers taught proper penmanship. Look at many samples to recognize individual styles. These change, too, with age.

6. **Do not automatically accept what someone else wrote on the back of a photograph as accurate.** Consider who wrote it, when, and what they knew or thought at that time. The mistakes or misrepresentations may be meaningful to family history, too, but you need to sort out which is which.

Warning

7. Do not permanently assume that your first identification of the people in the picture is correct. More research could lead you to different conclusions.

8. Note the photographer's identifying information, if any. This will usually tell you where a picture was taken. In city directories and town newspapers from that day you can locate the photographer's studio and narrow down the age of the photograph. In a group of family photographs, a switch in photographers may have resulted from a family move—very helpful information. Note the places and approximate times on a sheet of paper in order to start following family movements. Just as you might do with place names from censuses or deeds, check a map to see how close together the photographers' towns were and in what direction folks were apparently moving. One cautionary note, however: realize that photographers who moved from one place to another might have still used their old cardstock, with the old addresses printed on it, the same way that we sometimes continue using out-of-date business cards until we can order new ones.

9. Contacting the local or state historical society could get you more information about the photographer and timing. Some societies have collected the work of different photographers in their areas, partly to build a work-history of the artist.

10. Using the chart on page 96 or one of the sources available on the history of photography, figure out what type of photograph this was: a tintype, cyanotype, etc. More than likely it will be a cabinet card or *carte de visite*. Again, this will give you a time period. It also suggests information about family social habits.

11. Examine the contents of the photograph itself. Use a magnifying glass, or even two, holding one above the other.

12. Does the photograph appear to have been taken in a studio with false props and backdrops or in an authentic setting? If the former, you cannot be sure that any props are relevant to the people pictured. Sometimes oral history can clear this up. For example, in one of my mother's favorite photographs,

Oral History

Figure 1. Archibald Leslie Harper (author's grandfather) with his oldest son, John Leonard Harper, c. 1915, and with *The Adventures of Tom Sawyer*. Author's collection.

my grandfather and his young son (my uncle) sit smiling over an open book (Figure 1). She told me that they had taken with them to the photographer's studio Mark Twain's *The Adventures of Tom Sawyer*. This was the boy's favorite book for his father to read to him.

13. A man and his car. Such photographs proliferate in family collections and, thank goodness, automobiles can be easy to identify and date. Ask yourself whether the car may be a photographer's prop, as often evidenced by a painted backdrop. If you determine the year for that make of car, make sure that you examine the car's condition and other signs of the photograph's date, such as people's apparent ages. Folks did not usually trade or sell one car for another each year. Consider the meaning of the car to its human companions. Is it a family's means of recreation? What did it symbolize for the owner/driver? In his memoirs, my father described his car as his "first love." When he was dying, we showed him old family pictures to elicit pleasant memories for him. I will never forget the warm grin when he saw one of them and said, "It's the old Ford!" He seemed happier to see the "first love" than he was to see most of his relatives.

14. If the setting appears to be other than a studio, examine it closely and record your speculations. Perhaps it shows the arrangements in a parlor, revealing lifestyle clues and even helping to identify artifacts. Perhaps it shows how the farmhouse and buildings stood. Over time, continue to compare the setting and objects in the photograph with what you see in other photographs from the same family.

The photograph on the cover of this book came from a supplier to the publisher. I requested any identifying information that the supplier might have. Thus began an interesting research experiment. Several people became involved. Here is what we found so far.

1.   The supplier identified the photograph as "William H. McKernan, Brooklyn."

2.   Certified Genealogist Roger D. Joslyn searched the 1899 Brooklyn City Directory and found "McKiernan, Wm. H 61 Clifton pl" This was the closest name.

3.   Roger then searched the 1900 census. At 61 Clifton Place, he found the following family:

     McKiernan
Wm. H.	husb., b. Dec. 1868 in NY, m. 10 years, parents born Ireland
Agnes	wife, b. Apr. 1868 in NY, parents b. Ireland, 5/6 children alive
Mary	daughter, b. May 1890, in school, age 10
William	son, b. June 1891, in school, age 8
Thomas	son, b. July 1893, in school, age 6
Raymond	son, b. Aug. 1897, age 2
James	son, b. Sept. 1899, age 8 months

     The census also told us that McKiernan was a newspaster, living near other newspaper employees as well as neighbors who included two teachers, two clerks, and a pharmacist. All were renting their homes. The women neighbors with Irish names typically had numerous children but lost some. Families took in boarders, especially unmarried women relatives. Note that the first child, Mary, may have been conceived before marriage.

4.   Rick and I guessed the car was circa 1910. He looked through books that pictured old automobiles. He surmised that the car in the photograph was a Studebaker "A" Suburban from 1909 because of its appearance and even details such as the curved fenders, and the placement of the brake or shift handles. Whether or not this was correct, the model clearly was circa 1909–1910, based on comparisons with many models.

Adding ten years to the 1900 census to give the McKiernans the opportunity to buy this car of which the mister seems so proud, I compared the children in the photograph with the genders and ages of the census children as they would be then. They match, if the oldest child, Mary, was elsewhere when the photograph was taken. She would have been about twenty. Because she had reached adulthood, her being the only one absent could make sense, since the others would have ranged from ten to nineteen. The photograph also documents an additional four children since the 1900 census, who appear to have been born at the usual two-year intervals. I believe we have identified the family and gathered quite a bit of genealogical information on them. All of this is hypothetical and would take more research to prove, but it does illustrate what one can do with a photograph.

Figures 2 and 3. Compare the two panoramic photographs. Their size and shape suggests that they are related. With a magnifying glass, can you find the "Hotel Cayuga" in the town view? Its shape is distinctive, as is the taller structure behind it. So what is this town and where? Were the pictures taken in the same year? See the endnote for some answers.[2] Printed with permission from Rick W. Sturdevant.

15. If the setting is outdoors—a building, street, or town—examine and compare with other pictures that may be the same. Seek them in a historical society if you do not have them. Examine architectural styles. These speak not only to taste, but can also help date a photograph or identify the correct part of the country. See sources on architectural history in the chapter three bibliography. Also, see Loren Horton's articles listed in this chapter's bibliography.

16. There may be indicators of time of day and season of year in a photograph. For the former, study the direction of shadows or the degree of brightness. To determine seasons, study the development of leaves, flowers, and crops, the relative dryness of soil, and other clues such as clothing, outdoor furniture, or indoor bouquets. Is there snow on the ground or rooftops?

17. Is there printing anywhere inside the photograph? For example, one photograph of my grandfather shows him sitting in his office (Figure 4). There is a calendar hanging on the wall. My magnifying glass enabled me to see the year on the calendar. Even if the year had not been visible, one could judge by the position of the days in the month, comparing it to a perpetual calendar to determine the likeliest year.

18. Is there a picture within the picture? Sometimes an interior photograph reveals a portrait on the wall. Even better, you may find a copy of the wall portrait in the same family collection. Seeing that they match tells you much about who's who, whose home is pictured, the date, and what was important. You can also learn from funeral flowers. People photographed large wreaths and elaborate floral decorations at funerals. Sometimes, they placed a photograph of the deceased (taken when alive or dead) in the center of the flowers. Thus you can identify whose funeral it was and the

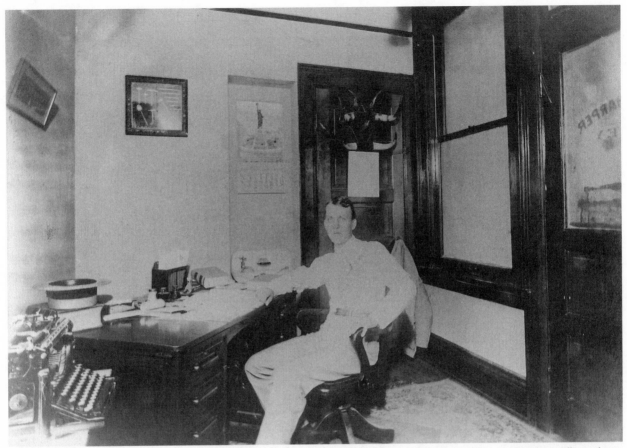

Figure 4. Analyze the clues in this photograph. The calendar is flipped to August 1911. The writing on the door tells us the office belongs to "HARPER" and his work is "_____EY." On the wall is a framed picture of mining tools, there is a long group photograph above the desk, and on the other door, cattle horns. He is wearing light colors and fabrics. His jacket has wrinkled sleeves. There is a straw hat on the desk. Perhaps it was a hot summer. The books, typewriter, and office supplies suggest work with records and writing. See the endnote to determine if you guessed well.[3] Author's collection.

date of the photograph. Sometimes families would have themselves photographed with the portraits of missing relatives or of themselves on the walls around them. Examine whether the hanging portrait represents someone in the group, someone at a noticeably earlier stage of life, or someone who is missing, presumed dead.

19. What are the people in the photograph wearing? Clothing can provide clues to time period, identity, economic status, gender (when small children are in doubt), ethnicity, age, season, and more.

20. Are the people wearing any jewelry or other distinctive artifacts that you can see with your magnifying glass? Can you identify the jewelry that is now in your possession? My grandmother had a favorite pin from a boyfriend. She wrote about it in her memoirs and noted that we could see the pin in the photograph of her taken at age sixteen. My mother (her daughter) knew which photograph that was. Although I never saw the pin itself (my grandmother lamented losing it), I was later able to spot that same pin in other photographs, even on my grandmother's wedding dress!

21. How are the people standing or seated in relation to one another and to

Figures 5 and 6. Analyze this pair of photographs. One depicts a Victorian child, and the other shows two adults and a boy in a parlor. What do they have in common, and what does that tell you about the family? What other clues can you find, and what do they tell you? See the endnote for some answers.[4] Printed with permission from Rick W. Sturdevant.

the setting? Does this reveal relationships, generations, or rank? Determine the size and relationships of a family from one photograph and it will help you speculate on the rest of the accompanying photographs. Ask each photograph questions: Were the old family members still alive when this was taken? Had the baby been born yet?

22. Study the faces. How old are the people pictured? Do you recognize them from one picture to the next? Do you see a family resemblance between them?

23. Compare a group photograph with the same family's collection of individual photographs. Can you match the individuals with their faces in the group?

24. Consider whether the photograph was taken in order to commemorate a family event. Describing the photograph may lead to a description of the event. Common family events to occasion photographs were marriages, engagements, anniversaries, birthdays, graduations, christenings, deaths, and funerals. Two types of wedding photographs were more common than today's bride-in-the-white-wedding-dress poses. One was to juxtapose individual photographs in matted openings on an elaborate preprinted marriage certificate. If you find one without the pictures, look through all of the family pictures to find the ones that may have once fit in the certificate. Otherwise the couple would pose together, seriously, in their best clothing, often one seated and one standing.

DEVELOPING A SIXTH SENSE

I feel I have developed a sixth sense for identifying people in photographs, one that you too can cultivate. Just as you have learned over the years to recognize in photographs your own parents, siblings, spouse, children, friends, and self, you can become that familiar with ancestors through photographs. **Historians' skills can assist you because the historian looks at the bigger picture: your family from the specific to the general and back again. The historian analyzes the whole, its parts, and the whole again.**

Technique

My favorite way to accomplish this, and to teach it, is to spread a large group of one family's photographs out on a safe, clean, dry, flat surface—usually a large table. When on my own in my house, I use the guest bed. Then think in terms of how you play solitaire or how you work a jigsaw puzzle. Look for whatever links pictures and group those photographs accordingly, even ranking by generation. Think of people's ages like card suits: the eldest is the king or queen, next generations rank lower, etc. In large group family portraits, folks tend to pose in family rank. Or, start as smart jigsaw puzzlers do: single out the easiest jigsaw corner, border, or color to recognize, look for its matching pieces, and work toward the most difficult. With family photographs, this means singling out the individuals of whose identities you are certain, then studying who is with them and at what ages. In either the solitaire or jigsaw method, often the easiest individuals to use as starting points are the eldest.

Children can be difficult. It helps, however, that proud parents thought them

the most photogenic. The more pictures that there are of a child, at various ages, and with companions, the more possible it is to identify the child. **Ask questions of the children's photographs.**

1. Does the child's sex seem difficult to determine? Both genders might have had long hair and curls from the 1880s through the 1910s. Both genders may have worn dresses during their first five years. A good rule of thumb, however, is that mothers almost always parted boys' hair on one side or the other, not down the middle, as they did with little girls. Boys normally did not wear jewelry, although ruffles and scalloped collars were acceptable. Christening gowns rarely varied by sex. Look back at Figures 1, 5, and 6. All of the children are little boys and, obvious or not, all are wearing short pants.

2. Does the one family have many pictures of one child at different ages? Was there just one child for a while?

3. Does another child join the first after a certain number of years? Does this match the genealogical information that you have for their ages and sexes?

4. Does the child wear identical clothing from one picture to the next?

5. Does the younger child start wearing the hand-me-downs of the first?

6. In a larger group, do the ages and genders of the children match the genealogical information? If so, can you begin to guess which child is which?

7. Do the children bear telling facial resemblances to their parents or to each other?

8. Does the child have striking facial features that you can follow from one picture to the next, even to adulthood? There are features that are so basic to our facial structures that they do not change. People also have the same preferences we have, particularly about hairstyles, that they are reluctant to change.

cut of jaw	shape and color of eyebrows
dimples	shape of face (round, angular)
distinctive nose	shape of mouth, lips
hair combed, parted, arranged a certain way	shape and size of ears
high forehead	wide-set or close-set eyes

9. As you try to follow a child's pictures to the matching adult, or to match the young adult to the elder, you sometimes will be surprised how little people's basic features change. Think what you already know about aging. Typical effects of aging that we all know and yet forget to apply to photographs include the following.

addition of eyeglasses	lengthening earlobes
darkening hair while maturing	receding hairline through life
developing beard, graying beard	thinning hair
graying hair, eyebrows in maturity	weight gain in middle age, thus rounder
increasing height and size in youth	
increasing wrinkles	

The sixth sense may only work, or work most reliably, when you have pictures of one family that have stayed together as a collection. Thus keep such groups or albums together and identify photographs, even your own recent ones, as soon as possible. Ask any relative or acquaintance to assist you, soon, with identifying photographs.

WHAT KIND OF PHOTOGRAPH IS THIS?

There were several popular types of photography during the span of your family history. On page 96 are some basic distinctions to help you identify and date the photographs that you find.

Know The History of the Art Form

\di'fin\ *vb*

Definitions

Sketches, painted portraits, and silhouettes were the only means our prephotography ancestors had of preserving their images. Many people painted portraits of one another. The best surviving collections are from New England. Portrait painters were called limners, and most of them were craftsmen who painted folk art without training. It was acceptable for women to sketch and paint, too. All of the prephotography methods of portraiture faded after the advent of the daguerreotype in 1839. Wealthy people might carry on their traditions of employing artists, but photography was available to almost everyone. Many early photographs, especially enlargements for framing, came to look like painted portraits as photographers altered them for color or clarity of line. In the 1840s to 1860s, photographers retouched lines often to prevent fading, a problem later corrected in their processing.

Daguerreotypes, introduced in 1839, were the first popular photographs. Because they are fragile, one usually finds them encased in wood frames. They fell out of favor because they could not be duplicated as the later forms could be. Do not assume that the picture in a lavish velvet and gold frame is a daguerreotype. People reused the frames.

Ambrotypes literally replaced daguerreotypes in the same frames sometimes. They are distinguishable because ambrotypes do not have the mirror surface. A magical feature of ambrotypes is that you can make some scratches disappear simply by replacing the sheet of black paper or fabric backing behind them, inside the frame. This is because ambrotypes are negatives on glass that turn to positives when backed with black. They look damaged when the black backing fades or deteriorates.

Tintypes were sharp images printed on metal. One can use a magnet to test whether an image is a tintype. Individual tintypes can be as small as a half-inch circumference, suitable for jewelry. Small tintypes traveled with many Civil War soldiers. I have seen family-group tintypes as large as 8″ × 10″! They are sturdy, but the surface images scratch easily. Some folks replaced ambrotypes with tintypes in the same cases. They were popular in 1920s and 1930s carnivals as cheap booth snapshots. Good or restored tintypes copy especially well.

Cartes de visite and cabinet cards were images glued to heavy cardstock because the paper was thin and would curl. *Cartes de visite* were small and intended for use as visiting cards. Many people gave them away and left them in silver card-receiving trays at homes that they visited. Copies were easily obtained, so

QUICK GUIDE TO COMMON TYPES OF PHOTOGRAPHS AND IMAGES IN AMERICAN FAMILY HISTORY

Type	Approximate Span of Popularity	Identifying Features
pen-and-ink or pencil sketches, painted portraits	c. 1780s–1850s esp. 1810s–1840s (until daguerreotypes)	esp. in New England, oil and watercolor
silhouettes	late 1700s–1820s	black snipped profile on white backing
daguerreotype	1839–1857	silvery, mirrorlike, often encased in gold and velvet, often hand tinted; must hold at a certain angle to see image; metal
tintype	1856–1938 esp. to 1890s	image on metal, often encased; image often scratching or peeling; very sharp resolution; tintypes were first lacquered black; brown was introduced in 1870
ambrotype	1854–1870s	underexposed glass negative on black backing, often hand tinted; not mirrorlike, rosy cheeks added
cartes de visite	1859–1914 esp. 1850s–1870s	2¼″ × 4¼″ size suitable as calling cards; revenue stamps on back indicate dating between 1 September 1864–1 August 1866
cabinet card	1866–1914 esp. to 1890s	4¼″ × 6½″ image glued to center of heavy cardstock
specific sizes of cabinet cards	1870–1890 1875–late 1890s late 1870s–1900 late 1870s–1900 no specific date	Victoria, 3¼″ × 5″ promenade, 4″ × 7″ boudoir, 5″ × 8½″ imperial, 7⅞″ × 9⅞″ panel, 8¼″ × 4″
glass-plate negative	1878–1940s esp. 1880s–1910s	negative film over glass squares; often peeling at edges
cyanotype	1842–1910s esp. 1890s–1910s	image with blue coloration throughout; same process as blueprints
postcards made from family photographs	1900–1920s	black-and-white standard-size postcards printed for addressing on back; recognizable as amateur poses
charcoal portrait or overpainting	1850s–1910s, esp. 1880s–1890s	large, often in elaborate frames, drawn or painted over enlarged photographs (you may find the original photo and recognize the person, hairstyle, and clothing); often multiple family members done together or separately at same time, typically 16″ × 20″
stereo views	1850s–1910s 1851–1867 1868 1879	double images on 3″ × 7″ cards for viewing in scope; three-dimensional flat and thin corners became rounded heavier type, curved, 4″ × 7″
studio black-and-white photographic portraits	1920s–1950s	closer views often in gray cardstock folders
cellulose nitrate film	1888–1951	has the word *nitrate* on its edge; this film is so flammable that it can spontaneously combust. Make copies and discard originals in accordance with local hazardous waste regulations. Store in freezer in the meantime.
cellulose acetate film	1937–1960s	while not dangerous, it will disintegrate; says *safety* on edges; copy immediately
black-and-white snapshot	1930s–1950s	from home cameras such as Brownies; developers would often print dates on margins, put a series together in a small booklet, or pink the edges
home movies		8mm or 16mm, transferable to video
color snapshot	1942–present	commonly 3½″ × 3½″, often with processing date on margin; colors fade within twenty-five years, faster with light exposure
Polaroid prints	black and white 1947–1963 color 1963–present	Polaroid camera could develop a print immediately

folks had duplicates. Thus your family photograph collection may feature nonrelatives among the *cartes de visite*.

There is one happy detail about *cartes de visite*. If you find some that seem to have postage stamps on the back, read the stamps closely. They usually picture George Washington and say "U.S. Inter. Rev," "Two cents," and "Proprietary." These were tax stamps to show that one had paid the tax required on photographs in the North during and immediately after the Civil War, specifically from 1 September 1864 to 1 August 1866. The stamps can help you date the photographs.

Cabinet cards were processed like *cartes de visite*, but came in substantial sizes ranging between 4¼″×6½″ to almost 8″×10″. These were the family portraits with a sepia tone that graced velvet-covered parlor albums in the 1870s through 1900. Albums were specially made with slots for *cartes de visite* and cabinet cards.

Glass-plate negatives print out beautifully on printing-out paper. Because they are glass, they are fragile. A plentiful supply of these, especially blank ones, suggests you may have had a photographer in the family.

Cyanotypes were most in use between the 1890s and the 1910s. They did not catch on because of their blueprint coloration. Some amateur photographers liked them because they were cheap and easy to make. Interestingly, a cyanotype will fade with sunlight exposure but will recover somewhat when put back in the dark. If you want to have a more useful image for framing or enlargement you can make black-and-white copies of cyanotypes by photographing them using a blue filter.

Overpainting was popular in the Gilded Age (1877–1900) and refers to a wide variety of touch-ups. Photographers retouched images for a host of reasons: they faded, clients wanted color and were happiest with vanity satisfied, or people wanted to frame large portraits. A popular 1880s–1890s version was to enlarge a photograph of a family member. Before later refinements, enlarging was a dissatisfying process in which the image became more faded and less defined. An "artist" would use charcoal or crayon to reconstruct the lines of your ancestors' faces. Often advertised as "life-size," the standard charcoal portrait seems to be 16″×20″. Folks tended to display them in elaborate wood and plaster, gilded frames. Watch in your collection of regular-size photographs for the originals. One way to spot overpainting is to compare the facial features with the clothing. Faces will be precisely drawn, but the clothing, collars, jewelry, and background will have a hastily drawn appearance.

Know the Tricks of the Photographer's Trade

If your ancestors appear stiff and unsmiling, it is because they were. Early daguerreotypes required between fifteen and thirty minutes for the proper exposure. Wet-plate negatives shortened the time in the 1850s and even faster plates became available in the 1870s and 1880s, but still the photograph was an ordeal. Early "photographists" (studio portrait specialists preferred this term) used headrests and supporting stands, similar to those that hold up collectible dolls on display. The room and clothing were liable to be hot. Flashing lights—whether mirrored sunlight or explosive flash powder—were alarming or annoying. Therefore, most ancestors did not smile. Also, photographists were trying to please clients who wanted photographs to display their character as well as paintings would. So they encouraged the clients to make serious faces. Even today, many people are sheepish about displaying their full-teeth smiles when having their pictures taken.

Photographers' backdrops were sometimes ridiculous paintings and the props were unnatural in people's hands. Photographers could order their props and backdrops from catalogs. Furniture such as fringed and tasseled chairs were also cheap photographers' stock-in-trade. Children were provided with dolls, bicycles, and fishing poles. You can even date photographs by the props: neoclassical elements such as columns, stair rails, and curtains were popular props through the 1860s and 1870s; rustic, outdoor nature props were a fad of the 1880s; and bicycling and sports symbols were popular by the turn of the century. Automobiles were also common as photographer's props and regardless of who owned them, they can help in dating the photograph. Photographers experimented with photomontage, placing people in the midst of crowds where they had not been. They retouched features to please the clients, leaving distorted, unnatural, and falsely colored reminders not to trust everything that we see.

RECORD PHOTOGRAPH IDENTIFICATION AND ANALYSIS

Inventory photographs so you do not lose the information you have deduced from one examination to the next. On your inventory form, use question marks liberally to indicate any doubtful information.

Dating Photographs and Extracting Social History Based on Clothing and Fashion

There are many books that will assist you in deciphering the clues offered by clothing in photographs. I have listed some of the best in this chapter's bibliography and in the general bibliography at the back of the book. Knowing what was in fashion helps you date the image. There are also, however, many social history revelations to be had from studying what people wore. As you study photographs, do not just look at when those fashions were worn, but why, how it felt to wear them, and what the style told people about each other.

Gilded Age wedding dresses were rarely white and frothy as they are today, especially in photographs. Brides wore their best dresses and traveling suits, trying to appear serious and dignified. Photographers discouraged everyone from coming to the studio in blinding white. So a wedding or marriage photograph would be of the couple, dressed in darker colors, posing in a studio with as much dignity as they could muster.

Frances Hodgson Burnett's 1886 novel *Little Lord Fauntleroy* was so popular that it dictated style for unlucky little boys for a decade or so. Boys of that time would have girlish, long haircuts with bangs and blouses with large, ruffled collars. Their dark breeches and frock coats would complete the dandified appearance. When you see this fashion, you can analyze what it meant about views

A USEFUL FORM YOU CAN REPRODUCE

For a full-size blank copy of the Family Photograph Inventory and Analysis form, see page 234. You are free to photocopy this form for personal use.

For More Info

For excellent charts and advice on identifying photographs by costume, see Maureen Taylor's *Uncovering Your Ancestry Through Family Photographs*, pages 63–72.

of boys and where it came from. You can also date the photograph as circa 1886–1900.

Consider regional variations, too. You may not find photographs of your cowboy ancestors to tell you what gear they wore, but a book will tell you what was typical so you can still describe that. In Tom Lindmier and Steve Mount's *I See by Your Outfit: Historic Cowboy Gear of the Northern Plains*, you can discover what men wore from their hats to their spurs, rather than relying on inaccurate movie stereotypes.

FAMILY PHOTOGRAPH INVENTORY AND ANALYSIS

Inventory Number (in Soft Pencil or on Archival Label on Back) __1069__

Date of This Record __January 28, 2000__

Recorder __Katherine Scott Sturdevant__

Location of Original Photograph __in recorder's possession__

Condition of Original __stained, yellowed, worn edges, fading__

Location of Negatives and Copies __same, plus copy printed in book by recorder, Bringing Your Family History to Life Through Social History__

Original Location __Maybelle Sturdevant home, Waverly, Iowa__

Notations on the Photograph __none__

Description of the Photograph (Type and Image) __Lafayette Sturdevant and camera on crude (homemade?) cabinet card, circa 1870?__

Photographer, if Known __unknown, except that Sturdevant was a photographer himself and for a time also had a partner__

Setting of Photograph __unknown__

Identifying Features (Artifacts, Clothing, Signage) __camera could be identified, clothing style__

People Appearing in Photograph (Identified and Unidentified) __Lafayette Sturdevant__

Analysis of Historical Significance __could reveal how early Sturdevant began photography, general value for early camera and example of an Iowa photographer__

Unsolved Mysteries to Research __age of photograph and Sturdevant by age of camera__

Keep paying attention to social history by examining clothing in photographs all the way to the present. For example, perhaps you will find a family member in a photograph wearing a zoot suit, studded leather jacket, bell-bottom pants, or a tie-dyed shirt. These are obvious statements of rebellion that one can analyze for personal and social meanings. See Ruth Rubenstein's *Dress Codes: Meanings and Messages in American Culture*.

It Helps to Know the History

General historical research about a time period or place can help you identify a photograph. Identifying the photograph through historical research can give you historical context for your family history. See the illustration of the "Landing of Columbus" in Figure 7. A photographer used cabinet cards that had this printed on the back. Why? Certainly it was not a photograph from 1492. Neither the photographer nor his subjects were Italian Americans. Historical research might remind you that the Chicago World's Fair, also known as the World's Columbian Exposition, was a major event for Americans in 1893, marking the year after the four hundreth anniversary of Columbus's discovery. The photographer dated his photograph for you! To verify, by the way, we also recognized the baby in the photograph on the other side (not shown) as one that was born in 1893.

Suppose you find the picture in Figure 8 of two identifiable relatives (the women) in front of their house with unknown children. On the back is written "Opal and her Belgian children." Note there is also a Red Cross banner in the window to your left. Try researching the most specific historical pieces of information: Belgians or Red Cross. A textbook reference or an encyclopedia would

Reminder

Figure 7. "Landing of Columbus," back of photograph of E. Louise Chandler, c. 1893, Frank Sturdevant Collection, in author's possession.

Figure 8. "Opal and her Belgian children," Opal Lovejoy, c. 1917. Woman on porch is Opal's mother Lillie Sturdevant Lovejoy. Also barely visible is a star banner in the window opposite the Red Cross banner, indicating a man in service. Frank Sturdevant Collection, in author's possession.

tell you that, during World War I, American women worked for the Red Cross and some temporarily took in Belgian refugees. Knowing your relative did this, you could now do more intensive research into her whole experience in order to be able to describe it in your family history narrative.

You may find photographs of dead children. Postmortem photographs were popular in the 1880s–1920s, and children were a common subject. This was not morbid by our ancestors' standards. They lost many children, and a photograph or a lock of hair was a souvenir in memory of an all-too-short life. Dead babies are relatively easy to recognize as deceased in photographs once your mind has allowed for the possibility. They usually appear asleep or unnaturally laid out.

For example, see the infant in Figure 9. He lies on a flat table that is draped with a white cloth. He is surrounded with flowers. There is no obvious reason for this situation other than that he was dead. The picture has no identification, although it seems to be a studio photograph datable to the 1910s–1920s. The baby, however, appears to be full-term and the flowers beside him appear to be narcissus, which would bloom in early spring, especially if forced by a florist.

Finding the memorial cabinet card (Figure 10) with the photograph (Figure 9) would answer almost everything. It reminds us that the sentimentality of Victorians

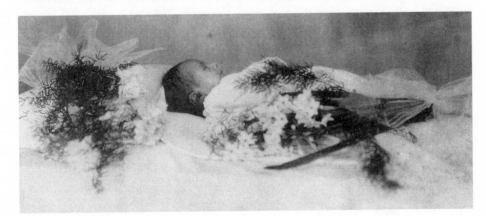

Figure 9. Postmortem photograph of a baby, c. 1921, believed to be Willard Sturdevant. Printed with permission of Wendell Sturdevant and Rick Sturdevant.

Figure 10. A memorial card for Willard Sturdevant. This particular memorial cabinet card was extremely popular. The Henisches included it in their book, *The Photographic Experience.*[5] It reproduces a sketchy version of Wilhelm von Kaulbach's painting *The Angel of Peace*. The verse and vital information on the card could vary; one could change the pronouns in the verse, for example, between male and female. The card could also include a photograph of the deceased child. The Henisches show a copyright date of 1888 or 1898. Families selected memorial cabinet cards from extensive catalogs and brochures kept by funeral directors and printers. The Sturdevant family even kept the brochure.
Printed with permission of Wendell Sturdevant and Rick Sturdevant.

carried over into the 1920s, because those born in the Victorian era were still child-bearing adults then. Little Willard (the name is misspelled "Williard" on the card) died in February, a good time to buy narcissus from a florist. If we had not found the cabinet card, however, the family lore, oral history, cemetery records, letters, and other genealogical sources would have helped identify poor little Willard.

Documentary Photograph

Historians, historical societies, and photograph archivists will tell you that simple portraits of individuals and groups are treasures, but are not the very best photographs for social history. Even better are photographs of people participating in work or recreational activities, of towns and buildings, and thus of social history as it happened. These can be your ideal social history photographs for researching

WRITING FROM A FAMILY PHOTOGRAPH AND MEMORIAL CARD

Maybelle Sturdevant deeply mourned the loss of her first of only two babies. Little Willard Edward was a full-term baby who lived only on his birthday, 26 February 1921. According to family tradition, he may have died of strangulation by his own umbilical cord. Maybelle gave him her father's and grandfather's first name. Frank gave him his own father's name as a middle name. When Maybelle and Frank buried him in the family cemetery, they did not provide a traditional aboveground marker, but instead embedded a metal vase—a canister within a canister—into the ground between family graves, so that fresh flowers would last longer for the baby. Around the vase's rim was engraved Willard's vital information. Maybelle proceeded to mark little Willard's life in any way that might keep him alive in memory. Among Maybelle's photographs was a postmortem picture presumed to be Willard surrounded by narcissus, even though it was February. The funeral card carried a poem about the "little treasure," who was "Gone but not Forgotten."

Maybelle and Frank were thrilled to have another son, Wendell Frank, on 30 May 1924. At some point later, probably on two separate occasions (because the frames do not match), Maybelle found two portraits of babies for sale in the furniture store. They were prints by the popular illustrator Bessie Pease Gutmann. One, called *A Little Bit of Heaven*, was of an infant sound asleep, looking for all the world like baby Willard gone to his eternal rest. It is the older of the two prints, sepia-tone rather than colored. The similarity between the Gutmann print and the photograph of Willard helps us identify the photograph just as it made the print appeal to the bereaved mother.

The other Gutmann illustration, titled *Awakening*, was a colorful print of a smiling, reaching, healthy baby surrounded by blue. Maybelle hung them forever above her bed. She called them "my two boys." Wendell grew up acutely aware of having lost a big brother. When he had his first son, he gave him the middle name Willard.[1]

---

[1] Rick Willard Sturdevant, conversation with author, 25 September 1999, Colorado Springs, Colorado; photograph believed to be Willard Edward Sturdevant, 26 February 1921, Waverly, Iowa, Frank Sturdevant Collection, in author's possession; memorial card for "Williard" Sturdevant, 26 February 1921, Frank Sturdevant Collection, in author's possession.

and writing your family history too. Think like a historian. When you have such pictures in your collection, strive to identify not only the people, but the places and artifacts. There will be clues to watch for in settings beyond those listed above for examining photos.

For example, examine the photograph in Figure 11. These are obviously men dressed and equipped for work. The large photograph has a handwritten label on the back that says "Barre VT Stone mason 1930s?" The handwriting appears to be an older person's hand. The type of photograph is a large, sepia-tone cabinet card. Thus the owner's guess at the date seems to be incorrect. Everything about

Figure 11. Unknown photograph from antique store with back label "Barre VT Stone mason 1930s?" Author's collection.

the photograph seems at least twenty to thirty years older than that: clothing styles and hand tools, for example. There is snow on the ground, rooftops, and men's shoes. See how they are displaying their tools and many are wearing aprons? Some of the aprons look makeshift, perhaps from burlap or flour sacks tied around their middles. Note their clothing, caps, and neck scarves. Also, note the sheds behind them on the left side. These look industrial, and one is built of light-colored brick and stone. Faded in the background are more buildings of light-colored brick.

What about the men themselves? For many, the break-time hobby was smoking cigarettes and pipes. Some sport twirled moustaches. There is quite a range of ages: a few middle-aged men, many perhaps in their twenties and thirties, and as many as one-third appear very young, a couple even barely in their teen years, if that. Very few carry any height; they appear to average closer to five feet tall than to six. In coloring and facial features, most of them also seem to have an ethnic commonality of some sort, with one or two darker exceptions. They work hard in cold weather and get dirty with a light-colored, dusty dirt (on their dark lapels).

One source I will recommend again and again is the Works Progress Administration's American Guide series from the Federal Writers' Project of the New Deal. I refer to these as the WPA state guides. For this series, government-employed writers compiled oral history and local detail to write a volume on every state, as well as many volumes on individual towns and special topics. Dating from the late 1930s and early 1940s, these books captured small-town America before its last series of radical changes. Each is written in a driving-tour format, so almost any little village along the route received at least a mention. The essays tend to be a somewhat literary effort to characterize each community.

Sources

To learn more about the photograph, I pull the Vermont guide—a used library copy—from my shelf and check the index for Barre. Armed only with what I know from the stone masons' photograph, I make a remarkable discovery. "Barre, the Granite Center," the guide tells me, is dominated by the granite quarrying industry "from the stark gray quarries on Millstone Hill to the long, somber sheds on the river flats." Brick and stone buildings, streets, statuary, and cemetery markers display the handiwork of the hundreds of "Scotch" and Italian granite-cutters and stone-carvers. The central memorial statue of the town was of Scottish poet Robert Burns, presented by the Scottish citizens in 1899. These "hard-working, hard-playing stonecutters" arrived starting in the 1880s and 1890s. Their fine granite work graced many monuments—the best stone being white or bluish gray. "Much of the carving and lettering is now done with pneumatic sandblast machines," the 1937 book continues, "but skilled stone-carvers are still found in all the finishing plants."[6]

One photograph and one history book, together, can offer so much family and social history. Although more genealogical and historical research is needed, the two sources together suggest setting, work, recreation, ethnicity, and chronology. We now have clues to explain the light dusty dirt, the handtools, and the ethnic appearance of the men. We can already imagine how, in a family narrative, we could describe the town, the plants, the quarrying, the craftsmanship, the child labor, the ethnic character, and leisure activity. We could probably consult a city directory to determine which company employed the ancestor, and then this WPA guide would also tell us something about that company. It all started with a documentary photograph.

PHOTOGRAPHIC ARTIFACTS
Our Ancestors' Version of the View-Master

Amongst your family photographs you may also find photographic equipment or mass-produced photographs. These are artifacts that the family purchased or received rather than pictures of the family. Yet they can be just as important to family history as any artifact. Social history will assist you with these as well. Perhaps your ancestor was a photographer. After all, the equipment was available in the Sears Roebuck and Montgomery Ward catalogs. Just as your VCR and stash of videotapes would reveal much about you to future historians, so, too, we can analyze our ancestors through their parlor entertainment. For example, we can try it with an artifact that many American families acquired starting in the 1880s.

Great-Grandpa's Stereopticon and Stereo View Cards

- We found an artifact in my parents' crawlspace. I knew it was a stereoscope or stereo viewer. If I had not known, the old Sears Catalogue would have told me. My reprint, *1902 Edition of The Sears, Roebuck Catalogue*, pictures an almost identical stereoscope for "24 cents."
- Family tradition says this was Great-Grandpa's "stereopticon," as my mother preferred to call it. She told me that her mother, Kate, and the whole family enjoyed it while growing up. My mother also remembered playing with it as

Case Study

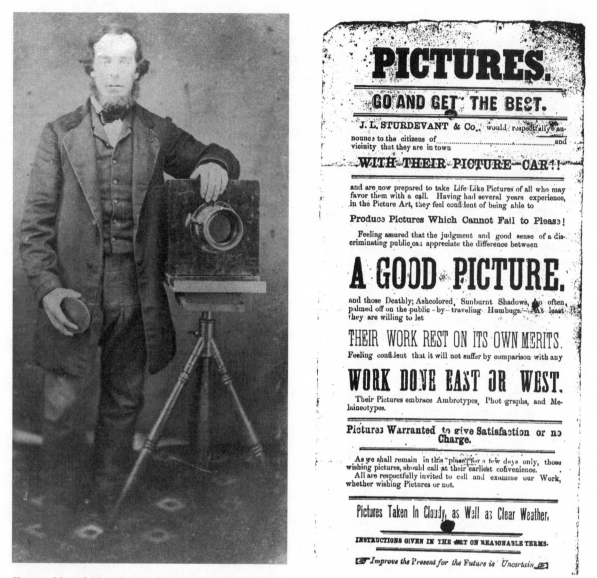

Figures 12 and 13. Lafayette Sturdevant, Rick's great-great-grandfather, worked at photography for a time to earn an income. Printed with permission of Rick W. Sturdevant.

a child. Her mother told her that Great-Grandpa fixed it when it broke. The packet of matching cards offers views of exotic places and comedic situations. There is also a card displaying a weeping mother kneeling by an empty crib.

- Comparison to other stereopticons in antique stores reveals that this one must have lost its original hood. The replacement hood looks homemade from a metal coffee can—the label "coffee" still visible. The replacement is well cut, though, and firmly attached. It is painted brown to match the wood pieces. There is also a fixture on the base that would have, at one time, fit into a pedestal. Alas, that stand is missing, too.

- Old newspaper ads confirm family tradition that Great-Grandpa was a tinsmith, making utilitarian things with metal. He had a shop selling hundreds of different household and farm implements.

- John Waldsmith's *Stereo Views: An Illustrated History and Price Guide*, tells us that stereoscopes of this sort were made between 1892 and 1908, the period when my grandmother (born 1881) was growing up in her parents' home. Waldsmith also notes that, during the height of the stereoscope's popularity in the 1890s, one "could be found in nearly every middle- and upper-income home in the United States." They were popular parlor entertainment. The stereoscope combined two pictures into a three-dimensional image just like the more modern View-Master. The same book helped me identify Great-Grandpa's stereo cards by the photographers' names. It was also through reading this book that I learned to call the replaced part a hood. The author points out that "Condition is the key in determining price. . . . All original parts increase the value." Thus Great-Grandpa's stereopticon is not very valuable as an antique for a collector (although priceless to me).[7]
- Handwritten family trees and family tradition indicated that Great-Grandma lost infants to death. The spacing between the births of her surviving children also suggests possible losses.
- Still another book, Harvey Green's *The Light of the Home: An Intimate View of the Lives of Women in Victorian America,* reveals that infant deaths occasioned melodramatic sentimentality in photographs during the late Victorian period.

WRITING FROM PHOTOGRAPHIC ARTIFACTS

Now, from examining artifacts, photographs, social history, family tradition, oral history, antique stores, and collector's guides, I can write the stereoscope into my family history to make the narrative more detailed, interesting, and meaningful. See the case study on page 108.

We Must Be Related to Abraham Lincoln—He's in Our Family Album!

Do you remember the photographs of movie stars that used to come with new wallets and picture frames in order to show us where our own pictures would fit? It was always funny to think someone could keep those Hollywood faces there and claim them as relations. This is a more serious issue for family historians who find famous faces in their family albums. I have known several people who, when they saw a famous person in the midst of a family album, asked me if I thought they could really be related to General Grant, Robert E. Lee, or General Tom Thumb, P.T. Barnum's circus midget. Of course, one could be. The easiest way to dismiss a family relationship is when the famous picture turns out to have been clipped from a magazine.

Occasionally, however, the famous person appears in one of our antique photographs, matching those of the rest of the family to the extent that they are all, say, cabinet cards, at least. For example, in the middle of one family album was a *carte de visite* that I recognized as General Tom Thumb. It was possible to duplicate photographs for distribution as early as 1854, so some photograph albums came with Tom or other personages inserted in their own slots. If anything

Case Study

Growing up in 1890s Kansas meant Kate had homemade dolls and makeshift toys. Any activity might become a game. The closest the children got to most manufactured toys was the Sears Roebuck or Montgomery Ward ("Monkey Ward") mail-order catalogs, dubbed "the wish books." Kate and her brothers pored over these big books often, especially in anticipation of Christmas.

One of Kate's favorite objects was the stereopticon along with the many sets of view cards they could order. Like middle-class families all across America, the whole family spent many hours viewing faraway places and funny situations through the viewer that made each double picture three-dimensional. Some of the stereo cards were for the adults only, however. These usually depicted other adults behaving in silly ways.

The children must have been sorry when the hood piece broke off of the family's stereopticon. Thank goodness their "Pa" was a tinsmith. He crafted a new hood from a coffee can that made it look like new. Never mind that the edges were a little sharp if you held it too close to your face.[1]

[In another section, I could write . . .]

Fannie must have mourned the loss of her baby. One clue to her feelings is a singular stereo card. Among the travel views and comedy series, "The Empty Crib" stands alone in its mournfulness. In the three-dimensional image, a mother kneels at the bed where her lost child once slept. Perhaps Fannie's daughter Kate understood the card better when she, too, lost one of her babies.[2]

---

[1] Unless otherwise noted, information is from family tradition as relayed by Barbara Scott. Stereopticon and cards in author's possession. See John Waldsmith, *Stereo Views: An Illustrated History and Price Guide* (Radnor, Pa.: Wallace-Homestead Book Co., 1991).

[2] Stereo card "The Empty Crib" in author's possession.

more than that, Tom Thumb's picture revealed a family interest in circus performers, not a surprise relative. His appearance, then, may give some social history to write, even though it does not give us the satisfaction of having famous kin.

It was customary when compiling family photograph albums to treat them as edifying books for the parlor table. Many families used the first few pages to display people whom they admired, the "stars" of their day. If a family placed General Grant or General Lee in the family album, that suggests their politics, which side they may have supported in the Civil War, whom they admired, and how familial they felt about such heroes. Go back to the genealogical charts; they may have even named a child after their hero, such as John George Lafayette Sturdevant (honoring both George Washington and the Marquis de Lafayette).

In *Homelands and Waterways: The American Journey of the Bond Family, 1846–1926*, Adele Logan Alexander presents a good example of family photographs that included a famous person's image. The very recognizable Booker T. Washington gave to Alexander's ancestors a picture of himself, which she found in an archival museum collection. She also found a group photograph that included a relative posing with Booker T. Washington. She relates her family's connection with Washington's Tuskegee Institute as an integral part of the family history. She also uses photographs and illustrations that are not from her family collection but illustrate aspects of its history. In her case, these include Civil War photographs of black sailors and their officers, ships, and hospital; events that ancestors experienced and buildings where they lived or worked; cemetery markers and monuments; and famous leaders whom her ancestors followed. These are excellent examples of how to use documentary photographs and pictures of famous individuals in a family history narrative that has strong historical context.[8]

Don't Dismiss Images of Strangers Found Among Family Photos

You may identify photographs in the family collection of people who bear no known relation to your family. One example found among family photographs in the Withers family trunk was "Aunt Mattie Sapplington," an elderly lady on a *carte de visite* (see Figure 14). Her name appeared in pencil on the back, with a corrected spelling as though spelling it did not come automatically. The photographer was "T.M. Wells, Decatur, Ills."

Hidden Treasures

I knew of no connection with anyone by the name Sapplington, until I went back over the family census listings on microfilm. In 1870 Illinois, the Withers family lived in Clinton. They had sold the Jacksonville-area farm after both the father and oldest son had died, the latter in the Civil War. These deaths had left the mother and three daughters alone. In the census I found Mattie Sapplington listed as living in the next numbered house. I still might someday find evidence that she was truly a relation. Unless or until I do, however, my theory is that she, as a neighbor, befriended Widow Withers and her daughters, and they befriended her. Her wonderful character shows through the *carte de visite*. Many older women were dubbed "Aunt" without being blood kin. The Withers family had originated in Kentucky, where this might be their custom.

As we do now—although perhaps less often—people used to send one another photographs and trade them with friends. When you visited someone's parlor, they might invite you to leave your photograph in their family album as a keepsake. Although you must determine whether a "stranger" was a family member, remember that they were not truly strangers to your ancestors. Think like a historian. Research these outsiders for family social history as well.

CITING PHOTOGRAPHS

Advice on citing photographs is only slightly less scarce than advice on citing artifacts. This is because style guides have assumed that one would either use a photograph as an illustration in a book, identifying it in a caption or with a figure number; or cite a photograph from another work being cited, listing the figure number at the end of the citation after the book's page number (see *The Chicago Manual of Style*, page 567, section 15.200).

Citing Sources

Figure 14. *Carte de visite,*
c. 1870, with "Aunt Mattie
Sapplington" written on
back. Photographer's label
identifies Decatur, Illinois.
Author's collection.

I am suggesting, therefore, something a bit radical. We should be citing photographs that we use as sources in our family history narratives. If you learn something useful from examining a photograph, the photograph is your source. You may describe an image after seeing it in a photograph, or you may even describe a favorite photograph itself, as part of the narrative. Whether or not you also reproduce the photograph in your narrative for readers to see, you need to cite it so that readers know where you got your information and everything that you know about that source.

Elizabeth Shown Mills, in *Evidence! Citation and Analysis for the Family Historian,* presents two examples of how to cite portraits in archives or private possession, along with annotation of the portraits' history. I have adapted her advice under the assumption you may be citing hundreds of family photographs. Because we are breaking new ground here, we may need to experiment. **Whatever method of citation seems best, follow it consistently. Consider the convenience of your readers first, and provide all of the information they need.**

If we have all of the pertinent information, we must choose whether to list the photographer first or the subject first.

Reminder

> T.M. Wells, photographer (verso), "Aunt Mattie Sapplington," Decatur, Ill., c. 1870 (Dickey Family Collection, original in author's possession).

or

"Aunt Mattie Sapplington," T.M. Wells, photographer, Decatur, Ill. (verso),
c. 1870 (Dickey Family Collection, original in author's possession).

If we conform to what is usual practice with book citations, we would list the photographer first because he is the "author" of the photograph. I believe that it makes more sense to list the subject first, however, because the subject of the photograph will more often be part of the family history and the subject is more likely to be known and important to us for our purposes. I put information that was taken directly from the back of the photograph in quotation marks because I am, indeed, quoting it. *Verso* refers to the backside of the photograph; *recto* would be the front.

The less you know, the more your footnotes must take on an explanatory quality. If the photograph does not provide reliable printed information, you will need to make clear when your details are speculation or supposition. It should be evident in every footnote that you are citing a photograph. Names alone are not necessarily enough.

"Papa's Cousin Helen Frick" (verso), probable overpainted portrait,
photographer unknown, location unknown but probably Kentucky,
"Taken in 1840," (Dickey Family Collection, original in author's
possession).

Chandler, Maybelle and Frank Sturdevant, photograph, photographer
unknown, Camp Cody, Deming, New Mexico, 1918, identified by Rick
Sturdevant (Frank Sturdevant Collection, original in author's
possession).

"Barre VT Stone mason 1930s?" photograph of workmen at granite yard,
c. 1900, origin unknown, original in author's possession, purchased at an
antique store in Colorado Springs, Colo., circa 1993.

What if the photograph is not of people? We can try to follow the same model, placing subject first.

Naismith farmhouse owned by Archibald and Janet Naismith, photographer
unknown, Straffordsville, Ontario, Canada, c. 1920s, identified by James
A. Scott (James Scott Collection, original in author's possession).

Goodland, Kansas, photograph of Main Street, photographer unknown,
c. 1895, copied by M.C. Parker (original in Sherman County Historical
Society, copy in author's possession).

In each case I have tried to begin the citation with the name of the important family member or place assuming that this is the key information most readers would seek.

Acquiring Family Photographs

In chapter six, we will literally address letters. When you start collecting family history, you should write to anyone anywhere who might have family photographs. Include in any such letter "Do you have any old family photographs?"

Idea Generator

or words to that effect. Offer to help pay for copies or to bring your equipment and make copies yourself. Offer to trade copies of what you have for copies of what they have. Offer to help supply archival envelopes for the pictures. If you learn that a relative has an old trunk, closet, garage, or woodshed, ask whether there may be family photographs there. Offer to help in the unpleasant task of cleaning out the possible treasure trove. Offer anything, but be cautious until you learn whether your relatives are comfortable with the idea or prone to shy away from even mentioning what they have. Relatives may suspect you of trying to take, keep, or wheedle them out of pictures they own and value. After all, you probably would hesitate to trust *them*. Always offer to make copies rather than take originals. Emphasize that you want the information those photographs hold, not necessarily the original photographs themselves.

Hidden Treasures

You may be surprised to learn you can sometimes find family photographs in the cemetery. It was (and still is) a custom for some to frame a picture of the deceased in a tombstone or to leave framed photographs on a shelf inside a crypt. Italian Americans are one group known for placing photographs on markers and in crypts. Again, respect is in order. If you have your camera and macro lens with you, you can make copies of the photographs to use later in the family collection. Certainly one should not remove the photographs, nor should one even photograph them without permission of the cemetery authorities. Such permission may be necessary anyway in order to enter a locked crypt.

Serendipitous Discoveries of Photographs

Tip

The best way to get people to share or give family photographs is to become known as the family historian who is the Keeper of Everything. Then they may send photographs spontaneously. To create this image for yourself, write those many letters and, over time, recommend ways for relatives to care for their photographs. Ask that, even if they do not send them to you, they make sure the photos fall into the safest hands. Appreciate anything they send to you, even if it is of lesser family history value, because they are trying to help. Be patient with the growing piles of "stuff" you acquire because you cannot separate the wheat from their chaff without risking your relatives' feelings.

Remember that someone else may have already staked out territory as the family photograph archivist. Figures 12 and 13 showed you that Lafayette Sturdevant was a photographer, even offering his services to the public for income. He passed this talent (and his other hobby, beekeeping) on to one of his grandsons, along with his old equipment and many photographs. The grandson then introduced his own son to both hobbies. Thus, a cousin of Rick's father, Keith Lovejoy, became a keeper of some Sturdevant artifacts. When this happens, consider how fortunate everyone is that a relative with expertise has conserved the family's photograph archives and is capable of printing out glass plates and sharing copies. Keith was a wonderful man who shared family history, photographs, and homemade honey with us. The moral: Do not covet a qualified relative's role as keeper of the photographs anymore than you covet his role as keeper of the bees.

When you are a would-be keeper, ask people to gather their photographs when you are planning a visit. **If you plan to interview relatives, you may wish to show them their photographs to trigger memories.** Suggest that they sit down with you and identify their photographs in soft pencil while you tape what they say. This catalogs the photographs but also encourages storytelling. People who are shy about oral history may be willing to go on tape just to help you get a record of who is in those photographs. Take your macro lens and copying equipment with you (see instructions on page 117) to make copy negatives on the spot.

Once you have established your role as the family repository, relatives and others will not only send photographs but will sometimes operate as researchers or photographers on your behalf. For example, my mother's cousin had the wherewithal to visit the ancestral home in Wales. She took good photographs of the overseas sites and sent me copies. Other cousins have done the same at family history sites throughout the United States.

One Sturdevant relative, Cousin George, was cleaning out his mother's house after she died. He had been in touch with us for several years, sharing family history back and forth. One day he called from his mother's house to say that he had found some old family photograph albums and wondered whether we wanted them. He said they were mostly Sturdevants and so he thought we should have them. Because the people in the photographs shared our last name, not his, he was even more willing to share—even though they were as much his ancestors as they were my husband's! (George and Rick are cousins of the same generation who share old Lafayette Sturdevant as a great-great-grandfather, but Rick descends through Sturdevant males and George through two females and changing surnames.) Lineage patterns may determine who are the keepers.

Be Careful About Mailing Irreplaceable Photographs

The story of George's albums was also nearly a horror story. Rick and I agonized over how George should send these albums. We even encouraged him to wait until we could meet. I tried to advise him how to package and insure them. Most people, I have found, will listen patiently to such fussing and do what they want to do anyway. So, George packed them up in a used Sears carton and shipped them off, first class but uninsured, and without padding to protect them inside. Good-hearted George had more faith in the post office than we had.

The box did not come and did not come. Then the post office attempted delivery and left a yellow slip requesting that we pick the package up. I will never forget my dread when I walked out of the post office, toward Rick, after they told me that they could not find the box anywhere. I called for days and was passed from one to another less-than-helpful postal employee. They wanted to check by code numbers and proper cubbyholes while I had a feeling it was right under their noses if they would do old-fashioned scouting. I finally asked, "May I speak to a postal clerk who has worked there for at least twenty years?" He was my savior. He patiently listened to my description, from George, of exactly what the box looked like. He then walked about the post office and came back to the phone. "I have it!" he said. "After you described it so I could just look for

Oral History

Warning

Tip

Mailing Precious Photographs Without Archival Supplies

1. Avoid encouraging relatives to mail photographs if they may have the only copies. It would be better to visit the relative in person. If visiting is out of the question, instruct your well-meaning relatives on the proper way to mail photographs.

2. Enclose the photographs tightly in Baggies brand plastic bags. (Not every brand of plastic bag or wrap is the right kind of plastic.) These will serve as makeshift archival bags to protect the photograph from all of the other supplies used in packing.

3. Tape the Baggies (with the photographs securely inside) to the center of a piece of heavy, corrugated cardboard. The tape should never touch the photographs.

4. Wrap the whole package of bagged photos on cardboard in brown wrapping paper, as well as you would wrap a gift, with tape.

5. Pad around the package with bubble wrap, tissue, or newspaper.

6. If this whole mass is tight, is not bending the photographs, and will travel well, then place it in a strong mailing carton with more padding so that it will not shift.

7. Mail first-class, priority, registered (not certified), or whatever is the safest, quickest way. Most of all, I would use "return receipt requested" in order to require that the carrier place the package in the recipient's hands. The post office now offers tracking services for Priority Mail. The sender can track packages using United Parcel Service or Federal Express, too.

8. Make sure that the box is accurately and specifically addressed. Also pack both the shipping and return addresses inside the box with the photographs.

9. Offer to pay for all of these supplies and charges, or even send the money or the supplies in advance to try to encourage proper shipping. People will do it their way if left to their own devices.

the box, I spotted it in no time. Someone had put it back in an outgoing basket by mistake!" It had been two weeks.

Perhaps it was just as well that we did not realize how precious the albums were until we had them safely at home. The three albums were of the Victorian style: heavy cardstock pages with slots for cabinet cards and *cartes de visite* inside velvet and leather covers. Here were some of the earliest photographs of the post-Civil War generation we had ever seen, including many of which we had no other copies. The albums rubbed a little in shipping, but the images were excellent because they had suffered little exposure. Each album had a masking-tape price stuck to it, as though someone had at one time tried to sell them in a garage sale—for about two dollars each! All of those Sturdevants, whom we could identify, almost became someone else's anonymous "instant ancestors!"

Sometimes you will locate family photographs through unlikely strangers in less likely places. One such person for me, Marion C. Parker, of whom I write in chapter six, was a gold mine and also another example of people too faithful in the post office. We found each other through a "scattershot" letter that I sent to the small town in Kansas that my mother's family helped found. Mr. Parker was a local historian for the fledgling Sherman County Historical Society in Goodland. He specialized in collecting old photographs of the early history of the county.

Mr. Parker found relevant photographs among the local history collections. So, through him, I acquired photographic copies of newspaper illustrations and pictures of family homes, buildings, and local history events. These are all wonderful for illustrating family history narrative. Such a generous person is always on the lookout for your interests, too. One day, an elderly attorney in Goodland was retiring and offered Mr. Parker the chance to go through his files in case anything there was relevant to local history. Mr. Parker then wrote me a letter.

The lawyer had handled the estate of my great-uncle, circa 1936. My uncle's wife, Kate, was a favorite aunt of my grandmother. Aunt Kate was a daughter of the Widow Withers discussed earlier in this chapter and a younger sister to my great-grandmother Fannie. Aunt Kate had died before her husband and they left no immediate heirs. My grandmother had lamented that her Aunt Kate's beautiful things had gone to some unknown nephew of this uncle. However, a file folder remained in the attorney's files when Mr. Parker looked. In it were old family documents from the Kate Withers side, which would have held little interest for the mysterious nephew. The documents included several photographs. Among them were my great-great-grandmother Martha Withers with her grown daughters and the young boy, Ira, the son who died in the Civil War. Ira Withers had become all but forgotten in the family history, but now this lawyer's old file gave us his tintype and his Civil War letters. His mother and sister had tried to immortalize him by saving these relics. Now Mr. Parker offered to mail them to me.

I could hardly wait to see them, but fussed about how best he should package and insure them. Shortly the precious letters and photographs arrived via first-class mail in a used stationery box, uninsured, from Kansas to San Francisco. **Hunt for family photographs anywhere, any way that you can; treasure the helpers you find along the way; and trust that their faith in the post office will be rewarded, because they will do what they want no matter how much you fuss.**

Reminder

Create New Family Photographs!

Students have told me that there are no older family photographs in their families. Of course, I always encourage folks to keep looking, because so many older photographs will turn up as you contact family members. In the meantime, however, you can build your collection of family history photographs in many ways. Suppose that you want photos to illustrate a family history book or to display.

Start photographing anything you find that is part of the family history: an ancestral home, the family farm or business, your ancestors' tombstones, family artifacts, or surviving relatives. These may illustrate your narrative, inspire your writing, and appeal to your sentiments when framed. These images will bring your family history to life for you each day, as will the three-dimensional artifacts.

Supplies

Obtain good cameras, film, and equipment for making new family photographs. Learn from a professional photo supply shop and by reading. You may want to consider taking a photography course at a community college. **Probably the best camera will be 35mm, manual rather than automatic, with a selection of lenses and filters and a tripod for stability. If you can afford an even better camera, seek an 8″×10″ or 4″×6″ format camera.** Store both black-and-white and color film in the freezer or refrigerator for longer shelf life. On trips, take back-up equipment such as batteries, film, and even a second camera. I have heard many horror stories from people who have traveled for family history. They took wonderful pictures of the house, farm, cemetery, headstones, and old people, then came home to discover there was no film in the camera! Triple-check for film in the camera, especially if multiple family members have been using it or if you have left the camera untouched for a while.

CARING FOR PHOTOGRAPHS
Storage

See Also

The general advice on care of artifacts and documents in chapter three also applies to archival care of photographs. There are, however, some special features of conserving photographs to add or emphasize. For older photographs and negatives, recommended humidity levels are generally lower than for artifacts: ideally 30 to 40 percent humidity. See the chart of photograph types earlier in this chapter for special care concerns for specific types of images. Wearing gloves is especially important when handling photographs.

Unless you are preserving a whole antique album, each of your photographs should have a separate container—envelope or sleeve—that is chemically stable (acid-free) to protect it from possible sources of damage. These are available from archival supply houses. I prefer clear sleeves because you can see the photograph without removing it from its container. These are made of Mylar type D polyester. When you write on the back of a photograph, use only soft pencil or acid-free, foil-backed labels with archival ink (so that the ink cannot bleed through). Write as little as possible, preferably just an inventory number, and include the rest of the information on your control form. Write on the back in the margins area so that if you accidentally press or bleed through it does not reach the image.

Archival supply catalogs offer special holders for negatives, including glass-plate negatives. The latter need four-flap enclosures that wrap around them. There are also special boxes with dividers and slots that hold glass plates in place and even have shock absorption to protect them from accidental blows.

Possibly the worst paper for photograph albums is the highly acidic black construction paper of 1920s–1950s snapshot albums. Unfortunately, I have seen many of these put together by creative young folks who even got special white

Warning

ink to write captions for their photographs. Similarly harmful are the "magnetic" albums of the 1960s–1970s with self-stick pages. These are not chemically safe, and sometimes you cannot remove many of the photos without damaging them. In either case, I recommend that you get a photographic copy stand and make new negatives of all of the photographs, even if you must leave them in the albums to do so. If you have a carefully captioned album, you will have saved the images without dismantling the book. You could even photograph the pictures with the captions as part of the new photographs. Otherwise, I would recreate the album information on paper. After copying the photos, store the original albums away from other items so that they do not rub better-quality papers the wrong way.

You may store the entire collection in acid-free albums with archival mounting sheets, papers, and mounting corners. Place everything in archival boxes on shelving on a main floor of the house instead of the attic or basement. When in boxes, it is better for most photographs to be stored vertically (on edge) rather than horizontally (stacked on their backs). They should be in containers that suit their sizes rather than too tight or too loose. To prevent permanent loss, consider storing the negatives separately from the copies or storing separate sets of copies in more than one building. Donating copies or originals to a historical society is one way to accomplish this.

A note of caution: **Antique family photograph albums, with their plush velvet or leather covers, are themselves artifacts that you should not dismantle.** The order of the photographs is a set of clues to which you will return for more information. If you fear that the pages are unsafe for the photographs, order some 100 percent rag-content, acid-free interleaving tissue paper from an archival supply catalog and place a sheet between every two pages. Remove from the album anything, such as a newspaper clipping, that is obviously doing real harm. Document what you have taken out, where it was, and where you put it.

Warning

Restoration

I have not experimented with restoration myself and am reluctant to recommend that you do. This is another case for the professionals and experts, in my opinion. The best summary of restoration techniques that I have found, however, is in the Time-Life book *Caring for Photographs*. Ask the nearest museum if they can recommend a local restoration expert. In addition to that, the best advice I can give is to realize that no photograph is ruined and every type of damage has a repair solution. So do not give up and do not discard the damaged pictures. Even when photographs seem terribly faded, chipped, scratched, stained, torn, or curled, there is something you can do to bring out the image, restore the color, hide the scratches, flatten the curls, or retouch the flaws. Remember, too, that you can scan a photograph digitally and change the digital image. I would take care, however, to record the difference between the original and a retouched version, lest the latter, somewhat falsified version, be taken for absolutely accurate.

For More Info

Copying Photographs

Many family historians cannot resist photocopying their photographs. After all, you can then share them cheaply. Most genealogists and historians are attached to photocopying machines. This is not good for your photographs, however, because the shot of light exposure and handling that a photograph receives from a machine is a concentrated dose of the very hazards from which you are trying to protect the photograph. The newer laser color copiers, although more expensive to use, make very nice copies of old black-and-white photographs. The copies are accurate and often have an appealing sepia tone. If you are going to expose old photographs to hazardous light, you may as well do the best job in one shot.

Tip

The best way to copy a photograph is to photograph it, creating a new, archival-quality negative (copy neg) from which you can have prints made. To copy, you need to buy or make a copy stand. It is essentially a plank of wood with a sturdy metal arm attached to hold your camera firmly, lens down. The best camera is an 8″ × 10″ or 4″ × 6″ format camera, but second best and more practical for most folks is a 35mm. With the 35mm, use Kodak Panatomic X black-and-white film. You will need a macro lens, lamps set at forty-five-degree angles to the copy surface, a light meter, and a gray board for underneath the photograph.

For instructions on copying photographs, see Thomas L. Davies' *Shoots: A Guide to Your Family's Photographic Heritage* or the AASLH technical leaflet "Copying Historical Photographs" by James H. Conrad. You may also wish to contact a local college for a photography course, asking whether the course includes training in black-and-white copy work. **If you donate original photographs to a historical society, they may make new negatives and provide prints to you for free or at a nominal charge.**

Money Saver

You may also turn to an expert for copy work. Start by telephoning the best, oldest photography shops in town. Ask them if they do black-and-white copy work. If they say that they farm it out to an individual, ask them who that is and how to reach them so that you can discuss your special needs. When you contact the photographer, you may find that person will charge you wholesale rates when you deal directly, rather than go through the shop. Whether dealing with the black-and-white copier or the shop, you need to ask the charges for copy negs and different-size prints. What you want most is the copy negatives. If needed, ask whether they can print from glass-plate negatives onto printing out paper and then make a copy neg from that.

DISPLAYING FAMILY PHOTOGRAPHS

Framing Photographs

It is best to frame copies only, not original family photographs. The originals should stay in archival envelopes. The copies, nicely enlarged, make beautiful framed artifacts. Archival or ultraviolet-filtering glass is very expensive and so are archival materials if you are going to use them for every family photograph. Understand that I believe in surrounding yourself with family photographs. So have copies made and frame these. Then you preserve the originals, the new negatives, and other copies archivally. There is no need to invest in archival framing for modern, duplicate copies.

I make sure, however, to preserve the original framing of photographs such as large charcoal overpaintings. If you see evidence of damage on an already-framed picture, such as spots on the edges of an image, you may wish to take it to a museum or historical society conservator. You may need to reframe the item using archival supplies. Removing old backing is a delicate operation, especially if there is labeling on it that you want to preserve. You should always remove any newspaper used as backing. You need to remove the newspaper for the safety of the picture, but preserve it to read the content. I would also photocopy the old newspaper before risking its destruction. Try to reframe the originals in the same frames, even though the frames are wood, to maintain historical integrity. You can introduce archival matting to keep the print away from the glass, then seal the back with archival paper and adhesive.

Hang Family Photographs on Your Christmas Tree or on Yourself

Many Christmas-tree ornaments today come in the form of picture frames for small photographs. The best place to find selections of these is an all-Christmas, year-round gift shop. Instead of filling them with recent photographs, put copies of ancestral photographs in them. They give a tree a Victorian look but also bring your extended family around you to start a new tradition. If you do not celebrate Christmas, choose frames that do not have a Christmas look and hang them on a wall or set them on a display stand.

It was a custom to make jewelry containing family portrait photographs from the 1860s through the 1880s. Lockets and brooches have been consistently popular for holding tiny photographs. Jewelry manufacturers today also make a variety of picture-holding brooches in Victorian designs. These even come with a copy of a Victorian photograph installed, looking for all the world like one of your ancestors. Try placing copies of ancestral photographs, presumably of people with whom you especially identify, in these. Wearing them will make you feel connected and will occasion conversation. If you are short on family heirloom jewelry, you will have created some. Traditional lockets are available in most department store jewelry sections in gold or silver. Brooches suitable for copies of old photographs are a bit harder to find. Try antique stores who have costume jewelry or jewelry by makers such as 1928 brand that specialize in old-fashioned designs.

USING HISTORICAL CONTEXT IN FAMILY HISTORY VIDEOS

If you enjoy working with your video or digital camera, consider using your family photographs as part of a family history video, CD-ROM, or multimedia project. This is also a good way to inventory your photographs and artifacts and to give them narrative that amounts to oral history. There are many fine documentaries about family history that serve as models of how to do this in social history context.

The Yasui family became the subject of both a published book-length family history narrative and a fine family history documentary film. The book, *Stubborn*

Twig: Three Generations in the Life of a Japanese American Family, is by social historian Lauren Kessler. The documentary film, *A Family Gathering*, was a one-hour contribution to PBS's The American Experience series.[9] The film was narrated by Lise Yasui, granddaughter of the patriarch and matriarch who were relocated to camps during World War II. It is a model of what any of us might do with our family histories. Woven together are still photographs of the family and their activities, home movies, videotaped oral history, and stills or newsreel footage of the larger events that affected them. The story line has plot, mystery, humor, and characterization. It is inspirational. I strongly recommend that you use the highest quality models for your family history work, such as this film.

Consider also the shelf life of whatever medium you decide to use for recording family history. Videotapes (and audiotapes) might survive ten years. If you transfer images to CD-ROM, estimates are that it will last fifty years or more if stored under optimal conditions. Archival paper is the best, about five hundred years. So printing out copies of old black-and-white photographs and making archival albums with them, though old-fashioned, may be best.

PHOTOGRAPH COLLECTIONS IN LIBRARIES AND MUSEUMS

Idea Generator

Most modern photograph collections, especially in local and state societies and institutions, will emphasize social history in terms of everyday life in that community or region. This is great news for your research. First, **such organizations may actually be keeping photographs of your ancestors, just waiting for you to find them.** For example, a photograph archivist at a state historical society will have been collecting photographs by any and all local photographers. Your ancestors may have stepped into the studio of a local photographer. The surviving photograph may even carry a label with your ancestors' names, or you may recognize them from other photographs (through your sixth sense) or by having met them yourself.

My Great-Aunt Daisy donated her husband's Spanish-American War souvenirs to the U.S. Army Military History Institute at Carlisle Barracks, Pennsylvania, just before I started to inquire with relatives about family history. At first I was disappointed to think that the memorabilia was out of my reach. Instead, I discovered that this had been a smart move on the part of Great-Aunt Daisy. The curators answered my written request for information by sharing with me (at their cost) photocopies of the diaries, records, and photographs, as well as descriptions of the artifacts that included a bugle. The items were safer in the archives and my access was easier.

A photograph archive will emphasize social history or documentary photographs of life as it was in the region or subject that the archive covers. A historical society's photograph archives may include images of local farms, including houses and outbuildings, families at work in fields, agricultural equipment, crops growing or being harvested, livestock, irrigation ditches, wells, windmills, and household chores such as laundry, churning, and gardening. In an urban area, an archive might have photographs that document social classes, organizational activities, transportation, neighborhood businesses, and ethnic group life. In the 1940s, the Works Progress Administration photographed every building in all five boroughs of New York City, for example. You might not find your own ancestors, but you will certainly find photographs that you can use about how people like your ancestors lived.

CHAPTER BIBLIOGRAPHY

1. Bennett, Mary. "Tips on Handling and Labeling Historical Photographs," "Tips on Storing Historical Photographs," "Tips on Storing Historical Negatives," and "Tips on Displaying Historical Photographs in Albums and Frames." 4 parts. *The Palimpsest* [now *Iowa Heritage Illustrated* of the State Historical Society of Iowa] 71 (spring, summer, fall, winter 1990): 1–4.

2. Burns, Stanley B. *Sleeping Beauty: Memorial Photography in America*. Altadena, Calif.: Twelvetrees Press, 1990.

3. Conrad, James H. "Copying Historical Photographs: Equipment and Methods." Technical leaflet no. 139. Nashville: American Association for State and Local History, 1981.

4. Crawford, William. *The Keepers of Light: A History and Working Guide to Early Photographic Processes*. Dobbs Ferry, N.Y.: Morgan and Morgan, 1979.

5. Dalrymple, Priscilla Harris. *American Victorian Costumes in Early Photographs*. New York: Dover Publications, Inc., 1991.

6. Davies, Thomas L. *Shoots: A Guide to Your Family's Photographic Heritage*. Danbury, N.H.: Addison House, 1977.

7. Frisch-Ripley, Karen. *Unlocking the Secrets in Old Photographs*. Salt Lake City: Ancestry, 1991.

8. Frost, Lenore. *Dating Family Photographs, 1850–1920*. Berwick, Australia: Valiant Press, 1991.

9. Henisch, Heinz K., and Bridget A. Henisch. *The Photographic Experience, 1839–1914: Images and Attitudes*. University Park: Pennsylvania State University Press, 1994.

10. Hirsch, Julia. *Family Photographs: Content, Meaning, and Effect*. New York: Oxford University Press, 1981.

11. Horton, Loren. "Interpreting the Image: How to Understand Historical Photographs." 4 parts. *The Palimpsest* [now *Iowa Heritage Illustrated* of the State Historical Society of Iowa] 71 (spring, summer, fall, winter 1990): 1-4.

12. Jones, Mary-Ellen. "Photographing Tombstones: Equipment and Techniques." Technical leaflet no. 92. Nashville: American Association for State and Local History, 1977.

13. Light Impressions. "Tips for Proper Negative Storage." Rochester: Light Impressions, 1985.

14. Lindmier, Tom, and Steve Mount. *I See By Your Outfit: Historic Cowboy Gear of the Northern Plains*. Glendo, Wyo.: High Plains Press, 1996.

15. Lipman, Jean, and Alice Winchester. *The Flowering of American Folk Art, 1776–1876*. New York: Viking Press, 1974.

16. Lipman, Jean, Elizabeth V. Warren, and Robert Bishop. *Young America: A Folk-Art History*. New York: Hudson Hills Press, 1986.

17. Nickell, Joe. *Camera Clues: A Handbook for Photographic Identification*. Lexington, Ky.: University Press of Kentucky, 1994.

18. Northeast Document Conservation Center. "Storage Enclosures for Photographic Prints and Negatives." Andover, Mass.: Northeast Document Conservation Center, 1989.

19. Reilly, James M. *Care and Identification of 19th-Century Photographic Prints*. Rochester: Eastman Kodak Company, 1986.

20. Ritzenthaler, Mary Lynn, et al. *Archives and Manuscripts: Administration of Photographic Collections*. Chicago: Society of American Archivists, 1984.

21. Rubenstein, Ruth P. *Dress Codes: Meanings and Messages in American Culture*. Boulder: Westview Press, 1995.

22. Ruby, Joe. *Secure the Shadow: Death and Photography in America*. Cambridge: MIT Press, 2000.

23. Severa, Joan L. *Dressed for the Photographer: Ordinary Americans and Fashion, 1840–1900*. Kent, Ohio: Kent State University Press, 1995.

24. Shull, Wilma Sadler. *Photographing Your Heritage*. Salt Lake City: Ancestry Publishing, 1988.

25. Sturm, Duane, and Pat Sturm. *Video Family History*. Salt Lake City: Ancestry Publishing, 1989.

26. Taft, Robert. *Photography and the American Scene: A Social History, 1839–1889*. New York: Dover Publications, 1964.

27. Taylor, Maureen. *Uncovering Your Ancestry Through Family Photographs*. Cincinnati: Betterway Books, 2000.

28. Time-Life Books. *Caring for Photographs: Display, Storage, and Restoration*. New York: Time-Life Books, 1976.

29. Tuttle, Craig A. *An Ounce of Preservation: A Guide to the Care of Papers and Photographs*. Highland City, Fla.: Rainbow Books, Inc., 1994.

30. Vanderbilt, Paul. "Evaluating Historical Photographs: A Personal Perspective." Technical leaflet no. 120. Nashville: American Association for State and Local History, 1979.

31. Wajda, Shirley. "A Room With a Viewer: The Parlor Stereoscope, Comic Stereographs, and the Psychic Role of Play in Victorian America." In *Hard At Play: Leisure in America, 1840–1940*, edited by Kathryn Grover. Amherst: University of Massachusetts Press, 1992: 112–138.

32. Waldsmith, John. *Stereo Views: An Illustrated History and Price Guide*. Radnor, Pa.: Wallace-Homestead Book Company, 1991.

33. Weinstein, Robert A., and Larry Booth. *Collection, Use and Care of Historical Photographs*. Nashville: American Association for State and Local History, 1977.

FIVE

Relative Talk: Oral History and Oral Tradition

Simply put, oral history collects spoken memories and personal commentaries of historical significance through recorded interviews.

—Donald A. Ritchie in *Doing Oral History*[1]

THE GENEALOGICAL INTERVIEW VS. THE ORAL HISTORY INTERVIEW

In our class on family history and genealogy, Sharon Carmack chose as a genealogical text the excellent *Shaking Your Family Tree: A Basic Guide to Tracing Your Family's Genealogy* by Dr. Ralph Crandall, director of the New England Historic Genealogical Society. It is a good, basic, introductory guide to the main types of genealogical records. We used it regularly and lamented when it became out-of-print or difficult to obtain. When he discussed interviewing, however, Dr. Crandall took the genealogical perspective, not an oral history one. See if you can ascertain the difference.

Notes

Endnotes for this chapter begin on page 222.

> Some people have a tendency to respond to specific questions with a "life and times" answer. In such cases, be careful not to interrupt, or you may lose much valuable information that such "free association" evokes. Try instead to redirect the answer through questions that will focus your thoughts more narrowly. If your relative has launched on a long discourse on, say, his father's career as a ship captain, you might return to the subject by asking him, "How many of his children were married when he retired from the sea?"[2]

If you followed this advice, you might indeed redirect the speaker to genealogical facts, but are those facts the best material you could gain from that interview? Stories about "his father's career as a ship captain" might be more revealing, harder to come by, more reliable in the sense of oral tradition, and the stuff of writing family narrative.

In the past, many serious genealogists have tended to reject most of the information gained from interviews with relatives as too subjective, unspecific, and unreliable for ordinary genealogical purposes. They have been right, as far as that valuation goes. If you are seeking reliable facts—names, dates, birthplaces, and the like—you know that people's memories will fail them on such detail. A

Oral History

Idea Generator

If you think all of your older relatives are gone and you cannot imagine whom to interview, think like a social historian. Interview the old neighbors who remember your family. Interview relatives your own age with different viewpoints and experiences, even your siblings or your spouse. I have recommended to older adult students that they interview their own children for an amazing experience full of revelations.

Step By Step

birth certificate or even a census record might be more reliable. If you are seeking the definitive answer to a nagging or controversial genealogical question, you know that any two different relatives can give you two different versions of the same story. Even the same relative may provide different versions at different times. Do not approach an interview hoping for definitive factual information, but rather for experiential accounts, impressionistic descriptions, attitudes and perceptions, and family tradition.

Many disappointed genealogists interviewed for the wrong reasons. **The oral historian, however, knows that an interview's treasure is not the trivia of who, when, or where, but the what, why, and how of family tradition.** Think of yourself as the competent journalistic interviewer—you will always have to check your facts, but what you are really looking for is that quotable summary, explanation, or opinion of the interviewee. Therefore you avoid closed-ended, yes-or-no questions. You ask open-ended questions that elicit thoughtful, explanatory responses.

An oral history interview is carefully planned. The oral historian tailors the questions to bring forth descriptions, characterizations, explanations, and analysis. The professional-quality oral history interview stands as a tidy package, a complete historical document in and of itself. Properly introduced, identified, and concluded, with a logical progression from one subject to the next, it is comparable to a recorded book. It is the account of the person being interviewed with minimal vocalizations by the interviewer. The copied and transcribed tape is archival material for the use of researchers. It provides quotable descriptions and observations for interspersing in one's family history narrative—to illustrate points, to carry on the narrative, and to inject humanity, humor, poignancy, and the opportunity to empathize.

For the parties involved, an oral history interview is often an intense, memorable moment of bonding and of coming to a greater mutual empathy and respect. During the late 1980s, many of my students were the right age to have Vietnam-veteran fathers. They frequently told me that interviewing their dads for class created an opportunity for their dads to share their experiences for the first time, and therefore for the students to understand their dads for the first time. Many students—especially younger women—have expressed similar results after interviewing their mothers. In family history classes and oral history project meetings, I have seen students discover themselves and each other by staging practice or demonstration interviews. An oral history interview can be a life-changing event for all concerned.

Before the Interview

1. *Ask yourself questions.*

Who do you want to interview and why? (Start with the oldest and most fragile folks.)

What do you want to know and what would be the best way to learn it from an interview?

When would be the best time?

Where is the best place?

Why is this important to you and the interviewee?

How will you go about it?

ORAL HISTORY GUIDELINES		
Before the Interview	**During the Interview**	**After the Interview**
1. Ask yourself questions.	1. Identify and introduce.	1. Process the tape.
2. Lay the groundwork.	2. Phrase questions carefully.	2. Transcribe exactly.
3. Do your homework.	3. Draw out gently.	3. Obtain releases.
4. Construct the questions.	4. Listen well.	4. Index, socially.
5. Learn the equipment.	5. Ad-lib follow-up questions.	5. Copy and distribute.
6. Prepare the place.	6. Conclude respectfully.	6. Evaluate and use the resource.

2. *Lay the groundwork.*

Request the interview, explaining what to expect in a nonthreatening manner.

Make the appointment, specifying the amount of time needed, a quiet location, and the need for the absence (or presence) of others.

3. *Do your homework.*

Gather background on your interviewee and the subjects you expect to introduce.

Research the basic outline of the person's life, read about his times, learn enough that you know what your subject matter will be. If you know nothing in advance, you will waste time and exasperate your interviewee.

4. *Construct the questions.*

Having a list of written questions can be comforting. I prefer having a list of topics to prompt me. It is always better, however, to be overprepared with topics and questions than to run out.

Practice asking what, why, and how questions—open-ended—rather than just who, when, and where questions.

Avoid writing a script, and especially avoid following one during the interview. Do not get tied to asking certain questions in a certain order or the interview may become stilted.

5. *Learn the equipment.*

See the list of equipment under The Oral History Tote Bag on page 129. Plug in the recorder and test its taping capabilities before you meet with the interviewee.

I prefer to use the built-in microphone of my tape recorder, as long as I can interview across a table. Hand mikes are unwieldy and sometimes intimidating to folks. If you are going to use a separate mike, a clip-on microphone works best and is least obtrusive.

Practice watching the recorder as unobtrusively as possible for indicators of when you will need to flip the tape. Remember that you can only flip it once, so prepare second and third tapes in advance. Plan to stop at a comfortable pause in the speaking, even if there is still a little tape left on that side.

Locate and organize any photographs or memorabilia that you intend to show the interviewee during the interview.

6. *Prepare the place.*

Make sure it will be quiet and comfortable for both parties.

Technique

If you are new to oral history and you have doubts about your own ability to conduct a satisfactory oral history interview, try this. Contact your nearest historical society, museum, or public library to see which has an oral history collection. Ask to sit and listen to a good taped oral history (perhaps while reading the transcript, if one exists) to hear what an interview is like, what works well and what does not.

Tip

Plan and arrange who will be there. Most guidelines recommend one interviewer and one interviewee.

My best interview experiences have been across kitchen or dining tables. These provide a surface for equipment and writing. The face-to-face distance between participants is just right. Kitchen tables are comfortable and familiar places, but their chairs are not so comfortable as to make someone sleepy.

Is there a good electrical outlet within reach of your cord?

Can you rule out obtrusive noises that could ruin the recording? (I have a friend who even asks to unplug refrigerators, but I have not gone that far yet.)

During the Interview

1. *Identify and introduce.*

    Identify the parties by name, the date, and the place at the beginning of the tape (after the tape leader has wound forward).

2. *Phrase the questions carefully.*

    Ask quiet, tentative, encouraging, sensitive questions. Keep them open-ended. Keep them short and simple, asking one at a time.

3. *Draw out gently.*

    Do not pressure or argue.

    If there is reluctance, speak as though you may be addressing a shy person.

    Nod, smile, furrow your brow, and mutter quiet "uh-huhs" to encourage the speaker.

    Never be judgmental toward anything the interviewee tells you.

    Start with uncontroversial subjects and work up to the more sensitive topics or events.

    Do not hesitate to leave pauses. Sometimes the interviewee will fill them spontaneously.

4. *Listen well.*

    Do not interrupt, argue, dominate, tell, or show off your knowledge. The point is to hear the interviewee's voice on the tape and almost never hear yours.

    Give your primary attention to the interviewee at all times through eye contact. Don't allow yourself to be significantly distracted by the equipment or anything else.

    Take notes, but briefly, of key things you must remember.

    By all means, don't you get visibly sleepy or bored! Rest well the night before.

5. *Ad-lib follow-up questions.*

    Jot down topics you want to come back to rather than interrupting the flow.

    If the interviewee uses words or refers to something unfamiliar, ask for a clarification or definition at some point. If you think the interviewee may have been mistaken or even dishonest, you may carefully probe.

6. *Conclude respectfully.*

    Be observant about whether the interviewee is tired or anxious to quit. Offer a break and ask the person whether they are comfortable continuing.

Most guides will tell you that one hour is long enough, but most of my best interviews have been closer to two hours. Be flexible but, most of all, attuned to the interviewee.

Conclude the interview with a clear statement on the tape that it is over.

Be enthusiastically grateful and state to the interviewee the importance of what has just happened and of the historical resource now created.

After the Interview

1. *Process the tape.*

Fill out complete labels for both the tape and its case and attach them immediately. Include the name of the interviewee and the date, "Oral History Interview," and preferably also your name and the place. As a favor to future researchers: give the interview a title or notation as to its main topic(s) or theme(s), such as "World War II Experiences."

Break the tabs on the tape that prevent someone from taping over or erasing.

Store tapes in environmentally sound spaces. Avoid any contact with magnets.

2. *Transcribe exactly.*

An oral history transcript should be absolutely exact, word for word, at least at first. The written transcript will serve as a printed record of exactly what was said, so that you or a researcher could quote from the transcript with assurance that your quotes would be accurate without listening to the tape. It need not include every "uh" sound. You may legitimately go back and clean up a transcript by removing the "uhs" and the useless repetitions of words and phrases. In your introduction, note that you have done so.

It is helpful for the interviewer to note in parentheses occasions where the interviewee made particular gestures or pointed to particular visual items.

You may type it script-style. It is helpful to number the lines.

This task is a pain and a chore. One hour of tape may mean five to six hours of transcribing. A transcribing machine, with pedals and stops, makes it both easier on you and the tape. Even with such a machine, most oral historians and projects fall behind on transcription.

Transcripts will become important later, when audio tapes deteriorate or your recollections of what the interviewee said and meant fade. They are useful when the interviewee mumbled or when background noises took over. It is easier to look up passages, scan, and copy a transcript.

You can hire a professional to do your transcriptions for you, at some expense for the many hours. See the Yellow Pages under lawyer or legal services, or court reporters.

3. *Obtain releases.*

I see this as a matter to conduct *after* most of my interviews, but many oral historians do it before. Read further for some discussion and see page 137 for a sample release form.

4. *Index, socially.*

To do a big favor for yourself and future researchers, index the tape and transcript not just by names, but by social history topics and historical events. See chapter eight for instructions in how to index your family history socially and a list of sample topics.

5. *Copy and distribute.*

Make backup copies of the tape (most modern stereo equipment has this capability). Keep at least one copy in a location different from where you keep the original, such as in your office, home, safe-deposit box, local historical society, or with other family members.

Make a copy for the interviewee, if that was the agreement.

Make a copy to donate to a local historical society or museum that has an oral history collection. You can stipulate rules about use and permissions.

Make gift copies for family members if that is appropriate (**see the Grandpa Gates example on page 137**).

6. *Evaluate and use the resource.*

Who will you interview next, based on revelations in this interview?

When and where will you do that, or shall you conduct another interview with this first person?

Why was this interview a success? What were its failings?

How might you use quotes and information from this interview in family history narrative?

See Also

THE ORAL HISTORY TOTE BAG

Just do it—now! This should be the motto for family oral history. With all our guidelines and professional standards, we sometimes form the dangerous habit of thinking we must wait for the perfect opportunity. If you wait, you may lose the opportunity through death, memory loss, or other circumstance. Think how many people you wish you had on tape, telling their stories and answering questions. The perfect moment is now.

One way to make interviews happen and avoid procrastination, is to have a ready-to-go container of everything you will need. I use a tote bag. I make sure that it always has in it everything I would need for an interview so that I can grab it with confidence. I take it on any trip to visit someone I may wish to interview, so it is there and ready should the opportunity arise.

INTERVIEWING FOR FAMILY SOCIAL HISTORY

The guiding purpose of family history interviewing is to obtain grist for the writer's and researcher's mill. A good oral history tape and transcript, left in an archive, will supply historians with quotable examples of what it was like in the times and places of the interviewee's past. If all you get around to doing is recording interviews and leaving copies with an archive, you will have made an immense contribution. The text of a good interview can make fascinating reading by itself, so you may even wish to produce a transcription to accompany your printed genealogy, if you get around to doing that.

Most of all, I recommend that you interview to gain material for writing

Supplies

THE ORAL HISTORY TOTEBAG
Rules

1. Use a tote bag with some printed emblem on it that will enable you to recognize it as your oral history tote bag. Mine has a reproduction of a World War II Rosie the Riveter poster on it that reminds me of the great interviews historians have done with surviving Rosies.

2. Keep the items listed below in the totebag at all times, ready for use, even if that means maintaining duplicate items for other purposes elsewhere.

3. If there are items that should not sit in the bag indefinitely, such as batteries, make sure you leave a note in the bag reminding you to replace them.

4. Every time you use the bag, check your bag inventory list before leaving.

Contents

1. tape recorder, standard desktop size, roughly ten inches long by seven inches wide by two inches high, with built-in microphone, counter and automatic level control (ALC)*

2. extension cord and/or adapter (cord may be a surge protector outlet strip)

3. fresh batteries

4. fresh blank tapes—more than you will need. When purchasing tapes, note the type designation on the tape wrapper and case. Type I is best for for voice, type II for music.

5. external microphone (clip-on or lavalier) with cord and any necessary adapter

6. earphones

7. instructions that came with recorder

8. camera (preferably disposable, because you will take your good camera out and forget to put it back, or forget film)

9. film and batteries for camera if it is not disposable

10. paper tablet

11. pens and/or pencils

12. magnifying glass for examining photographs, documents, and small artifacts

13. blank release forms

(continued on page 130)

14.   questions, notes, and/or other prompts for the particular interview

15.   inventory list of what should be in the totebag

Occasional Additions

1.   old photographs (preferably copies) to be identified or to inspire stories

2.   small artifacts or photos of them to be identified or to inspire stories

3.   copies of documents with information you wish to question

Equipment Back Home

1.   standard transcriber with speed and backspace controls, foot pedals and headset

2.   home computer for typing transcript

3.   audio equipment to dub tapes

4.   extra blank tapes for dubbing

* Note: It can be difficult to find this basic kind of tape recorder—instead of a boom box or other device that does everything except wash the dishes—in stores. I have had the most success with Radio Shack. It is good to have this model because it is large enough for quality, small and flat enough to stay in a tote bag, and contains no unnecessary, easily broken features. I wrap mine in a sheet of bubble wrap or a towel. I did learn one lesson the hard way: do not leave your tape recorder in an airplane or a car trunk during a record heat wave. I did this during a speaking engagement in Luling, Texas, and something inside melted or jammed, ruining the new recorder.

narrative family history in a social history context. As you will see when we discuss social history research, in order to build narrative context around your family history, you will need to explain family behavior and fill informational gaps with descriptions of the typical experience in the time and place of the narrative. If, however, you have interviewed a family member about those experiences, you can quote his or her own words. Doing this personalizes the account with firsthand recollections. Almost always, interviewees characterize social history experiences—such as economic conditions, work, social roles and attitudes, responses to world events, and fads and fashions—in ways that ring true to the general experiences already summarized in history books. Your interview documents—proves, if you will—the authenticity of the general human experience, while also making the story come to life with individual recollections.

Making sure that your questions elicit social history responses may require special development of those questions. **Go back to chapter one and study the Elements of Social History.** Chart those elements in some way that becomes a "cheat sheet" for you, a brief outline that you can study to remind yourself of the elements of life worth covering in an interview. If you are not used to thinking in social history terms, it may take awhile. Look at the questions I have listed on page 131, and their categories. Of course no one list could

See Also

QUESTION CATEGORIES FOR FAMILY HISTORY INTERVIEWING

Geography and the Physical Environment

1. Where did the family live and why?

2. How large was the city or town?

3. Describe the area, neighborhood, town, or farm.

4. Describe the home, its layout and furnishings.

5. Who built the home, when, how, and when/how was it ever altered?

6. What was the weather like? How did it affect the family's lives?

7. How did the change of seasons affect the family's daily lives and work?

8. Where/how did they get food, water, or fuel?

9. Where did the family come from before that?

10. Did any of them prefer one place to another? Why?

Economics and Employment

1. How did the family earn their income? Extra money?

2. What jobs did they have?

3. What training had they received for their work?

4. What did they think about their work?

5. What work-related organizations did they join, such as labor unions or farmer's cooperatives?

6. What was women's work like?

7. What work did children do?

8. What was the family's status in their society, including economic class and social rank? How was that reflected in the way others treated them? How did it change?

9. Who handled family finances? Why? How?

10. What material things did they buy?

11. Did they collect anything?

12. What problems did they have with money?

13. Did they disagree about money? Who won those arguments? Why?

(continued on page 132)

Reminder

If you cannot visit and interview the desired relative, or cannot do so immediately, you can adapt these questions to a letter or a telephone interview. In letters, however, limit and space the questions so that the list is not so long as to discourage a response. The results may not be a true oral history interview, even if the questions are asked by telephone, but the material will still be useful and is better than nothing.

Social Life

1. What friends and neighbors did they have? How did they interact with each other?

2. How did they relate to co-workers, colleagues, employees, bosses, or customers?

3. What were their attitudes toward business with different folks?

4. How did different folks display attitudes toward dealing with the family?

5. How did they have fun?

6. How did the children play?

7. What clubs did they belong to and what did the clubs do?

8. What kind of family events and food events did they celebrate and how?

9. What special characteristics of theirs, such as behavior or customs, would you attribute to their ethnic identities?

Personal and Emotional Life

1. How did they meet and court their partners?

2. What were their ideas about/experiences with other members of the opposite sex?

3. What did they believe about marriage?

4. How did they treat one another?

5. What do you know about their sexual lives?

6. What were their ideas about and practices for raising children?

7. Tell any private stories about family relationships.

8. What happened when the generations disagreed?

Personal Physical Life

1. What did they look like?

2. Who inherited those features?

3. What unusual habits did they have?

4. How was their health? What major illnesses or injuries did they have?

5. What did parents tell children about puberty or the "birds and bees"?

6. What was it like when women gave birth?

7. What was their medical care like?

8. What did they do to take care of their own ailments?

9. What meals did they eat? What kinds of food?

10. How did they keep clean?

11. What did they do to try to improve their looks?

Education

1. What schools did they go to?

2. What levels of education did they achieve?

3. What special skills or training did they have?

4. What did they think of going to school?

5. How were the girls treated differently than the boys?

6. What special stories did they tell about school days? Their teachers?

7. Did any of them ever teach school? What was that like?

8. How did the schools celebrate special holidays or events?

Religion

1. What church did they belong to?

2. How did they practice religion from day to day?

3. What were their beliefs about their own religion? About others?

4. In what church activities did they participate?

5. How did they react to differences of opinion that arose within their church?

Politics

1. How did they feel about being Americans? About citizenship?

2. How did they vote or participate in politics?

3. What did they do about or think of local politics?

4. What political organizations did they belong to?

5. What political issues did they care about? Why?

6. How did the local, county, state, and federal governments affect their lives?

(continued on page 134)

Military

1. Where and when did they serve in the military? In what branches?

2. How long did they serve?

3. What was camp life like each day?

4. What was their rank?

5. How did service affect them physically? Mentally? Politically? Economically?

6. What effects did being veterans have on them?

7. What were the family attitudes toward the war?

8. How did the war affect the family on the home front?

include every worthy question, and no one interview could answer all of these. But these are the types of what, how, and why questions that will bring out social history descriptions.

The best book for sample questions similar to my social history categories is William Fletcher's *Recording Your Family History*. Fletcher includes chapter after chapter of questions specifically designed for interviewees of certain ages and experiences. This is especially helpful if you are unfamiliar with twentieth-century history and do not have time to read up on it. My questions are generic social history ones that would fit any time period.

ETHICS AND CONTROVERSIES

There are several controversial issues surrounding oral history interviewing. For genealogists, there is the unreliability of each person's version of the facts. If your goal is to write family history narrative, this problem is not so significant. You will still be researching to confirm facts, and you will be interviewing others or checking records for alternate versions. Whether or not the facts check out, you can use the interview in your family history narrative. Uncle Bob's version or opinion is still Uncle Bob's version or opinion. You may quote and cite it as such, even juxtaposing it with alternative views, as part of an interesting family narrative.

Privacy and copyright can be controversial. Some people do not want some parts of their interviews quoted or shared. Oral historians disagree about how to handle requests to go off the record. Some insist that the interviewee sign a complete release *before* they start the interview. These oral historians fear that they might have wasted their time if the interviewee refuses to sign the release after the interview. Some interviewees want to force alterations to transcripts after the fact, or they will not sign releases. Some oral historians will not quote from someone else's transcript and insist on hearing the original tape.

Here are my own rules, shared with you as suggestions.

1. Explain the release form and the interviewee's rights before the interview,

Important

but do not require a signature until after. I believe that the interviewee has the right to consider the contents of the interview after it has occurred before signing a release.

2. Before the interview, explain that it would be good not to go off the record, or that it is not your practice to do so. Usually, if you reassure them that there is no need to be embarrassed about whatever they are recollecting, most people will relax. They can stipulate later, even in the release form, that use of particular information is restricted. Many closet skeletons that come up in oral history interviews have lost their scandalous quality as times have changed. It is your responsibility as the family and oral historian to be cautious and sensitive about how you use the confidences of your interviewees.

3. A transcript of a tape, like a transcribed historical document, must be as exact a replica of the original as possible. The transcriber must explain any changes from the original in an introduction or some other kind of annotation. For example, I might add punctuation to a transcript to imitate the natural pauses and intonations that the interviewee used. I would explain this in an introduction and perhaps bracket [!] what I added.

4. Ideally, the oral historian should show the transcript to the interviewee and have that person sign a release after seeing that transcript. This step gets overlooked because the first release seems adequate and because so many oral history projects fall so far behind on transcribing. It can be a risky step to show the transcript for approval, because people often want to edit themselves. You could turn this step to your advantage, however, as an opportunity to draw additional stories and information from the interviewee. If so, do not forget to turn on the tape recorder or take notes!

5. As to copyright (where the laws frequently change), both the interviewer and interviewee have rights to their recorded words, perhaps for many years. That is why you want the interviewee to sign a release, specifying that you may use the material in whatever way. The release form should have a place for the interviewer's signature as well.

6. Some people request the questions in advance of the interview. I explain that I prefer not to do this for fear it may curb the spontaneity of good oral history by allowing the answers to be prefabricated. I sometimes also say that I will not be writing out whole questions in advance. If the interviewee insists, one can offer the compromise of a list of topics that one hopes to cover.

7. Some oral historians will not interview more than one person at a time and some avoid interviewing in pairs or teams of interviewers. Multiple interviewers or interviewees can clutter up an interview. If they speak over each other or have similar voices, it is difficult to discern who is who on the tape.

But pairing can enhance an interview in some cases. Rick and I interviewed his parents together, and then I interviewed the two of them about their courtship of almost sixty years ago. It was wonderful to hear what each was thinking of the other at the time, and they helped each other to recall things. Rick and I interviewed his father about his World War II experiences, with which Rick was more familiar than I. I separately interviewed his mother about women's history topics. Taping a man and a woman as a pair eliminates the problem of recognizing taped voices. Having a pair of interviewers can mean you have both someone with background knowledge and someone new to the subject. A partner can also help monitor equipment.

8. I believe in donating oral histories to historical societies, even if one chooses to keep them for exclusive family use for a period of time. You, as the author of a family history narrative, may want to specify the right to first use of the material. If donors want sensitive material protected, say until after their own (or other people's) deaths, they can stipulate this in agreements with the historical societies.

9. Oral historians generally believe in audiotaping rather than videotaping—perhaps partly because we are used to the former. Tape recording is usually more private, less obtrusive, and less expensive. Tape recording equipment is more compact and portable. Either you or your interviewee might feel more self-conscious about being filmed as well as taped.

Tip

VIDEOTAPING TIPS

Videotaping is better than audiotaping in some instances. If you have a particularly special family member or group, perhaps you should catch them on film for at least one of your interviews. If someone uses animated body language or will refer to many visual items, then videotaping is ideal. Videotaping is the best method of interviewing multiple people simultaneously, especially if they are of the same sex, to resolve the who-said-what problem. If you take your camcorder when visiting someone to interview them, you can also videotape artifacts, photographs, and even the family household, farm, or town. If you are taking this equipment, treat its carrying case as you do your oral history tote bag, keeping everything you might need with it.

BREAK THE RULES IF NECESSARY

This Is an Emergency!

Important

There is an urgency to oral history interviewing. I can state this in a way that many genealogists will understand. Think how frustrating it is when you discover that some needed records burned in a courthouse fire. **Now, realize that older relatives will die or lose their memories more often and sooner than records will be lost in repositories.** If no one has interviewed Great-Grandpa or Great Grandma yet, and they have not written their memoirs, interview them now. Their memories are more valuable than most public records for writing your family history narrative.

If you suddenly discover that you are in the right place at the right time to grab a good interview, do so without advance preparation. If the only way to get it done is with others present or with unavoidable background noise, do it.

ORAL HISTORY AS A GIFT: GRANDPA GATES

Imagine capturing that special elder of the family while he (or she) still has his natural voice, his spark of wit, his stories intact, and his sharpness for answering questions. My grandparents died too soon for this. Rick was too late for three

Case Study

SAMPLE ORAL HISTORY RELEASE FORM

I ___Wendell Frank Sturdevant___ (interviewee) hereby give to ___Rick W. and Katherine Scott Sturdevant___

(interviewer) the original tape recordings and transcripts of our interview conducted on ___25 December 1999___

(date) at ___Home address, Cortez, Colorado___ (place).

I authorize ___Rick W. and Katherine Scott Sturdevant___ (interviewer) to utilize this interview, in whole or in part,

for history or family history projects, including the possible pubication of history or family history books and

articles.

I further authorize ___Rick W. and Katherine Scott Sturdevant___ (interviewer) to donate said interview, tapes,

transcripts, or materials derived therefrom, to a historical archive (to be determined) for future educational and

scholarly purposes.

I voluntarily relinquish any rights to this interview, tape, transcript, or material derived therefrom.

Signed ___Wendell Frank Sturdevant___
(interviewee and donor)

Signed _____
(interviewer and recipient)

Date ___December 25, 1999___

Date _____

NOTE: You and your interviewee may negotiate alterations to this form as you see fit.

of his grandparents, too. Then there was Grandpa Gates, Rick's maternal grandfather, who was a stoic, quiet little gentleman, always in vest and hat—and sharp as a tack at ninety years old. He had been a devoted husband, so we might have guessed (but did not care to) that losing his wife that year would initiate his gradual decline.

On the day of her funeral, back at his apartment, Grandpa started to tell the old stories. He was speaking to me with that sparkle in his eye that he had for young ladies. I reminded him that someday Rick and I wanted to interview him on tape: would he be willing? Yes, he said, and we had better do it soon. Darn it, I said, a great opportunity and no tape recorder. "Daddy has a tape recorder in his closet," his daughter, Carol (my mother-in-law), said encouragingly. This is what I mean about grabbing an interview when you can. I was flustered enough, with the spontaneity and the foreign recorder, that I forgot to start with an introduction, so the tape begins abruptly with Grandpa and me in a teasing tone.

This interview was precious. Grandpa Gates told all of his best life stories, from his earliest recollections through his whole life and work, with minimal prompting. His stories were about major events in the family history as well. He had a dry wit. At one point I said "Grandpa, are you enjoying this?" He said "No." "Oh, well do you mind if we keep going?" He said "No," and we kept going. There was no release form, no proper dating and labeling, no clearing the room, and there still is no transcript.

Gradually, over the next five or six years, Grandpa declined and then died. During that period, he lost some of his most memorable characteristics—his deep voice, his stature, his wardrobe, his wit, and his will—bit by bit. He went from his retirement-home apartment to the nursing care section. When they called us to say that his time had come, we gathered around his bed. He kept hanging on. Somehow someone sensed that it was his only daughter, Carol, for whom he remained alive. Rick took her for a walk. Grandpa Gates died while she was out walking, with just me and my father-in-law in the room.

Back at home, between his death and the funeral, I dubbed copies of the interview with Grandpa. I wrapped each. After the funeral, I gave one to each of his four children and Carol's six children. Foolishly, I looked forward to hearing right away how overjoyed each one was to have and to hear the tape. Instead, most said it would be awhile before they would bring themselves to listen to it. But later, one at a time, I heard from his children how much it meant to them. They had postponed listening because they expected a sad tape of the disintegrating man he had recently been. Later pleased, they said it was their dad, still at his best, just like he used to sound before he started failing, telling all of his best stories so that they would never forget them.

CITING ORAL HISTORY INTERVIEWS

When you quote from an oral history interview, you must cite it for what it is. Part of our effort to have our audiences take family sources seriously is to cite them as meticulously as we would any other sources. Historians and biographers have often been casual in citing oral history; many books simply refer to "many

---

SAMPLE ORAL HISTORY RELEASE FORM

**A USEFUL FORM
YOU CAN REPRODUCE**

For a full-size blank copy of th Oral History Release Form, see page 235. You are free to photocopy this form for personal use.

Tip

conversations with" in the acknowledgments, or offer a list of people interviewed in the back of the book without specifics of when, where, or how.

As with citing other sources, you need an author and title. Think of the interviewee as the author. The title is "Interviewed by Your Name," and you should include the place and date of the interview. Also include the current holder of the resulting tape or transcript that you used. **See page 85 in Elizabeth Shown Mills's *Evidence!***

See Also

[1] Wayne Gates, interviewed by author with Rick W. Sturdevant, Good Samaritan Retirement Home, Loveland, Colo., 4 February 1985, audiotape in possession of author.

To be still more precise and helpful, your citations should make clear what form the interview took and what form the record of it takes. So, for example, a "title" might be "Oral History Interview With . . ." A more accurate title in some cases would be "Conversation With Author . . ." or "Telephone Conversation With Author. . . ." The implication of the latter two is that you did not record them. To make clear what remains of the interview, state at the end of the citation whether the tape, transcript, or merely your notes or personal recollections still exist. As with all citations, keep in mind that you are indicating to the reader how to obtain the original record and how reliable it may be. See pages 106–107 in *Doing Oral History* by Donald Ritchie.

ORAL HISTORY COLLECTIONS IN LIBRARIES AND PUBLISHED ANTHOLOGIES

Library/Archive Source

Other people's oral history interviews are great resources for you as well. You can quote another person's words about a topic that fits your family history, giving your narrative still more firsthand authenticity and personality. In the bibliography at the end of this chapter, I have listed not only excellent guidebooks on oral history, but some collections and anthologies of oral history interviews. Consider researching whether there are oral histories—in the form of tapes, transcripts, or books in the stacks—in your libraries and archives that might give you needed information and quotable passages.

Oral history was first recorded on a large scale in America during the Great Depression and New Deal. The Works Progress Administration collected it in several ways: sometimes on tape, but sometimes reconstructed from the interviewers' notes. The WPA focused on the poverty-stricken South for evidence needed in the development of social policy. The WPA projects included gathering slave narratives, which are accounts from African Americans who could still recall their families' lives during or immediately after slavery. The WPA state guides (see page 104) also include material from oral history and tradition as reconstructed by the researchers. Each of these projects generated so much material that they inspired books and still do. Other sources of published oral history have emerged since, such as the works of journalist Studs Terkel, *Foxfire*, and Twayne Publishers. See the bibliography at the end of this chapter for some of the resulting books. Each time you use published oral history materials, evaluate whether the collector used professional standards. Often we have to accept the exactness of transcription on faith because the author(s) converted the interviews into more readable paragraphs of text. Read their introductions and annotations for indicators of their methods and standards.

FAMILY ORAL TRADITION

Oral History

We need to take family oral tradition (the handed-down stories) seriously, as a valuable source of private information, viewpoints, and feelings. Many genealogists, however, will reject oral tradition because of its tendency to take on tall-tale proportions. When historians ignored oral tradition while writing Native American history, it meant that we only had the white man's version, because Indians told their own history almost exclusively through oral tradition. For reasons such as this, today we see oral tradition's value, especially on subjects for which there would be no other record, such as the most intimate aspects of a family's life.

Number one on the list of "Ten Things to Avoid" in Christine Rose and Kay Ingalls's *The Complete Idiot's Guide to Genealogy* is "Don't just accept all the family traditions without careful investigation."[3] This is excellent advice in terms of genealogical detail; if you are seeking facts, by all means do not assume you are receiving reliable ones through family tradition. Nevertheless, *do* accept family tradition as just what it is—family tradition. When you are writing narrative, you can note exactly what the questionable parts are. Even obvious biases and exaggerations can add to the story, although it is your responsibility to call them to the attention of the reader if they are not obvious on their own. It may be best to quote family tradition rather than recite it in your own words. Tell the story in the speaker's own words and, properly cited or annotated, it stands on its own as what it is—a good story.

PUBLISHED FOLKLORE AS A SOURCE FOR FAMILY HISTORY

Scholarly, professional folklorists and local collectors of popular culture have produced many volumes of folklore. Some cultures have received more attention than others, not necessarily because they have more folklore but perhaps because their folklore is more colorful and has attracted a market. In the chapter bibliography I have listed some general anthologies of folklore and some volumes of specific groups' folklore. Consider reading those applicable to your ethnic and regional groups, then weaving some stories (as quoted from these sources) into your family history narrative where truly relevant.

Foodways have become an area of folklore much documented and analyzed. When I started researching foodways just a few years ago, it was difficult to find any books on food history—most turned out to be cookbooks. Now there are more and more histories and analyses of foodways. In the program for the 2000 Organization of American Historians annual conference, where there are many publishers' advertisements, I found eight new and forthcoming history books

WRITING FROM FOLKLORE AND FAMILY TRADITION

'Our family did not participate in a federal census in the country until 1981' read the email from my newly discovered cousin.[1] . . . How could I trace my family history when the family deliberately chose to hide itself?

According to family tradition, the seafaring Monjardins were prime blockade-runners carrying cotton from the Gulf Coast to Havana, Cuba and bringing back essential supplies for military and civilian consumption. . . .

After the war, fearing Union reprisals the Monjardin family became the Maygarden family. . . . They continued to live on and around Dauphin Island but tried to blend in even more, avoiding anything that might bring attention to themselves such as a census that ask[ed] questions about their past. A folk tale about census-takers coming to Dauphin Island says an evasive old timer told the government man, 'My family don't have no sense.' When asked about how many children he had the resident told the census-taker only that, 'Oh, dey thick as de woods.'[2]

[1] E-mail from Jerry Maygarden dated December 1997 to writer.
[2] Julian Lee Rayford, *Whistlin' Woman and Crowin' Hen*. Mobile: Rankin Press, 1956.

Quoted with permission from Sharon Swint, "The Secret," unpublished paper, c. 1998, copy in author's possession.

on American foodways from different publishers. Foodways (such as my recipe collection) may be the most likely type of oral tradition for us to locate, document, and write about in our family histories. **Consider family food traditions as a theme for oral history interviewing and family document collecting.** Research what the foodways might have been for your family's ethnicity and time to give yourself more material for your narrative.

CHAPTER BIBLIOGRAPHY

Oral History

1. Allen, Barbara, and Lynwood Montell. *From Memory to History*. Nashville: American Association for State and Local History, 1981.

2. Baum, Willa. *Transcribing and Editing Oral History*. Nashville: American Association for State and Local History, 1977.

3. Dunaway, David K., and Willa K. Baum, eds. *Oral History: An Interdisciplinary Anthology*. Nashville: American Association for State and Local History, 1984.

4. Epstein, Ellen Robinson, and Rona Mendelsohn. *Record and Remember: Tracing Your Roots Through Oral History*. New York: Monarch, 1978.

5. Fletcher, William. *Recording Your Family History: A Guide to Preserving Oral History With Videotape, Audiotape, Suggested Topics and Questions, Interview Techniques*. Berkeley: Ten Speed Press, 1986, 1989.

6. Mullen, Patrick B. *Listening to Old Voices: Folklore, Life Stories, and the Elderly*. Urbana: University of Illinois Press, 1992.
7. Ritchie, Donald. *Doing Oral History*. New York: Twayne Publishers, 1995.
8. Ryant, Carl. "Oral History and the Family: A Tool for the Documentation and Interpretation of Family History." *Annual of the New England Oral History Association* 2 (1989–1990): 30–37.
9. Scobie, Ingrid W. "Family and Community History Through Oral History." *Public Historian* 1 (1979): 29–39.
10. Sturm, Duane, and Pat Sturm. *Video Family History*. Salt Lake City: Ancestry Publishing, 1989.

Selected Examples and Sources of Oral History

1. Adams, Judith Porter. *Peacework: Oral Histories of Women Peace Activists*. Boston: Twayne Publishers, 1991.
2. Arnold, Eleanor, ed. *Voices of American Homemakers*. Bloomington: Indiana University Press, 1985.
3. Banks, Ann. *First-Person America*. New York: Alfred A. Knopf, 1980.
4. Coan, Peter Morton. *Ellis Island Interviews: In Their Own Words*. New York: Facts on File, 1997.
5. Federal Writers Project of the WPA, North Carolina, Tennessee, Georgia. *These Are Our Lives*. Chapel Hill: University of North Carolina Press, 1939.
6. Gluck, Sherna Berger. *Rosie the Riveter Revisited: Women, the War, and Social Change*. Boston: Twayne Publishers, 1987.
7. Krause, Corinne Azen. *Grandmothers, Mothers, and Daughters: Oral Histories of Three Generations of Ethnic American Women*. Boston: Twayne Publishers, 1991.
8. Manning, Diane T. *Hill Country Teacher: Oral Histories From the One-Room School and Beyond*. Boston: Twayne Publishers, 1990.
9. Mellon, James, ed. *Bullwhip Days: The Slaves Remember*. New York: Avon Books, 1988.
10. Morison, Joan, and Charlotte Fox Zabusky, eds. *American Mosaic: The Immigrant Experience in the Words of Those Who Lived It*. New York: E.P. Dutton, 1980.
11. Terkel, Studs. *"The Good War": An Oral History of World War Two*. New York: Pantheon, 1984.
12. ———. *Hard Times: An Oral History of the Great Depression*. New York: Pantheon, 1970.
13. Terrill, Tom E., and Jerrold Hirsch, eds. *Such as Us: Southern Voices of the Thirties*. New York: W.W. Norton, 1979.
14. Tucker, Susan. *Telling Memories Among Southern Women: Domestic Workers and Their Employers in the Segregated South*. New York: Schocken Books, 1988.

Examples of Published Oral Tradition and Folklore

1. Axelrod, Alan, and Harry Oster. *The Penguin Dictionary of American Folklore*. New York: Penguin Books, 2000.

2. Botkin, B.A. *A Treasury of New England Folklore*. New York: Bonanza Books, 1965.

3. Espinosa, Aurelio M. *The Folklore of Spain in the American Southwest*. Norman: University of Oklahoma Press, 1985, 1991.

4. Leary, James P. *Midwestern Folk Humor*. Little Rock: August House, 1991.

5. McNeil, W.K., ed. *Ozark Mountain Humor*. Little Rock: August House, 1989.

6. Welsch, Roger L. *A Treasury of Nebraska Pioneer Folklore*. Lincoln: University of Nebraska Press, 1939, 1984.

7. West, John O. *Mexican-American Folklore*. Little Rock: August House, 1988.

8. Zeitlin, Steven J., et al. *A Celebration of American Family Folklore: Tales and Traditions From the Smithsonian Collection*. New York: Pantheon Books, 1982.

Sample Sources on Foodways

1. Brown, Linda Keller, and Kay Mussell, eds. *Ethnic and Regional Foodways in the United States: The Performance of Group Identity*. Knoxville: University of Tennessee Press, 1984.

2. Camp, Charles. *American Foodways: What, When, Why, and How We Eat in America*. Little Rock: August House, 1989.

3. Hooker, Richard. *Food and Drink in American History*. Indianapolis: Bobbs-Merrill Company, 1981.

4. Levenstein, Harvey. *Paradox of Plenty: A Social History of Eating in Modern America*. New York: Oxford University Press, 1993.

5. Luchetti, Cathy. *Home on the Range: A Culinary History of the American West*. New York: Villard Books, 1993.

6. Mariani, John. *America Eats Out*. New York: William Morrow and Company, 1991.

7. Perl, Lila. *Red-flannel Hash and Shoo-fly Pie; American Regional Foods and Festivals*. Cleveland: World Publishing Company, 1965.

8. Neustadt, Kathy. *Clambake: A History of an American Tradition*. Amherst: University of Massachusetts Press, 1992.

9. Root, Waverly, and Richard deRochemont. *Eating in America: A History*. New York: Ecco Press, 1976.

10. Stern, Jane, and Michael Stern. *American Gourmet: Classic Recipes, Deluxe Delights, Flamboyant Favorites, and Swank "Company" Food From the '50s and '60s*. New York: HarperCollins, 1991.

SIX

Recapturing a Dying Art: Correspondence

I am really glad that you are improving in your writing but you must try to improve much in your composition, so that you can write a long and nice letter. The way to do that is to get a piece of paper and from day to day write some thing on it that you wish to write and at the end of the week get your paper and read it over carefully and select from it all of the matter that you think will interest the one that you are writing to[.] write to me in this way and I will answer.

—C. A. Brown to D. A. Keller, 1884[1]

Notes

Endnotes for this chapter begin on page 222.

Important

CORRESPONDENCE 101
Writing to Relatives and Family Friends

Personal letter-writing seems to be a dying art. Traditional newsy letters and correspondence courtesy are giving way to the quick convenience of no-frills E-mail. Ironically, the decline in letter-writing began well before E-mail's availability, so E-mail may even be reviving communication by written word. Before E-mail, many of us let family correspondence diminish into typed, annual form letters folded into preprinted Christmas cards. At least E-mail, among family members with access to it, can be frequent and friendly enough to serve as a documented conversation.

Recently, while my husband's parents traveled to visit relatives and friends across several states, my brother-in-law, Frank DeFranza, conducted an E-mail campaign to track their every move for the benefit of us siblings, cousins, and in-laws. This was reassuring to the worriers and amusing to the subjects of Frank's surveillance, Rick's parents, who have never touched a computer. There's the rub. **The generations whom you most need to contact for family history information are the least liable to be computer literate.**

Of course many senior-citizen genealogists are very advanced—much more than I—in their computer use. It will be the family members who are not that you need to contact first, however. When you initiate contact with an older relative, or one whose life is less technologically up-to-date than yours, you are establishing a relationship that you hope will bring your family history meaning, information, and artifacts. Therefore, although most advice about correspondence encourages brevity and getting down to just the facts, you may need to invest more patience, caring, and sharing in old-fashioned letters to older relatives. Consider: what might the relative want to get out of responding to you?

The older man, who may be retired and anxious to tell his war stories to anyone who will listen, may need you to take the time to care about what he thinks is important. The older woman, who may still religiously write cheery letters or holiday cards and who reads the obituaries each day, might want to share her family expertise with someone who addresses her with the niceties of proper letter-writing.

Know your audience and your intended effect, then write accordingly. Think like a historian. You are addressing letters to the historical figures about whom you will write: the last survivors of the disappearing generations who can recall meeting ancestors of the generations before. Or, perhaps you are addressing the branches that still lead relatively simple, rural lives and who thus keep family history the old-fashioned ways (thank goodness). **You want stories, descriptions, thoughts, and feelings more than you want names and dates.** Older minds are better sources for the former than the latter. Country kin live more by storytelling than do many urban folks, but listening takes time and patience. Write to older and more rural relatives for some of the meat to put on the factual bones.

Reminder

If you think that all earlier generations are dead in your family, you should still investigate whether there are older relatives after all. Even if they do not exist, you can initiate rewarding correspondence with others. Middle-aged generations will recall what the earlier ones were like, as well as some of their stories. Even though your own generation of first cousins and siblings had the same grandparents and even the same parents as you, you may be surprised at what different stories they picked up, or at least what different perspectives they have. My father, when in his seventies, told his older sister how he had resented the neglect and domination he had felt from his mother when they were growing up. He believed his mother favored his older siblings. His sister was shocked: "Well, we thought of you as the spoiled baby. You always got what you wanted!" she said.

Tolerance is always in order. Be prepared for correspondents to have different lifestyles and viewpoints. For example, their religious views may be extremely different from yours. The older or more traditional your relatives, the more likely it is for them to disapprove of your lifestyle or quote scripture at every turn. They may include prejudiced remarks in their letters. Just as you might do in person, politely avoid confrontation. Take these folks' views in historical context too. If the prejudices have to do with family, region, religion, politics, culture, or economic station, you may be learning from them about how some of your ancestors thought and spoke. Think like a historian. Do not judge.

Think of your ancestors' communities; write to their neighbors. Consider corresponding with people who are not necessarily relatives but who can inform you about your family history. The neighbors know everything in small-town America. Older neighbors may recall who lived where, what jobs folks had, their major life events, what they were like, and what people said about them. Waverly, Iowa, the Sturdevants' longtime hometown, has been like that. Folks still refer to houses by the names of those who lived there many years (and several inhabitants) ago. Thus, even though there are no Sturdevants (of that family, by that name) left alive in Waverly, the name is familiar to neighbors through local lore,

Idea Generator

HOW TO WRITE AN OLD-FASHIONED AND IRRESISTIBLE FAMILY LETTER

1. Consider using personal, attractive stationery, depending on the gender and what you know of the tastes of the recipient.

2. Consider handwriting the letter, especially the first one, rather than typing it. Some people, particularly if they are older or live in rural areas, find typed letters off-putting. Legibility, however, takes priority if your handwriting is a problem.

3. Remember that the recipient's eyesight could be failing. Write larger and clearer than usual.

4. Start with a warm and personal salutation. Use a nickname for the recipient that is familiar and appropriate: "Dear Aunt Sally" or "Dear Cousin John."

5. Ask questions of family concern about the recipient's health or major life events before you ask research questions. Genuinely care.

6. Recollect some memorable occasion or point of contact to remind the recipient who you are: "I will never forget the time my mother brought me to your house," or "I am your brother's granddaughter."

7. State a strong motive for the research you are doing: you are writing a family history. Again, do not begin the letter this way as though it is more important than salutations and concern.

8. Ask for the family information that it is most essential to get from the particular source to whom you are writing, such as stories and descriptions. Use the questions for oral history interviewing in this chapter or the Elements of Social History in chapter one, for ideas of what to ask. Use *what*, *why*, and *how* more than *who*, *when*, and *where*. Try asking about one person or one event at a time, rather than vaguely asking for "everything."

9. Write as you would speak if you contacted the relative on the phone or in person. Write simply and directly. Do not be formal. "I wish I could visit you, but since I can't, I hope you'll be able to write to me. It would be so nice. . . ."

10. Consider including a copy of a photograph, such as one that identifies you or a relative about whom you are asking. Perhaps make some color photocopies of the picture you will send so that you have them on hand for each letter to a new recipient.

11. Offer any appropriate way to assist the recipient's reply, such as a self-addressed, stamped envelope, photocopying costs, or a telephone number that they can call collect.

12. Encase the letter, beginning and end, with warm comments indicating how special it will be to hear back and how much you appreciate the recipient's time.

13. Reread and revise each letter before you send it.

14. Handwrite the envelope, at least the first time, with complete names and addresses.

Case Study

By way of a local genealogical society in Illinois, I learned that graves of my Dickey and Withers ancestors still existed in two small cemeteries: Maroa and Friends Creek. In my letter to the society, I referred to the names of two men, the B_____ brothers, who owned a chattel mortgage on the Withers farm in 1861. (I had obtained the original mortgage from M.C. Parker; see chapter four.) At the beginning of the Civil War, the Withers family mortgaged everything on their farm. During the war, father James Withers, uncle Alexander, and son Ira died. After the war, widow Martha Withers took her surviving children to town. A Withers daughter married a Dickey son and later became my great-grandparents, who moved to Kansas.

Among other resources, the Illinois society gave me the name and address of the current owner of the farm on which one of the cemeteries still sits. His name was also B_____. I wrote to this owner of the cemetery land. He was a descendant of the men who held the mortgage on my ancestors' farm in 1861! Through my Mr. B_____ I learned the history of the farm's ownership, which included the Dickey, Withers, and B_____ families. Through him and the society, I learned the tombstone inscriptions of about thirty relatives, many of whom I had not known before. I was surprised at the continued existence of both Dickey and Withers families in that part of Illinois after my grandmother's branches had moved on. One of the farms was still known by the name Withers, even though its last Withers owner died in 1941.

My Mr. B_____ was an extremely helpful, friendly contact. It was also meaningful that over one hundred years later he in rural Illinois and I in San Francisco were discussing the interlocking fates of our ancestors, whose only apparent connection was that his ancestors financed my ancestors' mortgage. I wonder what they thought of each other at the time?

house names, deeds, and cemetery markers. In such towns and rural areas, try writing to *anyone* who might know something.

FINDING AND USING HISTORICAL LETTERS AS SOURCES

Some of your best sources for information and quotable observations to use in your family history narrative are the letters written by family members. You may reproduce them in their entirety as part of your narrative, quote them here and there, or cite them as information sources. Think how much better a narrative will be if it contains the thoughts of the soldier or the pioneer in their own words.

Just as with artifacts and photographs, seek and gather such letters from home sources first. Organize them chronologically to read the order of events in them. If you have both "to" and "from" letters, such as your grandparents' wartime love letters, organize them (or copies or transcripts of them) chronologically to

Citing Sources

For how to cite letters (and E-mail messages) when writing family history narrative, see pages 80 and 87 in Elizabeth Shown Mills's, *Evidence!* A good rule of thumb for citing letters is to think of them as comparable to books: the author of the letter is as the author of a book, the title of the letter is "Letter to _____ (recipient's name)," the location of the writer is parallel to the place of publication, and the date of the letter is comparable to a year of publication. As with most unpublished documents and materials, a complete citation also identifies the current holder/location of the letter (or copy of it) that you used. Annotation in a footnote can also explain the relationships among the letter's author, current holder, and you, if these are not clear within your text.

read the running conversation. Treat them as antique paper documents, copying them and preserving them archivally. If you find one bundle of his and another of hers, one bundle "to" and one "from," you should copy or transcribe each, then put the copies in chronological order. Do not destroy the bundles as someone left them. Work from copies as much as you can. Use a magnifying glass or the enlarging feature on a photocopying machine to help read difficult handwriting.

Transcribe the letters that will serve as your sources. Use the same standards that genealogical guides recommend for transcribing wills, deeds, and other documents. Be exact and exacting. Transcribe literally every mark on the page—errors, cross-outs, and all. This should produce a typed, legible version of the letter that is so true to the original that you can quote and cite the transcription rather than struggle with the original every time. The original may fade, crumble, or even disappear.

MODERN LETTERS ARE HISTORICAL DOCUMENTS TOO

Your family history research correspondence can become historical documents for you to quote and cite. If they survive you, they can be someone else's historical archive. In between writing them and your death, however, even you may forget when or to whom you wrote a particular letter. Thus it is a good idea to make each family history letter a historical document that is self-contained, carrying with it all identifying information. See the advice on page 149.

Figuring Relationships

A key topic of discussion when you write to relatives will be "Exactly how are we related?" If you can determine this for your correspondents they will be impressed and appreciative. It may help you to "bond" and serves many people as a conversation piece. Several genealogical guides have complex charts for determining relationships. See page 75 in the revised edition of William Dollarhide's *Managing a Genealogical Project* and page 115 in the second edition of Emily Anne Croom's *Unpuzzling Your Past.*

Being a historian, I needed a chart that was more linear and that followed lines of descent. I have included my simple chart on page 150. It does not fit every need as thoroughly as others and is not as sophisticated. That is why I like it. By all means, move on to the more complex charts. Work out for the people with whom you correspond their exact relationship to you and they may take more of an interest in that than in the family history, about which they will tell you stories in the meantime.

Cutting Family Trees Into Jigsaw Relatives

Relatives will probably send you genealogical charts compiled by the well-meaning family tree planter. This enthusiastic arborist has made an elaborate chart that seemed just perfect for displaying relatives' names and dates so they could see the connections. Sometimes the chart is even in a tree design, with branches and limbs, or in some other artistic representation, such as a fan shape.

Step By Step

HOW TO WRITE HISTORICALLY USEFUL PERSONAL LETTERS

1. Write your complete address at the top right, of each letter that you write, in order to document authorship and place of composition.

2. Write the recipient's complete name and address at the top left, above the salutation. If only the letter (without the envelope) survives, some latter-day family historian will not necessarily know who "Dear Fred" is, let alone "Dear Aunt" or "Dear Papa."

3. Date every letter that you write, complete with the year written out in four digits.

4. Number successive pages and put an identifying header at the top right corner of each, such as "K. Sturdevant to M. McLeod, 10 May 2000."

5. Make clear in the letter your relationship to the recipient. For example, include a line such as "My father has told me that you were his favorite cousin. What did your mother say about what it was like to be sisters, growing up with my grandmother?"

6. Tell family history as well as ask for it. Although you must try to keep the letter from becoming overly long, telling at least one story or description in each letter means that you have documented a little bit of family history already. Later on, you will be glad for any family history that you documented. You can later cite your own letters as sources. Telling one version also may occasion alternate or additional versions from the recipient.

7. Identify people, places, organizations, and events by their full names whenever possible. Explain what something was if you suspect that younger generations or people from other places would not know. If you refer to someone or something in an "inside" manner, you leave a mystery for your descendants.

8. Reread and revise each letter before you send it.

9. Keep a copy of each letter that you send. Start an archive of your own correspondence copies, just as you should with the letters you receive.

Of course, the information may be inaccurate, citations are nonexistent, and it seems as though only the original planter could sort out the meaning of the branches and limbs. The careful genealogist might flinch at the unreliability, perhaps even worthlessness, of the chart.

However, the family historian, the Keeper of Everything, should see value in the hours and years of labor sacrificed by writers of family trees. You can put together the information from multiple family trees with a jigsaw method similar to the one I recommended for identifying photographs in chapter four (see also the technique on page 151). You can develop clues to further your research by

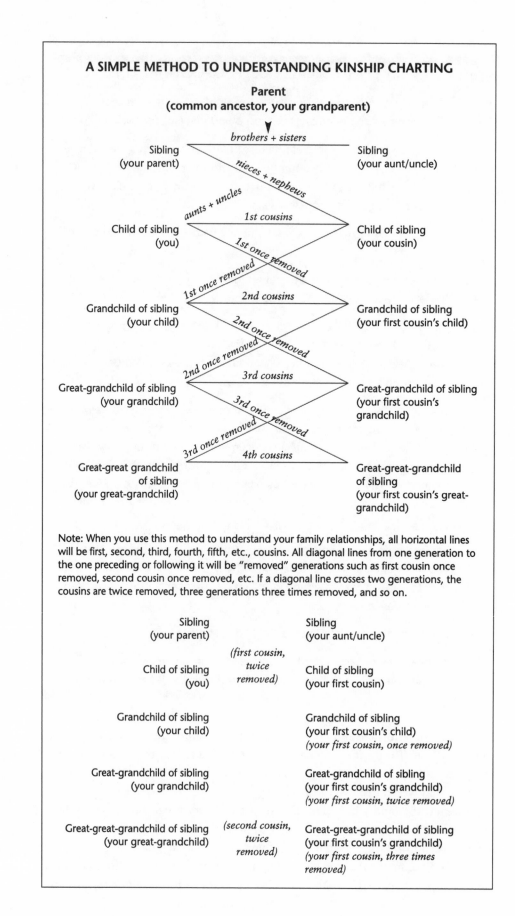

A SIMPLE METHOD TO UNDERSTANDING KINSHIP CHARTING

Parent
(common ancestor, your grandparent)

brothers + sisters

Sibling
(your parent)

Sibling
(your aunt/uncle)

nieces + nephews

aunts + uncles

1st cousins

Child of sibling
(you)

Child of sibling
(your cousin)

1st once removed

1st once removed

2nd cousins

Grandchild of sibling
(your child)

Grandchild of sibling
(your first cousin's child)

2nd once removed

2nd once removed

3rd cousins

Great-grandchild of sibling
(your grandchild)

Great-grandchild of sibling
(your first cousin's
grandchild)

3rd once removed

3rd once removed

4th cousins

Great-great grandchild
of sibling
(your great-grandchild)

Great-great-grandchild
of sibling
(your first cousin's great-
grandchild)

Note: When you use this method to understand your family relationships, all horizontal lines will be first, second, third, fourth, fifth, etc., cousins. All diagonal lines from one generation to the one preceding or following it will be "removed" generations such as first cousin once removed, second cousin once removed, etc. If a diagonal line crosses two generations, the cousins are twice removed, three generations three times removed, and so on.

Sibling
(your parent)

Sibling
(your aunt/uncle)

(first cousin,
twice
removed)

Child of sibling
(you)

Child of sibling
(your first cousin)

Grandchild of sibling
(your child)

Grandchild of sibling
(your first cousin's child)
(your first cousin, once removed)

Great-grandchild of sibling
(your grandchild)

Great-grandchild of sibling
(your first cousin's grandchild)
(your first cousin, twice removed)

Great-great-grandchild of sibling
(your great-grandchild)

(second cousin,
twice
removed)

Great-great-grandchild of sibling
(your first cousin's grandchild)
(your first cousin, three times
removed)

The name Sturdevant has its liabilities. People stumble over its pronunciation and spelling, even to the point of making it odder and more difficult than it really is: Sturdvit, Strurdegent, Storklevent, Sturdevansky. Yet, in genealogical research, it helps to have a rare, unusual name. Rick regularly receives letters and packages from people who "have some Sturdevants" in their family lines. Between six and eight different people have sent their ancestral charts in the last few years. I encouraged him to try a jigsaw method for putting these family trees together. One evening he fit together the last pieces in one of those "Eureka!" moments. You can do the same with dueling genealogical charts you have located for the same family from different sources.

Over a two-year period, Rick heard from several genealogical researchers. One was a man named Howard Mikesell in Oregon who was descended from Emeline Sturdevant Cave, a daughter of Rick's great-great-great-grandfather, Ira Sturdevant (the 1812 veteran and father of Lafayette). This correspondent found us over the Internet and telephoned to make sure we were the right Sturdevants. He sent a packet of materials and gave our address to another descendant. Nathan in Arizona had the long lost Sturdevant family Bible that had become legendary in the family, along with many other documents, copies of which he shared by mail.

Next, a co-worker of Rick's, Jerry Schroeder, called him at work one day and asked whether Rick had a Caleb Sturdevant, a Revolutionary War veteran and father of Ira, in his background. Jerry had just found Caleb in his own genealogical chart. Thus Rick and Jerry, who had known each other at work for several years, discovered that they have common ancestors! Jerry, of course, gave Rick another chart.

Next there was an eighty-four-year-old lady from Michigan who also wrote that she was a descendant of Emeline Cave. She obtained our address from cousins in the old Iowa hometown, Waverly. She sent her notes, which included her own reminiscences of meeting Rick's Civil War ancestor, Lafayette, whom she called "Uncle Laffy."

Finally, there was the other Kathy Sturdevant. She was sitting at her computer in Southern California one day and typed in a search request on her own name. Up came a reference to me as a genealogical speaker! So she wrote me an E-mail. The first time I saw it, I thought I had made a mistake on the computer and accidentally sent a message to myself. Then we started corresponding. I told her that I thought she might be distantly related to my husband, so she sent a packet from a genealogist in her father's family.

With all of this material, plus some research in genealogical collections at the Denver Public Library, Rick pieced together on a notepad each generation until he could figure out how all were related. All of this and more came from people spontaneously contacting Rick. Along the way many letters and documents turned up, loaded with valuable historical information about the family. There were the letters, recollections, and the long-missing Bible. Then there were the

(continued on page 152)

charts. By writing down and rereading, over and over, from one chart to the next, Rick figured out how they all intersected. This gave him shortcuts into censuses and vital records.

Research in genealogical libraries and books corrected errors and explained mysteries. Place names on the charts were also helpful new clues. The separation between the branch of Sturdevants that spawned one of our new correspondents and Rick's branch could usually be traced to a split between two brothers during the Yankee exodus from New England to the Midwest. Sharing with others, puzzling their charts together, and applying his historical knowledge and professional skills reinvigorated Rick's long-dormant enthusiasm (obsession) for intensive family history research.

such analysis. To spend your time on this takes a leap of faith in the earlier compilers, but for every misbegotten twig or bewildering knothole, you may find several healthy branches to climb.

It is a worthwhile project to mix and match multiple charts such as these and exercise your powers of deduction. Some of what you deduce will be correct and some will not. All will require further research to properly document it. Yet, think of the harm that would be done if you rejected family charts out of hand. They may hold the only surviving clues to solve family mysteries. They are a source of pride to those who send them. A good family historian must not alienate the human sources, who, in addition to their charts, have much else to offer.

Citing Sources

When you write your own family history, you can cite a family tree chart made by another relative as a source. Granted, it may not be your best, most reliable source, but if it is the only place where a piece of information existed, consider a footnote such as

[1] James Anderson, undocumented family tree chart, drawn c. 1945, copy in possession of author.

See Elizabeth Shown Mills's example of citing an "inadequately documented" family group sheet on page 83 of *Evidence!*

CORRESPONDENCE 102
Writing to Genealogical Records Agencies

Even if you are as fortunate in your family correspondence as the Sturdevants, you must next research in public records to prove what you've learned. Most genealogists are already aware of the "bibles" for records correspondence, and many genealogical guides offer good advice for the kinds of letters that one writes to agencies for information and records. These also provide sample correspondence logs for keeping track of your incoming and outgoing letters. See the general bibliography.

One of the most satisfying discussions of how to correspond is "Let's Write a

Letter" in Val Greenwood's *The Researcher's Guide to American Genealogy*. He uses clever reminders such as the LETTER formula: *L*imit what you ask, *E*asy to answer, *T*wo copies of every letter, *T*hanks, *E*xchange, such as paying expenses, and *R*eturn postage that you should provide.[2]

There are basic rules that we should all follow when writing for records. The same rules apply to any contact we have with any professional when seeking information on our families. See chapter seven for discussion of how to apply these rules during visits to libraries. I will address the rules and strategies as they apply to historical organizations, because these are least covered by genealogical guides and most known to me as a historian.

CORRESPONDENCE 103
Writing to Historians, Academic Librarians, and Other Professionals

"Send me everything you have on my family," wrote the beginning genealogist. In response, the historical society librarian pulled out the form letter that said "We regret that we do not have the resources to conduct genealogical research upon demand. We enclose the names of several genealogical researchers who may be able to help you for a fee." **The first deadly sin of the family historian is presumptuousness about how much others share our enthusiasm for our own families.** Assuming anyone would find our family history fascinating, we write paragraphs and pages of names, dates, and explanations so that the librarian will be better informed to conduct our research for us. Instead, we receive a letter stating "We regret that we do not have the resources. . . ." Indeed, the senior historical society or local history librarian has responded this way to this kind of letter so often that the mere words "I am doing my genealogy" may elicit a copy, just for you, of "We regret that we do not have the resources. . . ." Worse yet, the librarian who realizes a "send me everything letter" is a waste of time may file your missive in the canister intended for waste, without answering it at all.

Some of the advice for writing to genealogical records agencies applies to any organization or institution. You will see, however, particularly in chapter seven, that I am advising you to research in *historical* agencies and *scholarly* institutions more than you may have done. This will mean that you correspond with such agencies, too. The rules change somewhat when writing to a historical or scholarly agency. As discussed in chapter seven, scholars and the librarians who serve scholarly research sometimes look upon genealogy and its practitioners with disdain. Too many beginning genealogists have written letters that make unreasonable requests. Librarians are not there to do our entire family histories for us. Too many genealogists have wasted their own time and librarians' time by reciting their lineage. Think like a historian. Your family history and your research experiences are not unique. Disinterested librarians have heard it all before.

There are ways to engage historians, librarians, and historical institutions in your search. There are ways that they *do* have the resources to help you. Think like an enthusiastic historian; your family history, as a part of the social history of a place, truly is of interest to the scholars and librarians. If you put it in

Sources

Sources of addresses and information on how to contact vital records repositories and other organizations for genealogical research include *Ancestry's Red Book: American State, County and Town Sources* (Alice Eichholz, ed.), *The Handy Book for Genealogists* (George B. Everton, comp.), Juliana Szucs Smith's *The Ancestry Family Historian's Address Book*, and Elizabeth Petty Bentley's *The Genealogist's Address Book*.

Important

Tip

Reminder

County courthouses, vital records agencies, the National Archives, and many other public government offices will have special forms and fees for the records requests that genealogists are most liable to make. Visit their Web sites to learn in advance what forms and procedures you will need to use. Your first letters to such agencies should be brief requests for the forms and fees required to obtain certificates of birth, death, marriage, etc. There is no sense explaining what or whom you are researching to an agency that will simply send you the forms and fee schedule in response. Telephoning ahead is a relatively cheap and convenient way to find out fees, request forms, and prepare your requests so that they receive the best responses from agencies. Some agencies make it possible to download their forms online. Others will respond to your online inquiry by sending you the right form.

HOW TO WRITE TO A HISTORICAL AGENCY TO GET GOOD RESULTS

1. Do research to single out the agency most likely to have the specific information you seek. See the American Association for State and Local History (AASLH) directory discussed on page 157 or one of the genealogical directories on pages 223-225.)

2. Check (in the AASLH guide or others) whether the agency has a library, a full-time staff, and/or the other services that you need.

3. Determine whether the first step of your request might best be taken by telephone. A good telephone question would be to ask what the procedures or fees are for obtaining something.

4. Tailor your requests and expectations to the size of the staff and the nature of the collections.

5. Use the language of common courtesy: please, thank you, sincerely, etc. Include a concluding line thanking the recipient for her time and attention.

6. Seek the recipient's advice and acknowledge that they know their collection better than you do. Use language that indicates you are not certain whether they can help you or whether you might be asking too much: could, would, might, is there a way, how do I, can you recommend?

7. Ask for information by offering the *place* and *year* that you are researching. This is the most basic way that historical libraries are organized.

8. Introduce the letter with statements and requests similar to those discussed in "Good Introductory Lines" on page 156.

9. See "How to Write Historically Useful Personal Letters" on page 149 for basic advice on how to head and end letters with identifying information for your own records.

10. Form your inquiry in historical terms rather than genealogical.

11. As much as possible, avoid using the following terms. These may cause the librarian to consider you a tiresome amateur genealogist: *genealogy, family history, my family,* names of individual members of your family, *ancestors, pioneers.*

12. Do not bother offering a precise date (month and day) unless the piece of information you seek was a generally newsworthy event on that precise date. Precise dates about insignificant events also tip-off librarians that you may be the dreaded genealogist.

13. If you expect to need a long-term relationship with that particular library or repository, address the staff in ways that single you out as pleasant and memorable. Make friends. Indicate your enthusiasm and interest for the *history* you are learning, rather than for the private vanities of your own ancestors' names and dates.

14. Offer to cover postage and photocopying costs. If you fear that these will be too expensive, offer to cover them up to a certain amount and request that you be contacted if the costs are expected to go any higher. I prefer to offer to cover return postage rather than enclose a self-addressed, stamped envelope (SASE), because too many people do not bother to use the SASE, and it may not be the right size and postage anyway. Some researchers include a check for five or ten dollars to defray expenses, or refer to it as a donation to the library. I am not comfortable with this when I do not even know yet whether I will get a response.

15. Keep your letters to no more than one typed page each. The body of each letter should be no more than one or two paragraphs, or about half of the typed page, maximum.

that context and maintain it there, you have as good a chance as any academic researcher of holding the attention of the academic librarian or archivist. Examine the historical situation you are researching. What about it is dramatic, interesting, or shocking? Mention that to the person you are soliciting. Comment on how the individual situation you are researching seems to reveal trends. Ask the historian whether you are right to observe such trends.

Be realistic about how busy and understaffed a research institution may be. You are asking them to do you a favor. You may be one of hundreds of people who do so. If other genealogists have preceded you, the librarians and archivists may have formed a prejudice against the whole community of genealogists as people who make unreasonable requests.

If you learn to think of yourself as doing valid *historical* research, comparable to what a *professional* might do, you can present yourself as such and avoid the appearance of being the amateur, self-absorbed genealogist. (See my explanation of this stereotype in chapter seven.) I recommend to students in family history classes that they write or say "I am writing a paper for my college history course" sooner than say "I am researching my family history." If you are not a student, you can still convey a similarly objective purpose. Librarians and archivists who are used to working with scholars will be more receptive to any researcher who approaches with an awareness of scholarly standards. **Place your ancestors in a social or general history context, then ask for assistance researching the context, the topic, the place, and the time period, not the ancestor or family simply for its own sake.** Remember, too, that you can be spartan in expressing your motivations. There is no harm in getting down to the business of precisely what you seek, without even giving a reason. This is better than the opposite extreme of explaining your reasons at the risk of boring busy librarians.

Tip

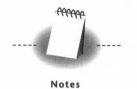

Notes

GOOD INTRODUCTORY LINES

1. I am researching the history of the town during the period of . . .

2. I am doing a study on what it was like to be a farmer in Middletown at the turn of the century. Do you have any suggestions of what may be available in your library?

3. I am researching the history of your area in about 1845. What would be good sources in your institution and how might I gain access to them?

4. I am researching the experiences of typical Polish immigrants in your community circa 1890. What resources does your library have that might help?

5. I am tracing the lives of a family that lived in Hartford in 1650. What sources in your collection would you recommend?

6. I am planning a research trip to your library. Could you please send me any brochures that will help me orient myself to the collections in advance?

7. I am looking for the records of the _____ sanatorium for the time period between 19__ and 19__. Can you tell me if the records still exist and how I might gain access to them?

Acceptable No-Frills or Very Specific Introductory Lines

1. I am seeking one particular piece of information. Can you suggest a source where I might find . . .

2. Do you have the source called . . .

3. In my research I have found reference to a tornado there in 1886. Can you locate or recommend sources that might verify and describe this event?

4. Do you retain Portland newspapers from 1875? If so, would it be possible to obtain, by mail, a copy of an obituary for Mary Williams from October 12?

Bad Introductory Lines

1. Please send me everything that you have on my family.

2. I am doing my genealogy. My family tree began with . . .

3. Please send me the history [or the book, or the file] of my family.

4. What do you have on my family?

5. Josef Klataska was my great-great-grandfather. He was born in . . .

6. My ancestors were very prominent in your community. I am sure that you must have . . .

Warning

The American Association for State and Local History's *Directory of Historical Organizations in the United States and Canada* (formerly titled *Directory of Historical Agencies in North America*) will suggest many local and state historical societies to which you may write. Most libraries will have a copy of an old edition, but a new one is due soon. Even an old edition can be helpful. Consider whether the address you will be using from an old edition is still the correct address (or phone ahead). This book is similar to the *Red Book, Handy Book*, and *Genealogist's Address Book*. There are some historical or genealogical societies that are listed in more than one book. The AASLH *Directory*, however, is dedicated to its audience of state and local historians and society staffs, and is therefore more comprehensive than any other directory of historical agencies.

For armchair family historians and correspondence purposes, the AASLH *Directory* offers many possibilities. Organized by state and then locality, it lists each historical agency with the information on page 158. Occasionally an entry is less complete because the information comes from mailed questionnaires.

The entries allow you to figure out, from a distance, what historical society is nearest to your family's home, what it may have for your research, and how reasonable it may be to make requests of its staff. This directory is comprehensive enough that you should find a society or museum in each town where your family lived, or at least in the nearest larger town, which will be the agency most responsible for collecting the local history.

Why Is It Worthwhile to Write Such Letters?

You will be amazed how much pertinent information awaits you (or your letter) in a historical society library or archive. Here are just a few examples of the kinds of resources you might access by mail with your patience, understanding of how to address the staff, and your reasonable *historical* requests.

- obscure local history books that include information about what life was like in your ancestors' day and sometimes even include your ancestor
- recently published scholarly history books on the area, whose authors have analyzed local history for you and given footnotes to sources you also could use
- hard-to-find books on local folklore and customs
- local newspapers, often complete runs on microfilm, that may be available by interlibrary loan
- complete runs of the society magazines, full of articles on people and events in local history
- photograph archives with donated collections from local families
- maps of local communities and rural areas from different time periods
- clipping files organized by local historical topics
- private papers of local families whose lives were like your family's
- genealogies published about local families
- oral history interviews with locals recalling life and events from your family's day

I am about to contradict myself, or so it may seem. I have earlier discouraged you from expecting the historical society librarian to find "the file" on your

Sources

A new edition of the AASLH *Directory* is overdue. The AASLH projects that the fifteenth edition will be available later in 2000. The new edition will have several improved features. One will be a topical index to the special themes and programs of the various agencies. If you are interested in a particular ethnic group, for example, the index will lead you to any society that specializes in that group. The new edition will also list Web sites and E-mail addresses for many of the societies and will be available for sale as either a book or a CD-ROM. There is no plan yet to put the entire directory online, although that may happen in about three years. For more information, contact Mitch Allen, publisher, Alta Mira Press, 1630 N. Main St., Ste. 367, Walnut Creek, CA 94596 or call (925) 938-7243 or visit <http://www.altamirapress .com.> Alta Mira is the publisher for AASLH now.

INFORMATION IN AN AASLH *DIRECTORY* ENTRY

Name of historical society

Street address

Mailing address and zip code

Telephone number with area code

Whether it is publicly or privately funded

Year of founding

Number of members

Number of full-, part-time, and volunteer staff

Name of its main publication

Special collections in the library and/or special public programs

Historical time period covered by its collections

Tip

family. As you become a better researcher and build rapport with information specialists, however, sometimes they will have a file on one of your family members. Many libraries maintain their own indexes of their holdings by names of individuals. This is especially true for names they have found in their local and state history sources. For instance, the Carnegie Branch Library for Local History in Boulder, Colorado had index cards with city directory information on John Harper's family from Victor, Colorado. When I wrote to them from San Francisco (before I could travel to access old Colorado city directories), I received from the Boulder library their extractions on my ancestors from a decade of city directories.

For another example, I was corresponding with Christine Marin, an archivist at the Arizona State University Library in Tempe, about other historical matters. She referred to her interest in Globe, Arizona, and copper mining. So I told her about my grandfather, Archibald Harper, being a Globe attorney and politician during the same period she was investigating. She sent me copies of extracts from Globe newspaper indexes that summarized stories about Harper's election campaigns and job appointments circa 1908–1915. Although extracts from directories and newspaper indexes mean I should go to the libraries and do my own in-depth research, my letters brought me some knowledge of what was available and the copies yielded some tantalizing family history information.

Writing to a College for a Piece of Its Own History

The academic atmosphere of any college or university may foster resistance to the average genealogical approach. Instead of seeing this as a negative, we can turn it into a positive. If a college played a role somewhere in your family history, you can use the same scholarly, professional approach that I have just recommended to request information from that institution. Most colleges retain archives of their own history either in their libraries, museums, alumni associations, or fraternities. To find an address, try *The College Blue Book*, the *HEP Higher Education Directory*, or *Baird's Manual of American College Fraternities*. As explained in chapter seven, the best place to find these and other publications is a college library.

One major advantage of college records to genealogists is that many of them—academic records, yearbooks, school newspapers, membership lists—are organized by individual students' names. **It is not unreasonable to ask about an ancestor specifically by name in this instance.** You need to give precise dates (or at least years) of attendance. In this instance, contradictory though it sounds, you may wish to emphasize your relationship to the graduate about whom you are inquiring. First, college librarians and archivists are alert to privacy issues and may not release what were once confidential records to just anyone. Second, in this case, they may find it endearing to be addressing a proud descendant of a long-ago graduate. Do not go overboard, however. Even keepers of college records may tune you out if you start telling long stories.

I knew that my grandfather had graduated from the University of Colorado Law School in 1905. We still had the photograph of his graduating class: fourteen men and one woman. (This long photograph is barely visible hanging above his desk in the photograph on page 91. It is the framed picture to your left.) I wrote to the law school for any information pertaining to this 1905 graduate. My letter obviously occasioned sympathetic interest. I received copies of his records, every yearbook entry about him, school newspaper accounts of him (and his 1904 marriage), and booklets and articles about what the law school was like at the time. One page even showed the same class photograph I had. If my grandfather had not identified each classmate on the back of his photo, the college brochure caption would have identified them for me. Especially meaningful were his classmates' yearbook comments characterizing what they thought of Archie Harper.

The law school archivist refused to share one thing: he blackened out the grades as confidential information! I wrote back to explain that my grandfather had been dead since 1965 and I included my mother's signature as his nearest surviving relative. They released the grades. "Papa" had nothing to be ashamed of in those scores of 90–100 but, ironically, his lowest score (80) was in history! The archivist also shared a list of the three known survivors of the law school, circa 1902–1905, with their addresses. I wrote to each and gained even more insight (and a delightful pen pal) from one gentleman, retired judge and Colorado water attorney William Kelly. He remembered my grandfather well. All of this began with one letter, a shot in the dark.

On page 160 is an example of family history narrative written from college records and newspapers combined with historical society materials.

Reminder

Consider this same approach with *any* institution, organization, or company. If it still exists, find an address, write a businesslike letter, and see if it has an archive. Ask also whether those records have beem moved to a nearby library or historical society. Perhaps there have been history books, articles, or brochures about what that institution was like. You may find family history records where people worked, went to school, conducted business, stayed in hospital, joined clubs, attended church, banked, or were prepared for burial.

CORRESPONDENCE 104
Scattershot Letters—Shots in the Dark

Before I used the Internet to find people, I used a simple zip code directory and an old student's habit of writing to chambers of commerce for tourist information about a place. Whenever a small town was important in my family history research, I would look up the town's zip code and address a letter to:

> Chamber of Commerce [Mayor or Postmaster might be more realistic]
> City Hall
> Town, State, Zip Code

Remarkably, it worked. My letter about ancestors living in that small town would capture someone's interest. The towns I tried with success were so small that my letter was an event to them. The towns were so small that the post office would attempt delivery to whomsoever fit the bill, and that person would carry the letter to the person in town who knew its history best. For each five tries that failed, there would be one that struck a gold mine of local and family history information.

Try scattershot letter-writing. Today you have access to directories, cheaper long-distance telephoning, and E-mail. We can use these the scattershot way, but also use the old-fashioned letters. Remember, small-town folks of earlier generations like personal, handwritten letters.

Steps for Scattershot Letter Writing
1. Determine the parameters of a small community in which your ancestor(s)

Step By Step

Case Study

Excerpts from "Nelle Arvilla Sanders and Andrew Jackson Seigle: The Cooper College Years." (Because they were lengthy and repetitive, I condensed the footnotes with the author's permission.)

Dr. C.H. Strong, who pastored the Second United Presbyterian Church in Sterling, taught Bible courses to Cooper students free of charge. Andy earned his best grades in his Bible courses, including a 98 for his first term in the preparatory school. The 1902 catalog indicates that Nelle studied the history of the kingdoms of Israel and Judah for her collegiate work, while Andy studied Mark and Acts in the preparatory school. Both made good use of this training when Andy pastored churches, and when Nelle taught Bible in her schoolrooms.[47-49]

Somehow Andy found time for other college activities. As early as 1902 he served as president of the Student Prayer Guild (which met Monday nights), played on the "Batteries" baseball team, participated in a "field meet" as a pole vaulter, won first prize ($5.00) in the Bible reading contest, served as a secretary and attended state meetings for the YMCA, and played football.[95-100]

During their courtship, Andy and Nelle received gentle teasing in the college newspaper, the *Cooper Courier*. As early as January, 1903, the "Locals" column (noted for gossipy tidbits) asks, "Who says Andy isn't engaged?" The following December, the *Courier* adds, "Andy Seigle left immediately after the [football] game for Cottonwood Falls. Andy must have some attraction to that place as he goes there frequently of late." A visit to Nelle's hometown, Cottonwood Falls, is noted again in the February 1904 issue, as well as in January 1905. The April 1905 issue confides, "Andrew Seigle made a short visit to his 'home' in Cottonwood Falls, recently."[127-131]

[47-49] Andrew Jackson Seigle, official Sterling College transcript, typed version, 1 June 1944, copy in possession of author; *Sixteenth Annual Catalogue of Cooper College, 1902–3*, Sterling College Library, pp. 15–16; Kenneth Porter Wiggins, ed., "College Days at Cooper Memorial, 1895–1898," *Kansas Historical Quarterly* 26:4 (Winter 1960), 383–409.

[95-100] *The Cooper Courier*, Cooper College, Sterling, KS, 13:3 (November 1902), 8; 13:9 (May 1903), 7, 10, 11; 14:1 (September 1903), 9; 14:5 (January 1904), 11; 14:3 (November 1903), 9; copies in possession of author, originals in Mabee Library, Sterling College.

[127-131] *The Cooper Courier*, 13:5 (January 1903), 10; 14:4 (December 1903), 9; 14:6 (February 1904), 11; 15:5 (January 1905), 12; 15:8 (April 1905), 13.

Quoted with permission from Sherry Nanninga Walker, "Nelle Arvilla Sanders and Andrew Jackson Seigle: The Cooper College Years," unpublished paper, 9 December 1998, pages 9, 17, and 21. Copy in possession of author.

operated, such as a neighborhood, town, or organization. If the community was or is too large or complex to try scattershot, consider whether you can reduce the community to a smaller one, such as the parish of a particular church or a local chapter of the larger organization.

2. Ask yourself the following questions.

   a. Does this community still exist within relatively the same parameters as the period you are researching? If not, try changing the parameters. If the community only existed that way in the historical past, then turn to the nearest historical organization, such as a state historical society, that may be maintaining the history of your community.

b. Do you already have a contact within that community? If you have one relative, friend, or other contact there, solicit that person to help you track down the local experts.

c. Is there a central address for someone in this community—a headquarters, library, post office, chamber of commerce, neighborhood association, organizational chapter office, city or county clerk, mayor, real estate agent, local historical or genealogical society, church, school, etc.?

d. Can you visit the site to conduct firsthand research? If not, write.

3. Write the letter with "hooks" to catch a response.

a. Single out a person by name (perhaps you can telephone ahead) or by title such as "Dear Mayor," "Dear Registrar," or "Dear Librarian," rather than "To Whom It May Concern."

b. Explain who you are and what you are doing in two to three sentences. Summarize who your ancestor or family was, only as the information relates to the community, in a brief paragraph.

c. Include something warm and friendly about the meaning of the community to your family history.

d. End with gratitude and offers to cover postage. Include a self-addressed, stamped envelope if you feel hopeful.

e. Limit the letter to one or two pages long.

f. Remember that this works when a small group of people, whose lives are not too "fast track," becomes excited by this interesting contact from far away. Keep the community you are trying to reach that small and keep your inquiry that friendly and interesting.

HISTORIAN EVERYMAN

The person whom you most hope to find when writing scattershot letters is that Unknown Soldier of family and local history, the one I call Historian Everyman (HE). This individual, male or female, is a special breed of local citizen. "Everyman" is a concept from literature and history that indicates someone typical of the common folk who travels among them, is trusted by them, and who understands what they are about. I came up with this title partly because I have an academic historian's reluctance to christen everyone who does history a historian. We scholarly and professional historians have tried to establish our profession's credentials by reserving the term *historian* for those with graduate degrees in history. (More snobbery, I know. Professional and certified genealogists have some of the same problem with generic use of *genealogist*.)

I am entirely comfortable with all of us being *family* historians. **The Historian Everyman, however, is a special breed. In a given community, he or she knows the local history and the histories of all of the local families better than anyone else does.** He or she probably serves as an unofficial guardian of the local cemetery and is often a charter member of clubs, chapters, and churches. The Historian Everyman keeps track of everyone in town with the best of intentions. Citizens

\di'fin\ *vb*

Definitions

speak this person's given name as if evoking a title that speaks volumes to them. Of course, the Historian Everyman is also likely to be a Keeper of Everything. If the town does not outgrow the Historian Everyman, the town can make its museum or historical society of what the Historian Everyman has accumulated. Sadly, if the town grows (or dies) too fast to care, the collections can die with the Historian Everyman.

If you miss finding a Historian Everyman because you simply do not take the time to write a few letters (some of which might go to waste), well, just consider what you might be missing.

Case Study

Historian Everyman One: Frank Sturdevant of Waverly, Iowa

If someone wrote or visited Waverly, Iowa in 1945 looking for local history or old local families, someone would tell the stranger, "See Frank Sturdevant." Frank was an accomplished historian without any academic training. He got that way by growing up with his Civil-War grandparents as his surrogate parents. He read. He joined. He was a veteran from a long line of veterans who decorated the graves of ancestors and their comrades every Memorial Day. He wrote thousands of letters to people all across the country. His letters inquiring about bits of family history still turn up when we contact the descendants of those to whom he wrote. As a young man, he traveled cross-country. In each town he would study the telephone book and knock on doors. Even his employment became part of this calling. After serving in World War I, he went to work for the post office as a carrier. He walked a route for almost thirty years, sharing the good news and bad with everyone as though he was a member of each family. Of course, he was also a Keeper of Everything.

So how would such a Historian Everyman assist you in your research? Frank's papers and memorabilia survive because his widow instilled the Historian Everyman instincts into their grandson, my husband. One example: During the Depression, Frank worked with the Works Progress Administration (WPA) on an Iowa Graves Registration Project. His special goal was to document each veteran's grave well enough to make sure that it had a proper tombstone and received proper memorial decoration. The WPA provided special file cards for recording the burial information. As he filled out the cards on these buried individuals, he turned each card over and added something of his own. In the tiniest of hands, he recorded every bit of family history information he knew about that individual, going back several generations, including war experiences. This is the kind of resource a Historian Everyman will have in his boxes and drawers. You will find it if you contact him or her, or if the materials go into a manuscript collection in a local history archive.

Case Study

Historian Everyman Two: M.C. Parker of Goodland, Kansas

If someone wrote or visited Goodland, Kansas in 1975 looking for local history information, someone would tell the stranger, "See Marion Parker." I did. What I mean is that I wrote one of my scattershot letters to Goodland because my great-grandparents had been among the first settlers in the area and the town.

The secretary of the chamber of commerce gave the letter to Mr. Marion C. Parker, who was one leader of a group trying to found a local historical society. He answered and became my first Historian Everyman. He generously copied and sent historical and contemporary photographs of the family homes and buildings, along with historical photographs of family members and local scenes. When he would search the newspapers for his own purposes, he would keep me in mind, copying every little newsy bit about my family. He found school records and deeds, political cartoons about my great-grandfather's role in a county-seat dispute, and even gave me an original antique county map because there were many surviving originals. He answered every question with authority.

I have already related his greatest find for me. In chapter four I told you about the retiring lawyer's file that contained my family's documents and photographs, circa 1855–1890. I have already related that this file included an 1861 chattel mortgage. It also included a letter, written by my great-great-grandmother to her mother after she arrived in frontier Illinois, describing her life there. There was a typed reminiscence of early Goodland by my great-great-aunt Kate Leonard. Historian Everyman Parker judiciously kept the original of this last item as rightfully belonging to the new historical society, but he sent me the rest of the original documents and photographs as belonging first to my family.

Mr. Parker surely helped others this way as well. I know of one case. Muriel Haase took Sharon Carmack and my college class in family history. Her husband's family had been German homesteaders near Goodland in the late 1880s. At my suggestion, she wrote to Mr. Parker. According to her student report of 2 March 1994, she received "a manila envelope with thirteen pages of newspaper articles, pictures from Sherman County history, and a map where these families homesteaded." He helped her research the mysterious death of a female ancestor, a woman who probably poisoned herself, while pregnant, after marital abuse. The articles both were revealing of community reactions to the case and the stuff of fascinating social history narrative.

The Sherman County Historical Society was founded in 1975 and is still growing strong, and when I visit there, they treat me like a minor VIP. Among its collections, especially of photographs, are those of M.C. Parker, the acknowledged senior expert.

Historian Everyman Three: Mary Tabor of Belton, Missouri

Case Study

If someone wrote or visited Belton, Missouri in 2000, looking for local history or deceased local folks, someone would tell the stranger, "See Mary Tabor." I learned of Mary because I work with her daughter Mary Ann, and each story that I heard made Mary sound like the consummate Historian Everyman. I interviewed her by telephone on 28 November 1999. Mary is, indeed, the unofficial Keeper of Everything, especially cemetery records, in her small town. Her training was her involvement in classic community activities: she was a welfare volunteer who visited local families, a United Methodist Church lady, and a widow with energy for projects. If you ever wonder about the authority of a Historian Everyman, think of Mary's example. She is not officially sanctioned as the local historian, unless you itemize who runs Belton and how they work with Mary. She works with her schoolteacher daughter, who is president of the local historical society. Mary is a docent for the local museum and a member of the cemetery board. Mary's brother used to be the mayor and works with the American Legion chapter to decorate veterans' graves. Mary has worked closely with multiple generations of the family of funeral home directors. She is a classic case. When a family history letter comes to the Belton city hall, someone is likely to carry it to Mary Tabor to answer.

A person such as Mary collects many records that could help you in your search if your family stopped over in her town. Since 1976, she has been recording all of the grave markers in the cemetery. Some of the older ones are becoming illegible, so her record is all that survives. She has the cemetery platted and has helped make sure markers are properly placed. In the last 24 years, when people have died, she put together obituaries, funeral programs, correct dates, participants, causes of death, and such for her own archive. Like Frank Sturdevant, she adds her own research to the cemetery gleanings. For older graves she has researched censuses, old obituaries, city hall and funeral home records, and clippings about school, church, and vital events. She has her own system (professionals will cringe) of recording information in her notebooks and on teacher's scrap paper. Yet she is a discriminating researcher, who notes the inaccuracies in census records and tombstone inscriptions. What will happen to her records and collections of everything remains to be seen. But if you wrote a letter to Belton, Missouri for family history information, Mary Tabor would surely write back.

SCATTERSHOT LETTERS OUTSIDE OF RURAL AND SMALL-TOWN AMERICA

Most of the best examples of successful shot-in-the-dark letters and of finding a Historian Everyman are from rural America. The same method can work, however, with urban neighborhoods and foreign countries. Follow the same steps listed above. One way to find an expert on an urban neighborhood is to locate, online or through your library, a recently published book about the neighborhood. The author knows the character, and perhaps the properties, of that subcommunity. Contact the author with questions within that realm of knowledge. Locate the nearest historical society and ask them to suggest people who are experts or long-time residents of the neighborhood. If you know folks in the neighborhood yourself, write to them, meet them, and interview them about life there. Consider reconnecting with neighbors from your own childhood to help you record the lifestyles that you and your parents experienced.

Tip

To find someone who can perform some of the functions of a Historian Everyman for you in a foreign country, ask all of your known relatives if they have any contacts with relatives in the mother country. For my immigrant ancestors from Scotland and Wales circa 1850s–1910s, there were remaining cousins in the homelands, even on remote islands, who could connect me with more relatives and portray aspects of their own lives that have not changed significantly since my ancestors left. A particularly interesting aspect of corresponding with them is that different versions of immigrant family lore have developed there.

These relatives also have documents and photographs. The key contacts for the whole locality may not be Historian Everymen, but they can bridge the ocean for you. If you lack even an initial point of contact, start reading genealogical research books on your particular ethnic origins. Their authors will point you to starting places for correspondence.

CHAPTER BIBLIOGRAPHY

Correspondence

1. Baugh, L. Sue. *Handbook for Practical Letter Writing*. Lincolnwood, Ill.: National Textbook Co., 1991.
2. Crawford-Oppenheimer, Christine. *Long-Distance Genealogy*. Cincinnati: Betterway Books, 2000.
3. Greenwood, Val D. *The Researcher's Guide to American Genealogy*. 2nd ed. Baltimore: Genealogical Publishing Company, 1990. 3rd ed., 2000.
4. Nickell, Joe. *Pen, Ink, & Evidence: A Study of Writing and Writing Materials for the Penman, Collector, and Document Detective*. Lexington: University Press of Kentucky, 2000.

Note: Remember to see the general bibliography at the back of this book for guidebooks that contain advice on correspondence and for directories mentioned in this chapter.

Handwriting

1. Kirkham, E. Kay. *The Handwriting of American Records for a Period of 300 Years*. Logan, Utah: Everton Publishers, 1973.
2. Sperry, Kip. *Reading Early American Handwriting*. Baltimore: Genealogical Publishing Company, 1998.
3. Stryker-Rodda, Harriet. *Understanding Colonial Handwriting*. Baltimore: Genealogical Publishing Company, 1986.

SEVEN

"Here Come the Genies": Braving the College Library

Regarding those in the genealogy field, if one of them gets you cornered . . . in between the library shelves, you will be subjected to the unspeakable indignities of hearing all about his hopelessly boring lineage, while you can bet that you won't even be allowed a minute to interject any of your brilliant reportage about your own far more fascinating predecessors.

—Laverne Galeener-Moore[1]

Notes

Endnotes for this chapter begin on page 222.

THE DREADED "GENIE"

Having spent many hours working (as an employee or a researcher) in the historical sections of university libraries, historical society libraries, archives, and public libraries, I learned about the unflattering stereotype of genealogists that library staff members sometimes whisper to one another. Usually, the staff does not describe the stereotype to the genealogists themselves, so you may not have heard it. If you were unaware of this stereotype and its consequences, I am sorry to be the one to bring it to your attention, but you need to know. It is ironic, but perhaps characteristic of human nature, that genealogists labor under a stereotype occasioned most by the casual beginner at the same time that the field has been so carefully professionalized to such high standards.

I first noticed some library staff members' negative attitudes toward genealogists at a historical society library about fifteen years ago. When they referred to "genies," the librarians usually rolled their eyes and shook their heads in disgust. At first this bewildered me because I respect librarians and office staff tremendously. These are the people who really run things; they know how everything works and where everything is. The ones who have been at their work the longest are like unofficial historians of their workplaces. Sure, I knew they could sometimes be impatient, but I also knew that this came from being put upon. Often librarians and secretarial staff know more about where and how to find information than the people above and around them do. Yet the people above and around them sometimes treat librarians and support staff as something less than themselves.

I also thought of genealogists as followers of a noble cause and just plain, pleasant folks. So I asked my librarian friends what they meant by calling those folks "genies." It clearly was a derogatory term as these librarians were using it. The derisive definition went something like this:

> Genies are people who come into the library thinking we're going to show them how to do their family histories. They always think it should be easier and simpler than it is. New ones have no idea where to start. They always behave as though we should drop everything and hold their hands through every step. There *are* such things as stupid questions, and genealogists always ask them. They think somebody has already published their genealogies and we ought to be able to pull them off the shelf. They think we should have been building files on their families, just for them, waiting for their arrival. They camp out all day yet never seem to be able to just sit quietly and do their own research. Sometimes they come in with their charts and expect us to make heads or tails out of whatever they could not. Worst of all, they can't resist telling long, pointless stories about their family histories. You don't dare go near them unless you have to because they'll start in, occupying your time with stories of their ancestors—not even good stories—as though we're going to care who their ancestors were, as though we haven't already heard the same stories thousands of times. I've seen so many of them now that I can spot them just by how they look when they walk in the door. They're usually older people, dressed for vacation, carrying too much stuff, talking too loud, and they have that "could you help me?" look in their eyes before they've even tried to do anything for themselves.

Of course, the library staff knew that these genealogists were basically good people who meant no harm. The librarian also knew that genealogists accounted for most of the numbers she reported every year to her employer, numbers that justified the existence of the research institution and of her own job. Behind the scenes, however, frustrated, overworked, and underpaid staff bemoaned the unsuspecting genealogist's arrival. Each moment of alienation might cause the librarian to be less enthusiastic about assisting "genies" beyond what was required. Meanwhile, those poor genealogists had no idea that they were fostering a stereotype that would interfere with their ability to get the best possible service.

Like every prejudice or negative perception, this genie image has festered and spread. About seven years later and across the country from where I first heard the talk about genies, I was researching one day in the historical/genealogical section of a public library, visiting with a librarian. This particular lady was thoroughly identified with the genealogical section and with the local genealogical society. A group of other ladies walked in at around 3P.M. The librarian leaned over to me and whispered, "Uh-oh. Here come the genies!" Startled to hear the expression from even this librarian who was a genealogist herself, I asked what she meant. She said, "The society has its meetings here this night every week. When they start arriving, I know I won't get any more work done until the next day. They demand all of my time."

The display of librarians' prejudice against genies I remembered most occurred in a university library. Professional genealogist Sharon Carmack and I entered a university library together to do a little research. Seated at the reference desk was my friend, the university librarian. I had already told her that Sharon and I were team-teaching classes in how to do family history in historical context. I wanted my friends to meet. I said to the librarian, "This is my friend Sharon Carmack, the genealogist with whom I'm teaching family history." As soon as the word *genealogist* came out of my mouth, the librarian pointed her index finger into her wide-opened mouth, as if to put her finger down her throat. She grimaced, blushed, and made that gesture that means, "I could just vomit," right in front of Sharon.

It still amazes all three of us to think that the librarian's distaste for genealogists had become such a reflex action that this professional would make such a gesture. To her credit, the librarian immediately thought better of it, tracked Sharon down, and apologized. She explained why she, as a librarian, had become disgusted with genealogists who presumed that there were the usual genealogical research materials (such as census microfilm) in a university library. Of course Sharon and I believed there *were* many family history sources in that library. Our whole message of "do your family history in historical context" was that genealogists *should* branch out into scholarly sources.

Ironically, a few years later, that same librarian became interested in doing her own family history. No one has been waiting more patiently to buy my book than that librarian. She calls herself a convert, who would rather do her family history research than almost anything else. You will find her at the Family History Center or the local genealogical society. She advises other genealogists how to approach librarians for the best service. She cannot resist telling you a good story or two of what she has found out about her family. She is compiling boxes of material. Anyone who knows her well cannot believe the metamorphosis. So times and attitudes have changed, but we family historians still need to cultivate a better image and build a proper reputation.

DON'T BE A GENIE
Ways to Avoid the Stigma and Get More Help

You thought that all you had to overcome in order to research in a university library was your own intimidation? I am sorry for having just told you something that might discourage you from going to the library. You must go. There is no better place to find social history and historical reference books to flesh out your family history, unless it is used bookstores—but that can consume your money and space too fast.

Some of the best information I have found on how to bridge the gap between library staff and genealogists was in a lecture by Charles A. Sherrill at the Federation of Genealogical Societies 1998 conference in Cincinnati. In "Where Do They Hide the Good Stuff? How to Get the Best Service From Librarians and Archivists," Sherrill, who is Director of Public Services at the Tennessee State Library and Archives, explained how better to solicit aid from the librarian, who may "cringe and break into a cold sweat" when she sees a long-winded genealogist approach. Sherrill's advice is similar to mine, but he brings the combined background of a long-time genie with graduate degrees in both history and library science. He knows what librarians may be thinking as they deal with genealogists.

Warning

For More Info

To obtain a copy of Sherrill's lecture on tape, contact Repeat Performance (see chapter bibliography). Be sure to indicate the title, speaker, place, and date of the lecture.

I am not exaggerating the problem. If we want to research our family history contexts in scholarly libraries to the greatest effect, we must overcome the understandable prejudices of the staff.

How to Request Assistance at Scholarly Research Institutions

Step By Step

1. Before a visit, call or write to find out what the institution offers, its hours, and the size of its staff. Some of this information is available in directories such as the *American Library Directory* or the AASLH *Directory*.

2. Present yourself as doing *historical* research into a *historical* topic. If you are researching historical context for family history narrative, that is a historical topic.

3. Don't tell any more about your project (and especially your family history) than is absolutely essential in order to get assistance.

4. Avoid words such as *genealogy*, *family history*, *genealogist*, *ancestors*, specific relatives, family names, specific dates, or any other obvious clues that you are a genealogist.

5. Do not display pedigree charts or other genealogical materials to the staff.

6. Do not force lengthy conversation, especially about yourself or your family, with a busy staff member.

7. Unless you are new and unfamiliar with the institution, do not behave as though you are. Take yourself quietly to the books or records that you need and begin working independently. Ask questions only after you have looked for some answers yourself.

8. As with oral history interviewing, use open-ended questions to obtain library assistance. In this case, open-ended means that you need advice. "Who would be the best person for me to see?" "Where do I begin?" "What would you recommend?" "How may I obtain this?" "I can see that you are very busy. When might be a good time to come back for further assistance?"

9. Librarians want to see that you have put in some effort and started on your own. Do not claim to be unable to find something when you have not even tried yourself.

10. Before arriving and after you have arrived, inquire about and study the rules, systems, organization, and layout of the library collection. Look for charts to the shelving system or instructions on the computer catalog screen. Attempt to help yourself with these guides before pleading confusion to a staff member.

11. Do not assume that the library has any particular item that you are seeking. Plan to do the extensive research that it will take to find such sources. Do not complain if something you wanted is not available.

12. Do not demand immediate attention. In case the staff is occupied with other patrons or business, bring along tasks with which to occupy yourself, patiently, while waiting.

13. Before you approach a staff member with questions, organize your materials and be prepared to ask only the questions that you most need to ask, as clearly as possible.

14. Ask a helpful staff person to show you where something is or how to do it rather than relying solely on written or verbal instructions. Thank the person afterward.

15. Behave appropriately for a library or archive: speak only when necessary in a low voice, follow rules about what you bring with you, respect the materials and facilities, and ask permission and/or read instructions before you begin using equipment.

16. Dress appropriately, although this may not mean what you think. If you are visiting a historical society from out of town, try not to look like a vacationer. Conservative albeit casual skirts or slacks and plain shirts are best. Avoid shorts, athletic clothes, sweatsuits, souvenir garments, revealing cuts, outlandish colors, and faddish styles. Wear shoes and stockings. If you are going to a college library, on the other hand, remember that for the last twenty to thirty years, many students and faculty have worn blue jeans and other plain, casual clothing. The more you fit in, the more comfortable you will be and the more aid you will receive.

17. When you are leaving, thank the staff for the use of the facility and for any assistance they provided. They will remember you next time as you begin to build that positive relationship that will help you in the future.

18. When you get to know the library staff better, and they have seen that you are a careful and courteous researcher, let on gradually that you are a genealogist and have high standards. We all need to chip away at the stereotype.

19. Don't tell them that you know about this stereotype.

THE COLLEGE OR UNIVERSITY LIBRARY

Now that you know about the dreaded genie stereotype and how to avoid being the living proof of it, you will want to go to academic libraries (colleges, universities, and state historical societies) to uncover the wonders of social history. To locate college or university libraries, you can use *The College Blue Book* or the *HEP Higher Education Directory* (see the general bibliography). Also, most colleges now have Web sites. Or, if you are starting with a place of interest and then wondering whether there are nearby colleges, try telephone or zip code directories, both of which will list area colleges. Telephone directories usually also list each separate departmental phone line at a college, such as the library circulation desk. The *HEP Directory* will name administrators, such as library staff.

There is even a knack to picking which college in a particular locality might have the best books. The best books for scholarly, reliable social history context are newer ones, published since the 1970s. Thus the best libraries are those who have had money to spend in the last twenty to thirty years. The best library will be one motivated to order books for its students to use in their research papers, theses, or dissertations. Public libraries, two-year community college libraries, technical college libraries, and even historical society libraries are not serving that same audience. **Although any library may have something useful to you, the large, liberal arts university library is most likely to have up-to-date, academically**

Library/Archive Source

FINDING THE BEST LIBRARIES FOR SOCIAL HISTORY PUBLICATIONS: QUESTIONS TO CONSIDER

1. Is it the largest public college or university library in the area?

2. Is it a liberal arts college that would be likely to offer a history program?

3. Does the college offer four-year degrees in history (B.A.) and preferably graduate degrees in history (M.A. and/or Ph.D.)?

4. Is it a private liberal arts college, which may have a more generous budget for book buying? This can mean that it stocks books for its undergraduate students that are comparable to those a graduate school would have.

5. Is it a private college with an "agenda," such as a religious college, whose book buying may discriminate to favor its special interests or viewpoints? Does that agenda match your research goal?

6. Even though it is the largest in the immediate area, is there a still larger university within one or two hours' distance that is wealthier or more prestigious than the local campus? If so, go to the larger.

7. Does the college library have a collecting emphasis within history, such as regional history or history that relates to other important departments at that college? Does the emphasis match your needs?

sound, scholarly monographs based on detailed research in original records. Within communities, libraries tend to compensate for their neighboring libraries. For example, if a public library specializes in one topic when ordering books, a nearby college library, especially one with limited resources, may specialize in others. You will want to determine those emphases in order to know where to go, depending on the topic.

Before you visit the college or university library, you may wish to seek some instructions by mail, phone, or Web site. If you have never been to that campus, and especially if you are at all uncomfortable about going, advance knowledge could help. See if that college library's catalog is online for searching in advance.

After you arrive in the library, make yourself comfortable as you familiarize yourself with the potentially intimidating surroundings. Sit at the computer catalog for awhile. They are user friendly and will lead you to the right call numbers and shelves. Go to the stacks. Going to look through the books (rather than picking them off the screen) is old-fashioned but it still works best. You will not realize what wonderful, useful material exists in many books unless you stand in front of the history shelves and pick up one after another. Check their indexes and tables of contents, but also browse through the pages. Sometimes an indexer has left out the very topic that you are seeking.

Reminder

**PLANNING A VISIT TO THE COLLEGE LIBRARY:
QUESTIONS TO ASK IN ADVANCE**

1. Where is it located and what is the best way to get there? (There will be traffic.)

2. What are the library hours? (These will vary with semester schedules. During exam weeks and the last week of a semester, access may be restricted.)

3. Where should you park and do you need to arrange a way to pay for parking? (Most campuses have parking problems, designated sections, stickers, and other sources of confusion. Most have visitors' parking, but rarely is it intended for the family historian who could be researching in the library all day. There may only be twenty-minute meters.)

4. Is there a way for a nonstudent to obtain checkout privileges? (Remember that you are doing historical, not genealogical, research. Often a driver's license or local public library card is necessary.)

5. Are there public photocopying machines? (If so, bring plenty of change.) How much is each copy?

Library Privileges and Interlibrary Loan

Go to the circulation desk at the college library. Ask (politely) about library privileges. Will they allow you to check out books with a library card or some form of identification? How many and for how long? If the university library is restricted to students and staff, is there any category of privileges for authors or independent researchers? Perhaps you need to see the director (at her convenience, of course) or write a letter. Remember to be gently solicitous, not pushy. Remember to present yourself as a historical researcher, not a genealogist. You want in! If you have any legitimate avenues to special privileges, use them. Any time that I work for a college or university in any capacity, I seek staff library privileges there as part of my compensation and benefits.

When you want to find the best interlibrary loan services, it is better to ask a researcher who has used them than to ask the library staff. Many libraries will methodically fill out their request forms so that you think you will receive the books, but they must file the forms in W for wastebasket, because they never report back. If you call, they are still waiting for something to happen. Other libraries will pride themselves on the prompt and inspired service they offer. **The smaller library with less funding is more likely to develop its skills in interlibrary loan than the big, sprawling library that buys what it needs.** Thus a community college or public K–12 school library could outdo universities on its interlibrary loan, just as the remote, small-town library might outdo the urban public branch. If you plan to do a lot of interlibrary loaning, make friends with your librarian. It is harder for a busy staff to give the runaround to a client they have come to know well. Remember, you are researching and writing a historical book.

Tip

THE HISTORICAL RESEARCH PROCESS
ADAPTED TO FAMILY HISTORY

What you research, how, and what you do with the results can follow the same patterns, processes, and guidelines of any historical research. You can use the same methods and sources that a history student, graduate student, professor, or other professional historian might use. This will help keep you thinking of your family story or ancestor in historical context, enabling you to locate useful sources.

Most advisors on genealogical research will tell you to start with yourself and work backward. You learn accepted methods of filling in prescribed charts. You must prove and document every connection from relative to relative, even more so if you are working on your "papers" to get into a lineage society. Those who take these instructions too literally might become obsessed with that particular name, date, or record needed for the next link. Do not let the links chain you down. **Historical research starts with hypotheses and allows for them at every turn (as does advanced genealogical research).** One opens one's eyes to possibilities and potentials as one tries to imagine the whole picture of life in earlier times, rather than just the names and dates.

Step By Step

1. Select a topic for historical research. This may mean reformulating a genealogical question into a historical one. As I have suggested before, think collectively and in larger patterns. Your ancestors were not unique.

   GENEALOGICAL QUESTION
   Why did great-great-grandfather move from Kentucky to Illinois in 1850?

   HISTORICAL QUESTION
   Was there a mass migration from Kentucky to Illinois in the 1850s, and, if so, what sorts of people moved and why?

2. Determine whether your historical question may be too narrow or too broad to research in the kind of library available to you. For example, the historical question above is actually somewhat local to the history of Kentucky and Illinois. There would be suitable sources in the historical society libraries of those states, but not necessarily in libraries elsewhere. Perhaps you need to start with something broader. You may be adjusting your topic frequently as you research.

   NARROWER HISTORICAL QUESTION
   Was there a mass migration from Kentucky to Illinois in the 1850s, and, if so, what sorts of people moved and why?

   BROADER HISTORICAL QUESTION
   What major events and trends were going on in America in the 1850s that might have influenced migration patterns from the South to North?

   You could begin to answer this broader question with almost any general American history textbook or a history of that time period in America. As you survey broad overviews like that, you will learn more about specific topics, enabling you to research the narrower questions more readily.

3. Formulate a hypothesis, a possible answer to your research question, and test it as you do more research. For example: A migration from Kentucky to Illinois in the 1850s could have had something to do with the controversies that were leading to the Civil War. Do not become so focused on your

hypothesis that you neglect evidence that contradicts it. You may reformulate your hypothesis many times.

4. Evaluate your sources as you go using the methods in this chapter. Adjust your hypothesis based partly on the relative reliability of your sources.

5. Collect, record, and organize the research results to a high scholarly and professional standard so that the results will be more convenient for your own use and more acceptable to your colleagues or audience. Use the methods in this chapter.

6. Analyze the research results to determine how they answer your question. If they are inadequate, either continue research in additional sources or change the question.

7. Incorporate your conclusions into your family history narrative. Remember that you may use words that indicate uncertainty, such as "perhaps" or "may have been." You may also cite sources and examples that *suggest* a conclusion without absolutely proving it. You can rely on the opinions of the authors of your sources to speak for you. See chapter eight on writing techniques.

8. Keep going and do not hesitate to start over. Most historical research involves juggling all of the above steps in reference to several topics simultaneously and repeatedly.

Social History in the Catalog

Most college and historical society libraries now use the Library of Congress (LOC) cataloging system. These call numbers begin with a letter. On page 175 is a quick starting guide, although all categories break down further. Use this to take you to the right shelves on your first visits so that you do not start asking questions until after you have settled in.

Smaller and older public libraries, as well as the Church of Jesus Christ of Latter-day Saints (LDS) Family History Library in Salt Lake City, may still use the Dewey decimal system. Its call numbers begin with a number. They become extremely long and one has to read them carefully to find a precise book. All of these categories break down into many subtopics.

Family Social History Catalog Keywords

Any library catalog will direct you to topics when you provide keywords and subjects. Thinking of what those might be for your family history can be difficult if you have been focusing purely on genealogical research. Family names will not be good keywords in university libraries. Look back to my Elements of Social History in chapter one for some ideas. Of course, you will be doing this research after you have learned basic genealogical information about your relatives. Then you might choose keywords relating to the ethnic group, the geographical location (if that is important to the part of the family history you are investigating), or rubrics such as "social life and customs." Many libraries retain a directory to their keywords to guide you.

LIBRARY OF CONGRESS CATALOGING SYSTEM

A General works, encyclopedias
B Philosophy, psychology, religion
C History-related fields such as genealogy, heraldry, and biography
D General and world history
E American history, for example

51–99	North American Indians
185	African Americans
186–199	Colonial period
201–298	Revolution (American)
351–364	War of 1812
401–415	Mexican War
441–453	Slavery
458–655	Civil War

F United States local history and western hemisphere history
G Geography, anthropology, folklore, and customs
H Social science, economics, sociology
J Political science
K Law
L Education
M Music
N Fine arts
P Language, literature, and writing
Q Science and math
R Medicine
S Agriculture
T Technology and crafts
U Military science
V Naval science
Z Bibliography, library science

DEWEY DECIMAL SYSTEM

000–099	General works, encyclopedias, bibliographies
100–199	Philosophy and psychology
200–299	Religion
300–399	Social sciences, education, customs
400–499	Language
500–599	Science and math
600–699	Technology, agriculture
700–799	Arts
800–899	Literature
900–999	History, biography, geography, such as

971	Canadian history
972	Mexican and Caribbean history
973	U.S. history
974	Northeast states
975	Southeast states
976	South central states
977	North central states
978	Western states
979	Far western states, Alaska

Sources

SCHOLARLY BOOKS FOR SOCIAL HISTORY CONTEXT

There are thousands of social history books to offer you contextual background for your family history writing. One recent phenomenon in the genealogical community was David Hackett Fischer's *Albion's Seed: Four British Folkways in America*. More than any single history book, *Albion's Seed* attracted genealogical attention as a new tool. By synthesizing masterfully all of the literature up until his writing (1988), and by adding his own social history perspectives, Fischer provided a key to the everyday culture and folkways of colonial Puritans, Scotch-Irish, Quakers, and English Virginia planters. I was pleased to see the attention this book received. I had been reading Fischer's work since graduate school and always liked his ability to *characterize* past societies by analyzing their folkways.

Of course, applying this book, or others like it, to one's own family history is controversial, too. Some genealogists are uncomfortable with speculating on whether social generalizations apply specifically to their families when there is no precise proof. Historians have less difficulty with this. Their findings come from scanning records and literature holistically. They trust well-documented scholarly research. If you are uncertain whether the general history applies, you can still present it as what was typical of those folks at that time. *Albion's Seed* is a good example of a book that will help you do this. There are many more.

Perhaps the best social history of the family for your starting point will be Steven Mintz and Susan Kellogg's *Domestic Revolutions* (see the general bibliography). This book surveys the history of families in America from colonial times to the 1980s. After reading it to discover the special social history areas that may be part of your family history, your investigation of sources may become increasingly specific to the narrower topics that you need. See also the Everyday Life in America series discussed in chapter two.

There may be more social history books for the colonial period of American history—especially for New England—than for any other period. This is partly because the Ivy League graduate schools and university presses of New England published many dissertations as monographs. Many of the New England monographs have been town studies. For some of these, see the community history section of the chapter bibliography for chapter eight. *Albion's Seed* already takes in most of these studies from the 1970s through the 1980s. Yet, if you have family history in Puritan New England, you still need to investigate books by Edmund Morgan, John Demos, Philip Greven, Richard Bushman, Laurel Thatcher Ulrich, and Robert A. Gross. Demos's *A Little Commonwealth: Family Life in Plymouth Colony*, for example, would be a must if you have Plymouth ancestors. It would provide a picture of how those ancestors related to one another in their small spaces.

If your family history included Quakers (members of the Religious Society of Friends), there are many monographs to help you discover their lives, culture, beliefs, and practices. For very reliable and readable introductions to these ancestors, read Margaret Hope Bacon's books, such as *The Quiet Rebels* or *Mothers of Feminism*. The best family-centered history of early Quakers is Barry Levy's *Quakers and the American Family*. This would help you discover your early

Pennsylvania ancestors' lives in regard to marriage, childraising, land use, inheritance practices, division of labor, women's roles, and more. There are also many books that follow Quakers to various locales, such as *Quaker Nantucket* by Robert J. Leach and Peter Gow, and *Sojourners No More: The Quakers in the New South, 1865–1920* by Damon D. Hickey.

If you are descended from wealthy Southern plantation families, you are in luck, in terms of sources. These folks were so elite that they left many primary records and have been the subject of numerous books. There is a publishing trend of family histories that are transcribed, collected letters and papers held together as a volume. Some examples are the books in my general bibliography by Margaretta Barton Colt, Robert Manson Myers, and Mary Clay Berry. If you have a large enough collection of family papers, these might be models of how to tell your family history by editing and annotating family documents. There are also many published Southern plantation diaries, most notably that of Mary Boykin Chesnut (edited by C. Vann Woodward), to give you a window into the private lives of antebellum Southerners.

Each of the above books on Southern families would serve as an excellent model for your work as well as give valuable information. Books that might help you analyze what was typical domestic life in this culture include some superior studies of women and children's roles in plantation life such as those by Carol Bleser, Kathleen M. Brown, Catherine Clinton, Elizabeth Fox-Genovese, and Sally G. McMillen.

It is more likely that your ancestors were poorer or more middle-class people than the plantation owners. If they were backcountry settlers, folks who moved to the frontiers of early American society, there is a good body of historical literature to help you understand them and their lives. Some of these are historical geographies, such as James T. Lemon's *Best Poor Man's Country* about Pennsylvania or the *American Backwoods Frontier* by Terry G. Jordan and Matti Kaups. This kind of cultural geography does not just describe the place, but the whole experience of our ancestors within it. If your backcountry kin were Scotch-Irish, their colorful culture appears in *Albion's Seed* and also the books of James G. Leyburn and Grady McWhiney.

If you have Civil War ancestors, there are fascinating social histories of the common soldiers' experiences. These would help you capture the day-to-day lives of the average soldier, who is more liable to have been your ancestor than the famous general. For this kind of book, see the general bibliography under authors such as James M. McPherson, Reid Mitchell, James I. Robertson Jr., and Bell Irvin Wiley.

If you have Native American (American Indian) heritage, there are hundreds of books to assist you with that historical context. First, however, you need to pinpoint the specific tribal society and location of your Indian ancestors. Indian family history offers its special challenges and many folks just vaguely believe they have that heritage without any specific knowledge. Some Indian cultures have received scholarly social history treatments, and some have not. If not, you can still find historical sources about your group of Indian people. The Cherokee, who tend to be the Indian culture most cited by genealogists as theirs, have

Definitions

The practice of editing and annotating historical documents into a published volume is part of a field called *documentary editing*. Usually applied to famous families and individuals, it, too, has its own precise standards and methods. I will be publishing more on how to apply this field to your family papers in the future. Meanwhile, see my article in *APG Quarterly*, Mary-Jo Kline's book, and Michael Stevens and Steven Burg's book, listed in my general bibliography.

Library/Archive Source

Do not neglect specialized encyclopedias and other volumes in the library's reference section. These offer quick-and-dirty introductions to events and people about which you can then do in-depth research. Try *The Encyclopedia of American History*, edited by Richard B. Morris (and later Jeffrey B. Morris) for chronological summaries of historical events and trends.

Sources

There are complete citations for the social history books discussed here, along with others, in the general bibliography at the end of this book. See also Sharon Carmack's books, *A Genealogist's Guide to Discovering Your Female Ancestors* and *A Genealogist's Guide to Discovering Your Immigrant and Ethnic Ancestors.*

Notes

Printed Source

been the subject of much publishing. See *Cherokee Americans* by John Finger or *Cherokee Removal*, edited by William L. Anderson to help you understand the different bands and the tragic history that separated them. Modern social histories do exist for some tribes. See, for example, Morris Foster's *Being Comanche* or *A Hopi Social History* by Scott Rushforth and Steadman Upham. To identify *any* Native American culture, see the Smithsonian *Handbook of the North American Indian*, in the chapter two bibliography.

Black or African-American history has been well covered socially. In the general bibliography, see books by Adele Logan Alexander, John Blassingame, Elizabeth Fox-Genovese, Eugene Genovese, Herbert Gutman, Jacqueline Jones, Susan Tucker, and Deborah Gray White. For sources on black soldiers in the Civil War, see Dudley Taylor Cornish, Joseph T. Glatthaar, and James McPherson.

Immigrant history has been a burgeoning field throughout the thirty years of social history publishing. You will find your ethnic group in some of these books, at least in the general works such as Roger Daniels's *Coming to America* and the *Harvard Encyclopedia of American Ethnic Groups*, edited by Stephan Thernstrom. Then look for the hundreds of individual social history monographs for specific immigrant groups and even their subthemes.

There are topics within American social history that have received good general treatment, such as the history of poverty (see Robert Bremner, Jacqueline Jones), childhood (see Bremner, Elliott West), education (see Lawrence Cremin and Andrew Gulliford), and especially women, as already indicated throughout this book. If your family is strongly identified with a particular city, town, or region, there are probably social histories about it. Use the Elements of Social History, this time as a list of topics to investigate in libraries and bookstores.

It should be clear: **the supply of social history and other historical sources to help you build context around your family's own history is voluminous and constantly growing.** I have mentioned only a very few areas of publishing and have barely scratched the surface in each case. Library and bookstore research will introduce you to hundreds more and, if I did not mention the topic you seek, the same research will probably turn up similar sources for whatever topic that is.

OTHER RESOURCES IN THE ACADEMIC LIBRARY
Periodicals

Most libraries subscribe to periodical journals and magazines. University libraries will tend to subscribe to professional and scholarly journals. In history, each of these may contain articles based on intensive research in the same kinds of materials genealogists use, such as town records and censuses. The article topics may seem humorously esoteric sometimes, but that makes them ideal when your ancestors lived in the little worlds that the articles describe.

Historical society libraries will tend to subscribe to the popular history magazines and scholarly journals of their home state and a few surrounding states. In most cases, it has been the state historical society that has published state history periodicals. Therefore, state historical society libraries are likely to have complete runs of the old state history journals, often bound as books and indexed for you.

Sources

SAMPLE ARTICLES IN SCHOLARLY HISTORICAL JOURNALS

I have taken these examples from periodicals off my own shelves to show how immediately one can find social history with the potential to serve family history purposes.

Joyce D. Goodfriend and Dona K. Flory, "Women in Colorado Before the First World War," *Colorado Magazine* 53:3 (summer 1976), 201–218.

Thomas Hine, "The Rise and Decline of the American Teenager," *American Heritage*, (September 1999), 70–82.

Susan E. Klepp, "Revolutionary Bodies: Women and the Fertility Transition in the Mid-Atlantic Region, 1760–1820," *Journal of American History* 85:3 (December 1998), 910–945.

Michael A. McDonnell, "Popular Mobilization and Political Culture in Revolutionary Virginia: The Failure of the Minutemen and the Revolution From Below," *Journal of American History* 85:3 (December 1988), 946–981.

Leigh Block Turner, "On Being a Child in a Little Mountain Town," *Colorado Heritage* (summer 1991), 2–18.

Special issue of *Colorado Heritage* on Buffalo (black) soldiers in the West, (spring 1996).

State history magazines follow certain patterns. In their early years, many of these magazines were not scholarly and tended to glorify the pioneer generations (who were often the founders and benefactors of the historical societies that were glorifying them).

During the twentieth century, state history journals became more scholarly. Some societies split their publications into two or three periodicals—a scholarly journal of essays, a glossy pictorial magazine, and perhaps also a children's history magazine and/or a newsletter for members. The state societies usually hold all of these publications to a high standard of accuracy, even if their popular magazines forego footnotes. Journal names have also changed to symbolize new approaches. Unfortunately, some of the better scholarly state history journals have folded altogether. Their old issues are still available, however, in state historical society libraries.

INDEXES AND REFERENCE GUIDES

America: History and Life

The best index to all scholarly history articles published in a given year, especially for including social history articles, is *America: History and Life*. *AHL* staff scan thousands of journals for entries. It is available in most college and university library reference sections, in book volumes, and now CD-ROM, as well as on the Internet (for paying subscribers) at <http://serials.abc-clio.com/faq.html>. Its

Sources

Sources

SELECTED STATE HISTORICAL SOCIETY PERIODICALS

Annals of Iowa

Annals of Wyoming

Arkansas Historical Quarterly

California History

Colorado Heritage (formerly *Colorado Magazine*)

Delaware History

Hawaiian Journal of History

Idaho Yesterdays

Indiana Magazine of History

Journal of Arizona History

Kansas History

Minnesota History

Montana, The Magazine of Western History

Nebraska History

New Jersey History

Pennsylvania Magazine of History and Biography

South Carolina Historical Magazine

Tennessee Historical Quarterly

Wisconsin Magazine of History

publisher, ABC-Clio, started printing this resource in 1964, with a retrospective Volume Zero (0) that abstracted more than six thousand articles for 1954 to 1963. Your college library may maintain the entire run of *America: History and Life* in book form, at least up until the library had to decide whether to switch to a digitized version, probably around 1996 or 1997.

No format beats the new online version because it comprehensively indexes all of the years. But I will provide instructions for the print version because you are more likely to have access to it in your library. Beginning in 1974, the volumes came out annually in four parts.

Part A: Article Abstracts and Citations
Part B: Index of Book Reviews
Part C: Bibliography or Index of All History Publications
Part D: Annual Index

In 1989, these increased to five volumes annually, with the index still being last. The additional volume contained citations of reviews of films, videos, and works on microfilm and microfiche.

Through the abstracts you can determine whether an article is worth looking up for information relevant to the historical context in which your family lived. *America: History and Life*, as its title implies and its years of "birth" suggest, is heavily oriented toward social history in its selections. The annual index lists the articles, books, and dissertations from the abstracts, reviews, and bibliography under social history headings that will help you discover the latest writing on subjects relevant to your family history.

The old book form of *America: History and Life* can be challenging to use at first. It is, after all, a compilation of what has come out only during one year, rather than an index of many past years grouped together. So, if you are seeking scholarly writing about a precise topic, say, Polish immigrant life in New York City and Chicago, you need to look at each year's index for articles, books, and other materials that might have come out that year. It makes sense to start with the most recent years and work back. More recent articles reflect the latest research and methods, are generally easier to locate, and presumably draw upon the scholarship that appeared in previous years. There are five-year indexes to the print versions, but libraries seem to have collected these only sporadically.

AHL is an index to sources, not the sources themselves. So be patient. Look up your social history topics in volume D, read the abstracts in volume A, narrow down the articles that seem most worthwhile, then look those up in the history periodicals where they were published. **If your library does not have a particular periodical, an interlibrary loan search will often yield a photocopied version of the article from a library possessing that periodical.**

Tip

Step By Step

How to Read a Citation in the *AHL* Index

There are user's guides in the introductory portions of *AHL* volumes, but it is still daunting for the beginner. To explain one example, say you start in an Annual Index.

If the citation in the Annual Index (Part D) is "14A:888," that means go to volume 14 (which is the same volume as the index that you are using because the volume number refers to the set A–D that came out in a given year). "A" means that you go to volume 14's Part A: Article Abstracts and Citations. The 888 is the item number in part A, not a page number.

Once you get used to *AHL*, it is a timesaver. It indexes all of the scholarly historical writing from all sources, which frees you from having to search multiple indexes, or the periodicals themselves, for needles in haystacks. The abstracts summarize enough about each article to help you reduce your list of likely resources and shorten your search. The Web version is much more convenient than the CD-ROM or the books, especially because it is comprehensively indexed from the 1964 beginning.

The Harvard Guide to American History, (edited by Frank Freidel), was the best guide to scholarly history articles until it stopped listing on 30 June 1970. You will still find its hardbound volumes in the reference section of an older college library. Volume 1 is topically organized and volume 2 chronologically organized. Remember that it will help you locate older articles about historical events and personages, but it predates the intense interest in social history.

The *New York Times Index*

Microfilm Source

One of the most convenient sources for looking up an event in your family history is the *New York Times Index*. The *New York Times (NYX)* is a very reputable national newspaper and is indexed. The index has been published annually since 1913, with entries beginning as far back as the newspaper's publication: 1851. **Many public and college libraries keep it and the newspaper itself on microfilm so that students of history can read the contemporary accounts of famous events.** You may not have access to the local newspapers of your family's past unless you are willing and able to travel, but you can start closer to home with the *New York Times*. One way to use the *New York Times* itself is to read the microfilmed news pages for the days and period when your ancestors lived to see what was happening generally. The index can help you, however, to pinpoint some specific family history.

Sources

Ask yourself: Is there an event that affected my family or in which my family participated, a singular event, one that was newsworthy? Even though it was a local event, if it was interesting enough, the *New York Times* might have picked it up as a small story, perhaps for the story's drama or human interest. This practice is similar to the way a national television news broadcast might show a story on an individual person, family, or town. **Local stories summarized in the *New York Times* from around the country or the world could include elections, murders, noteworthy deaths, natural disasters, fires, extreme weather, scandals, heroic deeds, unusual marriages or births, disease epidemics, and so on.** After using it for a while, one develops a sixth sense about what would be in the *NYX*. It can ease your next search in the local newspapers, even though they are not indexed. For example, if you know of an event to look up in the *NYX Index*, such as a bad 1886 Kansas tornado that your grandmother described, and you find it in the *NYX Index*, then you would have the date and other particulars. Now you could go to the local, unindexed Kansas newspaper for that date and find the tornado described in more detail.

Most four-year colleges and universities should have the *NYX* general index. Some might also have the *New York Times Obituaries Index*, 1858–1968, with a 1969–1978 supplement, and some might have the *Personal Name Index to the New York Times Index*, 1951–1974, with a 1974–1993 supplement. Your ancestor would have to have been somewhat prominent to be in the obituaries index—which lists about 400,000 names—and that listing, under "Death," would take you to the general index, then to the newspaper. The *Personal Names Index* is also an "index to the index," and your relative is likely to be there if he or she was in a headline, large or small. If you do not find your entry in a *NYX Index*, try several different angles of the story you are researching: type of event, people involved, place, etc.

Newspapers as Historical Sources

Newspapers offer a wonderful window through which to see the contemporary spheres for our ancestors' lives. For a summary of the genealogical use of newspapers and an impressive list of finding aids, see James L. Hansen's, "Research in Newspapers" in *The Source: A Guidebook of American Genealogy*. See the discussion of primary sources on pages 188–191 for the concerns about biases and accuracy in newspapers. Start with the *New York Times* if you do not have access to the local newspapers you need. When you do gain access to the newspapers of your ancestors' lives, see the advice in chapter eight for using newspapers as a source of community history context.

Special Collections and Archives

Library/Archive Source

Many college and university libraries have special collections departments. These are often historical archives of materials related to the local area's history, college history, the papers of local authors and celebrities, and the donations of local families or businesses. The special collections may be where you would find local oral history interviews, tapes and/or transcripts. It may also be a photograph archive. There may be surprise packages there too. For example, if a local donor just happened to collect World War II posters, sheet music, or antique buttons, the special collections department may have become the holder of some of the best collections in the country of World War II posters, sheet music, or antique buttons.

Special collections departments usually use archival supplies and rules to protect their original artifacts, documents, and rare books. They may restrict who may enter, when, and for how long. They may limit access by bringing the materials that you request to you one at a time. You will have more access and success there if you respect the environment and ask before you act. You may well find materials from local history or other families that offer you quotable passages about life in that area.

Government Documents Sections

Warning

Many public and college libraries have government documents sections. The librarians there may be especially wary of genealogical inquiries. **Some genealogists assume that government documents means census microfilm or military records that might save them a trip to the National Archives.** These government documents sections, however, have been collecting government reports, statistical abstracts, and the like. The government function here is to group data about national trends, publish analytical reports, and disseminate them to libraries for researchers on those issues. That does not mean that these government documents are worthless to family historians, of course.

Take our example of the census. At the National Archives or the Church of Jesus Christ of Latter-day Saints (LDS) Family History Center you may look up your particular ancestors on census microfilm and discover their names, ages, genders, nationalities, educational achievements, and degrees of wealth. In the government documents section of a university library, you can read abstracts and analysis that tell you how typical they were, what their neighbors were like,

Notes

BEST RULES FOR NOTE-TAKING

1. Know as well as you can exactly what you are researching and what you will need.

2. Do not abbreviate in ways that even you will forget how to decipher.

3. Outline themes and subthemes rather than just listing. See page 209 for an example.

4. Make sure it is clear whether you are quoting or paraphrasing the source.

5. Keep careful notes of source citations and page numbers beside information and quotations.

6. Double-check, word for word, that you have copied quotes exactly.

7. Keep track of whether a passage is a quote within a quote.

8. Jot down the library call number with the notes in case you need the source again.

---

why they were there at that time, and all of the other collective data about people like them. You need not sit at the microfilm reader counting these numbers yourself. The government did it for you. When you ask the library, keep the request generic, to a town or area of life, without mentioning your family.

HOW HISTORIANS COLLECT AND ORGANIZE RESEARCH RESULTS

There are several ways that historians collect information from sources so that they can use it in their writing. Some of these are similar or identical to how you may do it as a genealogist, some are not. Many may seem old-fashioned. Naturally, historians are good at being old-fashioned. By all means, do whatever works best for you *after* you have experimented with whatever might work better.

The classic way that historians take notes, or claim to take notes, or used to take notes, or tell their students to take notes, is on index cards. My doctoral mentor made me do it this way. I had to show him regularly that I was doing the notecards and doing them properly (his way). You should have at least two separate 3″×5″ notecards for every one source (book or article). On one card, you write the particular quotable passage or piece of information that you are extracting from the source, with brief citation information. On the other card, the "bib card," you write all of the bibliographic information about the source that you would ever need to make a footnote or bibliography. Thus you can organize your research results by stacking and shuffling cards. Some people love this method. If I were going to use it today, I would graduate to at least 4″×6″

cards for the notes ($3'' \times 5''$ is fine for bib cards) and I would entertain myself by using pretty colors.

Another way is to photocopy the pages that you will want from sources. This makes sense if you expect to use much more material from those pages than you care to copy onto cards. Also, you can then write the complete citation information on the margins or backs of the photocopies. Or, you can photocopy the title and copyright pages. This is desirable because the complete citation information is attached to the material (unlike the card method). If you decided that you wanted to use more of the material on those pages than you originally expected, you have the entire pages in your possession without returning to the library. Of course, photocopying can be expensive and bothersome, especially in a library. Some libraries provide scanners now, but one would not want to spend all afternoon using the one and only scanner, nor would everything scan well. With photocopying and scanning, remember not to abuse copyright by copying whole books.

My preferred method of note taking has always been to use regular, lined notepad or binder paper ($8\frac{1}{2}'' \times 11''$). On the first sheet, I write all of the citation information for the source. I number my pages as I go. I write every piece of information that I want, and some shorter quotations, on the sheets, with the page number(s) for that information in the left margin of the notepaper. I start a new page of notepaper for each separate source, but I may have many pages of notes from a particularly useful source. One of the advantages of notepaper over cards is that, like photocopying, you attach the whole citation to the notes. You can also write all the notes from a given source together instead of on separate cards, and you can file notepaper with like-sized photocopies, manuscript pages, letters, charts, etc. in topical files or binders instead of having to maintain your notes separately in index-card boxes. It is harder to lose tablets and paper than index cards.

I was so much more comfortable with notepaper that, even when my doctoral mentor insisted I do index cards, I tried, but then secretly went back to notepaper. When he demanded to see more notecards, I recopied the information from my notepaper onto index cards just to please him! The one advantage to cards over my notepaper, however, is that the cards do limit you to writing one or two pieces of information each. You can move the cards around to organize them topically. As you use my notepaper method, however, where there are many different pieces of information on the same pages, you may use several methods to organize those pieces.

1. Use different color highlighter pens to remind yourself, say, that one piece of information belongs in chapter one but you will use this other quote in chapter four.
2. Write in the left margin of the page, beside each piece of information, where you shall use it. Designate a topic under which it fits.
3. If you intend to dispose of the rough original notes after use, check off or cross out each piece of information after you have recorded it in its permanent spot. This method forces you to use each piece of information somewhere in your writing before you throw the original notes away.

Warning

Tip

Nowadays, of course, many researchers will take their laptop computers into libraries and use them for note taking. If you prefer to do this in a college library, **keep your laptop with you at all times or invest in a lock and chain**. A laptop or notebook computer will be very attractive to thieves. I prefer to travel with a laptop for composing my writing, not for researching. A laptop is not that portable, especially if you have developed tendonitis of the wrist from carrying tote bags full of books and papers. With a laptop you are always looking for outlets. It is much easier to always carry a tablet, especially for spur-of-the-moment research opportunities. Remember, in the library you will be getting up and down and going through aisles during your research in order to look through books.

While taking notes, I constantly remind myself to get everything that I might need about each topic. **I even use the old-fashioned journalist's reminder: who, what, when, where, why, and how.** Have I recorded for myself all of the explanatory and identifying information I could possibly need from that book or article? As a historian, I tend to organize my notes by historical themes, such as "Gates family: Depression days on the farm" rather than just names of individual ancestors or family branches. I would outline those topics, as they became apparent, in what would serve as an evolving table of contents for my future book. Historians tend to maintain chronological order, overall and/or within each topic and subtopic. Keeping and adjusting the order in which you will use your research results for your writing will help you when you sit down to compose.

EVALUATING HISTORICAL SOURCES FOR FAMILY HISTORY

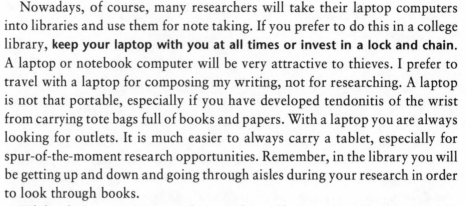

Technique

Historians and genealogists evaluate their evidence constantly. One could always discover an error or bias in one source or another. **Historians ask several questions when checking evidence.**

1. Is the evidence consistent within itself or does it contradict itself?
2. Do the pieces of information make sense when taken together?
3. Do other sources corroborate or contradict the evidence?
4. What are the biases of the reporter(s) of the evidence?
5. Could someone have concealed or distorted evidence?
6. Could the evidence have an agenda behind it, such as propaganda?
7. Is the source of this evidence reputable so that my use of it will also be so?

When you are planning to use historical sources for building context in a family history narrative, you need to ask questions of these sources beyond what historians generally ask.

1. Will this evidence relate directly to the example in my family history?
2. Is this evidence quotable, so that I can work into my narrative some testimony that supports what happened in my family?
3. Do I need to group this evidence with more of the same from multiple sources in order to make a general statement about what was common to all families like mine?

EXAMPLES OF HISTORICAL INFERENCE IN FAMILY HISTORY NARRATIVE*

More than twice as many men died during the Civil War from disease as from battle wounds. Hiram Grady died en route to Vicksburg. While records are silent as to cause of death, it is most likely that he was one of the hundreds of thousands who experienced infection and primitive medical care. Doctors did not yet understand "germs" and how they spread. The most frequently used medications were painkillers and purgatives. . . .

→-◄

Like most women of her day and circumstances, Mary gave birth to another child every two years. Why she skipped this six-year period and then recommenced having children at two-year intervals is a mystery. The family remained in the same home. There was no known military conflict at the time and John continued his regular town activities. The only unusual event seems to have been John's bankruptcy at the beginning of the six-year period. It was not until five years later that advertising appeared for his new shop in the town newspaper. Could Mary have been postponing the addition of more mouths to feed? Women of her time did privately exercise birth control by several methods. . . .

*I have composed these examples for this purpose based on typical examples I have seen over the years.

4. Does this evidence refute or confuse my hypothesis? If I stay with my theory about my family, should I use this evidence as a disclaimer, say, in a footnote?

Historical Inference

To *infer* is to conclude from evidence, to deduce, to recognize the logical consequences of something, and to draw conclusions based on a premise and accumulated facts. If you infer something, you move from one idea or judgment that you have already acknowledged or proven to be true to another that logically follows from the first. You state your inferences directly, rather than just implying them. An *implication* is indirect and is intimated without your making an open commitment to the idea.

Historical inference means to call upon historical knowledge of people, cultures, events, trends, causes, and effects to interpret the people or action at hand. For family historians who are researching and writing narrative family history, historical inference can be a means to include both the particular knowledge of the individual and family and the contextual knowledge of the times in which they lived in order to interpret the people or action in the narrative. You may already have the knowledge to make inferences, particularly the knowledge of your own family. You may not, on the other hand, have enough *historical* knowledge to infer. Then the solution is to research the times and topics so that

you might draw inferences about what was common and likely.

In writing family history narrative, you may need inference

- to explain a mystery so that you may research further or describe it in writing;
- so that you do not mislead readers that you know something is fact when you do not;
- to move a narrative along without the interruptions of an unsolved mystery or a presumptuous conclusion;
- to provide the historical context that makes a family story come alive.

Steps Toward Historical Inference in Research

1. Pinpoint a mystery or area of ignorance about your family history.
2. Speculate and hypothesize about the solution from your own knowledge.
3. Speculate from family sources.
4. Write down these speculations.
5. Determine potential sources that might provide historical background or explanations.
6. Find those sources and match the information to your mystery.
7. Examine and question those sources and record the possibilities.

Primary and Secondary Sources

To be able to draw conclusions or infer from your history sources, you have to have good reason to trust those sources. Historians trust their own scholarly research, if completed and documented to a high standard. **The best scholarly research is based on original research in contemporary records (from the time period, such as censuses, court records, or city directories) and other original sources (firsthand accounts). Original, contemporary, firsthand records and accounts are what the historian calls "primary sources."** These are the raw materials for constructing historical narrative and analysis. **"Secondary sources" are the history books and articles, preferably scholarly, that synthesize and analyze material from primary sources and other secondary sources.** Scholarly standards require that an author demonstrate thorough knowledge of all of the relevant primary sources *and* secondary literature on the chosen topic. A third type of source is the tertiary source. **A tertiary source is based entirely on other secondary sources. It summarizes and simplifies what others have said for a more popular or beginning audience.**

Historians and genealogists diverge somewhat on these definitions and standards. The genealogist uses original records to determine smaller facts or pieces of information, say about one person or family rather than a community or society. Therefore, genealogists have had a tendency to use the term *primary source* more narrowly, to refer to one which originated with someone directly involved with the event, near the time of the event. For many genealogists, this means that any source that does not fit this definition is therefore secondary and its information suspect. Genealogists might simultaneously label the same single record as both a primary and secondary source because some of its information is firsthand and some secondhand, while all records, in their entirety, would be primary sources to the historian.

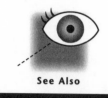

See Also

See chapter eight for steps to expressing inference in your writing.

\di'fin\ *vb*

Definitions

For More Info

Val Greenwood provides an excellent discussion of critically evaluating genealogical evidence on pages 65–78 in his *Researcher's Guide to American Genealogy*, 3rd ed. Elizabeth Shown Mills's *Evidence!* contains a sophisticated analysis of how genealogists (and anyone) should evaluate sources on pages 42–58.

To further clarify (or perhaps add to the confusion), genealogists have added a layer of definitions. Primary evidence or information originates with someone who directly observed or participated in the event at the time. Any other account becomes secondary evidence. (Elizabeth Mills differentiates between *original material* and *derivative material*.) When a genealogist examines a death certificate, if the doctor wrote the cause of death and signed his name in matching handwriting, a genealogist might assume that the doctor was in attendance and competent to diagnose, making the written cause of death primary evidence. If the certificate includes birth information about the deceased provided by his surviving children, that would be secondary evidence because the informants were not present at their father's birth. If the birth or death certificate is not the original one, but a later abstract made by a vital records clerk, it would no longer be primary to the genealogist.

Labeling each piece of information in a document as primary or secondary, however, could accidentally foster too much or too little faith in that evidence. Even the doctor's diagnosis and signature may not be primary evidence. I have been present at the deaths of my parents and two of my husband's grandparents. I was amazed at how the information for filling out the form developed. In none of these four deaths was there a physician personally in attendance. All four died in care facilities where their doctors had not visited them for weeks or months. Sometimes the mortician ran over to the doctor's office to get a signature and cause of death—one to three days later and from the physician who had not been keeping up his visits. Other times, a nurse or staffer signed the doctor's name and filled in the cause of death. When the health-care professionals listed causes of death, they chose somewhat haphazardly from a list of possibilities, sometimes posthumously diagnosing the deceased without enough knowledge or examination. In these instances, with my husband and myself present, the supposed secondary information such as birth and parentage was confirmed by knowledgeable family historians. The doctor's information—which genealogists might single out as some of the only primary information on a death certificate—was actually secondary. The only piece of information on these death certificates that was primary by the genealogical definition and wholly accurate, in all four cases, happened to be date and time of death.

Historians realize that all of these elements can affect the reliability of a record. Yet historians do not normally change their use of *primary* and *secondary* just because the sources may not be good, reliable sources. **Primary sources are first-hand accounts and records, period.** An oral history interview is a primary source, even if it is published and even if the interviewee is telling family traditions a century old. **Secondary sources are the published observations of historians and other researchers, usually written in third person, supposedly objective, and, if scholarly, very reliable.**

Newspapers test the historian's definition most. As firsthand, contemporary accounts, they are primary sources. Yet historians, even long before they used scholarly social history, have been acutely aware of the biases of newspapers. Even the Founding Fathers had party-organ newspapers that were deliberate propaganda. Thus newspapers have been one example where the historian is

189

EXAMPLES OF PRIMARY SOURCES
(by the Historian's Definition)

artifacts   memoirs
censuses   military records
church archives   oral history interviews and transcripts
diaries   organizational records
government records   photographs
letters   tombstones and cemetery records

EXAMPLES OF PUBLISHED PRIMARY SOURCES
(by the Historian's Definition)

city directories   published letters
newspapers   published memoirs
published collections of transcribed   published oral history interviews
   and annotated records of agencies   or excerpts
published diaries   published photographs

---

tempted not to call them primary just because they can be so faulty. So in many scholarly history books, historians have listed newspapers separately in their bibliographies rather than place them under primary sources or secondary sources. If a historian were using newspapers in ordinary family history for uncontroversial notices of local people's activities, the historian would comfortably consider the newspaper a primary source. Some genealogists, on the other hand, would call all newspapers "secondary," simply because they are published and possibly not eyewitness accounts.

Publishing trends, methods, and standards contribute to the differences between genealogists and historians on what is primary or secondary, and what is reliable or not. When a historian uses primary records heavily to write a scholarly history book or article, that historian is most often a scholar creating the best-quality secondary sources in history. In genealogy, many hobbyists have compiled extracts or transcribed from original records—such as tombstones, censuses, vital records, and town records—in order to publish that information, without analyzing or synthesizing it. These authors thus provide a valuable service to genealogists who cannot easily travel to obtain the originals. Because so many of these record compilers have not used standardized, accepted methods, however, genealogists suspect any such compilations of being faulty. Thus the genealogist would call a published transcription of records a secondary source, whereas the historian might call it a published primary source.

An interesting turnabout happens when a genealogist or historian views a published genealogy. To a genealogist, such a book is a secondary source, published, and sometimes not produced to a high standard. To a historian, a published genealogy might be a published primary source, especially if it is old and reproduces the contents of original records. If unaware of the high standards of modern genealogy, the historian might assume that any apparently detailed and organized genealogy is a reliable source. Fortunately, this naivete might not matter much because the historian is usually looking for confirmation of broad trends by scanning any local genealogies along with all other available sources. Both genealogists and historians, of course, would cross-check their facts in multiple sources.

Does the labeling matter? Only as a reminder to examine the reliability of sources. **If historians are less particular about defining** *primary* **than genealogists have been, it is because historians usually look through collections of records on a whole group.** The historian rarely cites an individual vital record or page of census microfilm. Many scholarly histories simply list in their bibliographies the entire census year(s) or record collections. So the genealogist's method is more precise and helpful to others who want to know about or track down the precise records used. On the other hand, the historian's greater readiness to categorize more impressionistic materials—such as artifacts, photographs, interviews, and memoirs (no matter when they were written)—all as primary sources is useful in opening our eyes to the potential seriousness of previously dismissed family history sources.

Reminder

Scholarly Secondary Sources

As you use secondary sources for your historical context, think critically about how reliable they may be. **The best are usually the scholarly sources, the works of academic experts based on years of painstaking research in both original records and published literature. Very often we call these books scholarly** *monographs* **because each book takes on one single, somewhat narrow subject and does so comprehensively.** It might amaze you how esoterically narrow some of these book topics are, but that can be good for purposes of your research.

Definitions

The trick that I teach my students to help them recognize a scholarly source is to look for voluminous footnotes or endnotes, which show that the author did painstakingly detailed, original research. These notes should often cite primary sources. If the book or article lacks notes but has a bibliography instead, and especially if the bibliography lists published books without records, documents, theses, or articles, it may not be a scholarly source in the sense we usually mean. It is more likely a tertiary source.

Tip

BUILDING YOUR OWN HISTORICAL LIBRARY

Historians, like genealogists, are often "bookhounds" and "bookaholics." Nothing seems a better way to spend time and money than to scout bookstores. Plus, we also *need* to order the latest monographs on our pet topics. My main reason (excuse) for buying books is that they are not otherwise conveniently available to me. Only the largest and best-endowed libraries will be buying the majority of the newest scholarly books. In most places I have lived, I was used to having a major university library nearby. When I moved where there was not one, I simply had to buy the latest books for my teaching and writing.

Then there are the older, hard-to-find history books about that very piece of your family history not covered anywhere else. Many topics have become passé for current publishing or unpopular with readers. Libraries that do still have the old books on these topics will withdraw them from their shelves because they

Case Study

Suppose that, among your male ancestor's belongings, you find pins with tomahawks on them or a headstone in the cemetery with what seem to be Indian symbols. Do not assume Native American heritage. It could be that your ancestor was a member of the Red Men, a fraternal organization. At an antiques store recently, I found *Official History of the Improved Order of Red Men* (Charles H. Litchman, ed.).[2] This book was priced at twenty-five dollars in the antique store, although it had been withdrawn from our public library, where it had been rebound in library binding. Thus it would have been a cheap find at a library sale but, even with its devaluing library features (torn-out card pocket, marked pages) it was not so cheap at the antique store.

The Red Men, like most fraternal organizations, had elaborate rituals, symbolic code names, and a high degree of seriousness about it all. A book such as this would help you identify any surviving paraphernalia, understand references in family documents, and learn much about your ancestor's social behavior and attitudes. The Red Men adapted Indian names and stereotyped Indian customs for their ceremonies. In this society, founded in 1813 or 1833, your ancestor may have been a Past Great Icohonee, who assembled at the Grand Council Fire of the Wigwam of Brother Hickory Sapling (Andrew Jackson) to celebrate the anniversary of Tammany Hall (a Democratic Party political machine). It is ironic that the party of Andrew Jackson, a fierce Indian killer, would inspire an organization that claimed to emulate the "noble savage." Remember that an antiquarian book, though it shows you what people thought at the time, should not stand alone. Modern scholarly history will help you analyze deeper meanings.

Money Saver

are old, obscure, and seldom used. **Thank goodness, withdrawn library books usually go on sale to the public cheaply at library sales.** If they are very old or unique books, book dealers may snatch them up and you must follow them to the used bookstores and pay higher prices. Antiquated books can be priceless sources for bits and pieces of your family history.

You may especially want to own the books about a very prominent topic in your family history. These books may have special meaning to you and be ones that you will cite and quote often in your work. (See the example of *The Cripple Creek Strike* in chapter one.) My father-in-law's experiences in World War II offer another meaningful example. He was in the Battle of the Bulge and became a Nazi prisoner of war. Rick began collecting all the books that had been published on this subject. Some were readily available and cheap. Others were extremely scarce, but he found them over the Internet. He will refer to and quote these as he writes his father's life into a publishable family history. Sharing these books with his father, who pores over them, has allowed his father to work through historical experiences that he had repressed for many years. The books have also inspired many detailed recollections, which we are preserving through oral history interviews.

Your Own Family History Library
Tips for Locating, Affording, and Keeping

Tip

1. In every town that you visit, seek out the used bookstores in the Yellow Pages. Make used bookstores the special souvenir-hunting destinations of your visits.

2. If you want to buy a book about, or relevant to, a particular locality, try to buy it somewhere else. For example, a history of Brooklyn will be much cheaper in a used bookstore in New Orleans than in New York. Western Americana will be cheaper where there is no special section for it, such as in Florida.

3. Bargain with book dealers when the prices seem too high.

4. The best used bookstores are large and have frequent turnover of titles. These stores depend on volume sales, and thus modest prices, more than on selling antiquarian books at rare-book prices.

5. Become friends with the bookstore owners in your hometown who acquire the most books of the type you want. They may start watching for the books you seek.

6. Go to library sales, where books will sell for small amounts or by the bag or box. Some libraries have semi-annual bargain sales. Some have a section constantly devoted to sale books. The books they withdraw for sale are often about obscure, old topics perfect for answering family history questions. Sometimes they have old magazines: I acquired a complete run of *Salt Magazine* at our regular public library sale.

7. Contact publishers such as scholarly university presses for their catalogs. They will have frequent discounts and major reductions in annual sales.

8. Use Internet companies to locate a particularly rare book that you seek, as well as for regular discounted book shopping.

9. Watch used and new bookstores for publishers' remainders at lower prices. Often recent scholarly books become remainders.

10. New bookstores will often have competitive discounts on bestsellers, hardcovers, or in annual sales. Inquire whether you can apply the new-book or sale discounts to books that you special order through the bookstore. If they will allow this, then order through them the books that you have seen in catalogs. This way you will avoid paying full price plus shipping charges. Usually when you special order books, the store will allow you to examine the book, after it comes in, before you decide to buy. Comparison shop among catalogs, bookstores, and online dealers.

11. Remember to check bookstore sections other than history. Social history books will often land in a sociology or "culture studies" section, including women's studies and African-American studies. Older social history books often fall under Americana. "History of . . ." books will often sit on shelves relating to the "of" part rather than on history shelves. Most bookstores will have special sections for their local and regional books, separate from other distant history.

12. Inquire about discounts for teachers, for people who pay cash, for society members (especially in society and museum shops), for senior citizens, and for regular customers.

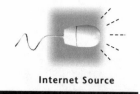

Internet Source

For locating used books on-line, I use <http://www.abebooks.com.> For new books, I use <http://www.amazon.com.> For new, used, and out-of-print books, try <http://www.barnesandnoble.com.> Another good source is Powell's Books at <http://www.powells.com.> There are other used-book sites coming and going. When you are searching for a hard-to-find book, remember to keep checking. The lists change over time. If you definitely want a book that you see on abebooks.com, order promptly or it may disappear. I inquire about an abe book online but ask dealers to hold for a check. I use credit cards only when required and to order from another country. The dealers claim it is safe to send a credit card number if you split it across two messages.

13. To determine the content and value of newer books that you hear about, see *America: History and Life* or the historical periodicals for reviews of recent books.

14. Historians also learn about the newest scholarly history monographs through attending the annual conferences of major organizations such as the Organization of American Historians or American Historical Association. These conferences have large book exhibit halls where publishers offer discounts. If you do not attend, you will still see the best new scholarly book advertisements if you request the conference program books from the organizations or if you read the ads and reviews in the organizations' periodicals (available in college libraries).

15. National genealogical conferences also have large book exhibit halls and publishers' discounts. Visit these conferences when they come within your reach for the valuable sessions. You will find that more and more of the books for sale are oriented toward social history and historical context for your family history.

16. If you buy many books while traveling, plan to ship them home. I take a roll of sealing tape and other portable supplies so that I don't have to buy expensive ones elsewhere. Hotels and conferences usually have cartons.

17. The books that you purchase might be tax deductible. If you need your professional library to conduct your money-earning professional activities, including paid lecturing, teaching, or commercial publishing, you may be able to itemize the books that you buy.

18. Follow the advice in chapter three about archival conservation of books. Avoid mildew. Cover dust jackets with Mylar covers as libraries do.

19. Treat valuable used books as investments. Do not write in them, turn down pages, or stick in bookplates. You may someday want to resell them or trade them.

20. If your collection is large, consider separately insuring it.

21. Locate a furniture store in your area where you can purchase good but inexpensive wooden bookshelves in floor-to-ceiling sizes. You need solid-wood shelves that will not sag over time.

22. Organize your books topically on the shelves so that you can find them and see what you have on a given topic.

23. Catalog your own books using a computer database.

24. When your library has become so large that you cannot recall what you already purchased, start carrying with you a list of books you already have, particularly those in any series or topic that you wish to flesh out.

25. If you have come this far, you are a goner, a true book addict. Consider buying a bigger house.

CONCLUSION

Social history research opens up whole new worlds to genealogists. It reveals more layers, more concentric circles, the larger spheres in which our ancestors operated, and it broadens the challenge and excitement of researching our families. We all want our families to have been important and to become important in what we write. Importance means more than fame. It means that our families were part of historical events, trends, and patterns all of the time. Historical context can teach us so much more about our ancestors. Our family histories, when published or disseminated, can teach people about history. In the next chapter we will write about our families in that historical context, and thus present future generations with a more meaningful record of their families' past.

CHAPTER BIBLIOGRAPHY

1. Benjamin, Jules R. *A Student's Guide to History*. 7th ed. New York: St. Martin's Press, 1998.
2. Booth. Wayne C., Gregory G. Colomb, and Joseph M. Williams. *The Craft of Research*. Chicago: University of Chicago Press, 1995.
3. Mann, Thomas. *The Oxford Guide to Library Research*. New York: Oxford University Press, 1998.
4. Metter, Ellen. *Facts in a Flash: A Research Guide for Writers*. Cincinnati: Writer's Digest Books, 1999.
5. ———. *The Writer's Ultimate Research Guide*. Cincinnati: Writer's Digest Books, 1995.
6. Sherrill, Charles A. "Where Do They Hide the Good Stuff? How to Get the Best Service from Librarians and Archivists." 1998 Federation of Genealogical Societies Conference, Cincinnati. Audiotape available from Repeat Performance, 2911 Crabapple Ln., Hobart, IN 46342; (219) 465-1234; fax (219) 477-5492; http://www.repeatperfomance.com.

Internet Resource Guides for History and Genealogy

1. Crowe, Elizabeth Powell. *Genealogy Online*. New York: McGraw-Hill, 2000.
2. Helm, Matthew, and April Leigh Helm. *Genealogy Online for Dummies*. 2nd ed. Foster City, Calif.: IDG Books Worldwide, 1999.
3. Howells, Cyndi. *Netting Your Ancestors: Genealogical Research on the Internet*. Baltimore: Genealogical Publishing Co., 1997.
4. Kardas, Edward P., and Tommy M. Milford. *Using the Internet for Social Science Research and Practice*. Belmont, Calif.: Wadsworth Publishing Company, 1996.
5. Kemp, Thomas Jay. *Virtual Roots: A Guide to Genealogy and Local History on the World Wide Web*. Wilmington: Scholarly Resources, Inc., 1997.
6. Michael, Robert Ashley. *The Houghton Mifflin Guide to the Internet for History*. Boston: Houghton Mifflin, 1996.

7. McClure, Rhonda. *The Complete Idiot's Guide to Online Genealogy.* Indianapolis: Alpha Books, 2000.
8. Roberts, Ralph. *Genealogy via the Internet: Computerized Genealogy.* Alexander, N.C.: Alexander Books, 2000.
9. Stull, Andrew T. *History on the Internet: A Student's Guide.* Upper Saddle River, N.J.: Prentice-Hall, 1997.
10. Trinkle, Dennis, and Scott A. Merriman, eds. *The History Highway 2000: A Guide to Internet Resources.* Armonk, N.Y.: M.E. Sharpe, 2000.

EIGHT

My Conclusion Is Your Beginning: Writing Family History

It is, nevertheless, difficult to stop telling about people we have not only come to know but come to love, as we read their letters, pored over their accounts, and looked at their pictures.

—James Oliver Robertson and Janet C. Robertson[1]

Notes

Endnotes for this chapter begin on page 222.

Writing a family history narrative in historical context using all varieties of historical sources, especially social history, is just what many genealogists have wanted to do. They tell me that they have been wanting something *more*. They want to relate to their ancestors and capture what life was like. For some, this means experimenting with fiction. Yet that would be a difficult turn to choose after years of training yourself to be a conscientious researcher with high professional standards of proof and truth. Why not choose to write a narrative that can be as interesting to read as fiction, yet will use historical standards, methods, and resources in addition to the genealogical ones, placing the family in the context in which it truly lived?

Folks who come to this idea from the direction of genealogical training in standards of proof become uncomfortable with the idea of connecting precise genealogical data with historical descriptions when they cannot *prove* the connection. Uninitiated genealogists often mistake the context idea for permission to fictionalize. Many librarians or historians squirm because they see the old "genie" stereotype and are thus skeptical about whether folks can do what I am suggesting. They may be unaware that sometimes genealogical standards are even more meticulous than historical ones, as in precise citation of sources.

So here is what I am proposing that you do. Write your family history, or portions thereof, in narrative book or article form. Take a step beyond genealogical charting. You can construct a narrative by researching the historical context in which your ancestors lived. Historical background, particularly the social history of the time and place, answers questions, explains behavior, and fleshes out the otherwise skeletal family record of names, places, and dates.

As you write this narrative, integrate your particular family history into the larger social history context, generation by generation. Each subsection should include both genealogical and historical information. It should rely on both genealogical and historical sources. The bibliography and notes should properly document all sources used. The book should have a creative title and theme or thesis about the family history. As a historical essay, it should be nonfiction, and should use past tense. It should identify and keep clear the who, what, when, where, why, and how. There should be few instances of difficult terminology or references that go unexplained. You can develop plot and use historical inference where appropriate. You should include some description of character, setting, and material culture. From the new sources and methods that we have discussed in this book, you could write your family history in a form that people would enjoy reading, researchers could use, and publishers could disseminate. Best of all, when you have found the right sources, the narrative starts to write itself because it grows closer and closer to the truth—it is your family, as they lived, part and parcel of American history.

Step By Step

WRITING FAMILY HISTORY HISTORICALLY: BASIC GUIDELINES EXPLAINED

1. Consider the possibility that everything about your family history fits into a broader historical context that you can narrate. Consider it twice. Everything fits into a historical context. You may not have found the right one yet, but it is there waiting for you to find it. There is a place for everything and more than one reason why each thing happened. Human nature and experience follow patterns. They are not unique. Finding the appropriate context means understanding your family, its background, its motives, and its prejudices. It means telling a story rather than reciting facts. It means a more meaningful family history for you and your readers.

2. Historians use conceptual frameworks. Since genealogy and family history can be so complex, try a conceptual framework approach to your book. In historiography, where we study the whole body of writing about history, we analyze and critique history monographs partly by figuring out their conceptual frameworks and whether these hold up. This term essentially indicates the complex thesis, outline, and method that interlock to hold up the whole structure of the book. In your family history, determine what the themes and subthemes might be. For types of themes, return to the Elements of Social History and the subfields charts in chapter one. As you continue to compile research and evidence, consider whether a preexisting conceptual framework might help you. Community history is a good example.

3. Remind yourself of the elements of a complete story: *who*, *what*, *when*, *where*, *why*, and *how*. Ask yourself whether each story, paragraph, or thesis statement addresses these thoroughly. In historical exposition, these elements take on a particular character. Think like a social historian. Do not assume that stating who, when, and where always means identifying a precise individual, date, and place. It does mean being explicit, thorough, and clear at all times. Yet *who*, *when*, and *where* might expand to include the groups of which your family was part, the times in which they lived, and the

Idea Generator

COMMUNITY HISTORY AS A CONCEPTUAL FRAMEWORK

A specialty in history that might give your family history a theme or even a conceptual framework is community history. During the social history decades, community history has become a sophisticated social science field, too. It is a far cry from the old-fashioned town histories that you find on some genealogical library shelves. Community history focuses on concepts within the community framework: defining what the communities are and how people relate to each other within the community and from one community to another. See the chapter bibliography for examples of recent scholarly community history.

Questions to ask to determine whether community history might work for your family history include

a.   Did your family live for an extended period in the same town?

b.   Did they move from town to town, even founding towns, and seem to reestablish the same patterns, with variations, in those towns?

c.   When they moved as groups, did they ever form a kind of colony within another town, as modern Americans sometimes do when employers station them in foreign parts?

d.   Did they relate to a "cast of characters" in each town, individuals with set roles or other families who also moved in chain or group migrations?

e.   Did they form other kinds of communities within their towns, such as voluntary associations (clubs), chapters of fraternal organizations, church groups, and political parties? What were their activities?

f.   Did they have smaller communities, such as neighborhoods, with their own characteristics within larger communities?

g.   Were they living in or near ethnic enclaves? How did they interact?

h.   What were the institutions that kept the communities together, such as meeting places, life-and-death events, social entertainment, or communications media (gossip, newspapers, telegraph, telephone, and E-mail)?

i.   Did a workplace become a community in itself, such as a college, hospital, law firm, or other institution might?

j.   Did members "network" across town or across long distances to build a kind of community, as isolated women on the plains might do through club meetings or as like-minded people do today by electronics?

k.   In a crisis, how did the community cope as a group? For example, did men from the community go to war together while the community homefront waited and supported the soldiers? Did the whole community have to deal with the epidemic that killed some of your relatives?

(continued on page 200)

l.   As you research records for your family—censuses, town histories and records, cemeteries, military unit lists, newspapers—do you see patterns of the same people and activities, so that you could simultaneously research your family and the community?

m.   If towns and neighborhoods are not the spheres that bring community to your family history, or to one branch of it, ask about alternative communities. Did the relatives live within an extended family that worked like a community? Did the slaves develop a kind of community in their quarters or across plantations? Did people in a particular trade or profession form a community among their own kind?

You begin to see how you could research your family, research its surrounding communities, and find plenty of material to write an interesting narrative if you are telling the stories of both. You would also be creating a special resource for other historians and family historians. Based on good research, you are calling attention to the spheres in which your ancestors really operated.

Newspapers for Context

Old, small-town newspapers are an excellent source for community history. Even though historians and genealogists correctly suspect newspapers of having biases and inaccuracies, the community historian looks at a newspaper from a different, more holistic perspective. Accidental inaccuracies matter less and bias is helpfully revealing.

Printed Source

All parts of the newspaper become precious when studying the community. Analyze the small-town newspaper with a variant of literary analysis, taking it apart piece by piece, to see its themes, audiences, and biases. The advertisements will display the dominant economic activity—is it rural? Agricultural? Trade?

All members of the small town took their turns in each part of the newspaper. One time they were in local news, returning from a visit to the next county or speculating on whether the rain would hurt the rhubarb. The next time they were running for local public office or carrying out civic duties and disputes. One member of your family was getting married while the next had just given birth. When they had a party, the whole town needed to see the guest and gift lists. When tragedy struck, members of your family offered their eyewitness accounts along with others. The family advertised its business and the newspaper advertised the family's failures. Obituaries and other vital-event stories in the old small-town newspapers had real character and social detail. The only problem with this kind of newspaper research is that it can engross you for months. Since that is a given, however, why not spend that time simultaneously developing the conceptual framework to write your family history in community context? Remember that if you want to build community context around your ancestors and represent the communities in which they truly lived, you must do community-oriented research. You must be aware of and record findings about the whole cemetery, the whole newspaper, the whole town directory, the whole membership list, etc.

Tip

whole spheres in which they operated. *What* becomes larger, *why* becomes deeper, and *how* becomes more complex.

Who, What, When, Where, Why, and How in Social History Context

Important

	TRADITIONAL, FACTUAL	SOCIAL HISTORY CONTEXT
Who	a name, an individual	a group, class, community
What	what did he/she do	what happened around them, events and trends
When	a date	a time period, an era that has a theme
Where	a place name	the character of a place, community, region
Why	individual causes	group motives and exterior influences
How	how did he/she do it	how did everyone around them do it

4. Draw conclusions after presenting evidence that leads to those conclusions. Both genealogists and historians want you to "show your work," as math teachers used to say. So do not just announce the explanations that you have determined through your research. Reveal them gradually in the narrative, so that readers see them unfold and believe them with you. If, however, it would be purely intrusive to explain a source or a research effort in the midst of your narrative, then use footnotes, endnotes, or other ancillary matter for these explanations.

5. Use sources critically. Be aware of the relative reliability of different types of history sources. Make sure your readers know that you are aware. With proper disclaimers you may use any source available. There is no need to reject any source that you wish to use. When you question and evaluate the sources and find something dubious, you should indicate this, at least in your footnotes. In your narrative, you may even write "as he later claimed" or "his version was" or "according to this source," especially if that source is a legitimate part of the narrative, rather than an intrusion.

6. Do not fictionalize or state as fact anything that you cannot know. **Please do not resort to fiction as a way to document your family history.** One writes good fiction because that is the goal and purpose of the project, not as an easy way out of research. I have seen students tell a family story as fiction to exercise their literary skills, and do well. I have also seen them figure: "If I don't know what happened, why not make it up?" Good-quality fictional literature is wonderful, but very few people can write it. There is no need to fictionalize your family history because, if you do your homework, you can write it interestingly using historical evidence. As soon as you insert fiction, readers wonder whether they can trust you to tell the truth. If you break faith with us, your family history is no longer a reliable source. Some writing devices look so much like fiction that you will have to take special care to footnote them as to their real sources.

Warning

Warning Signs That a Family History Author May Be Fictionalizing

- The narrative contains extensive conversation from long ago ("he said," "she said,") that is not, or could not be, from an oral history interview.

- The author writes, "he thought," "he wondered," "he wished," "he felt."
- The author describes ordinary scenes including ordinary behavior—behavior that would not normally have been recorded historically—as though they are happening before our eyes: "Rachel looked out to the horizon, longing for . . ."
- The characters see and hear things as though they are happening: "Hearing the footsteps on the cobblestone walk, he turned . . ."

If I saw these writing devices in a family history paper, I would comment "How do you know?"

7. As in good history teaching and writing, avoid boring, trivializing recitation of factual minutiae. Instead, aspire to storytelling and analysis. Genealogies are recitations of small facts linked together. Who would care to read genealogical summaries for fun, interest, or learning? Good narrative history is creative nonfiction. It entertains and it makes you think. We do not need a paragraph like the following amidst good narrative passages.

> Charles Joseph Morgan and Virginia May Miller were married on 2 December 1897 in Albany, New York. Their first son, Charles Joseph Morgan Jr. was born on 12 October 1898 in Albany. Their second child, May April Morgan, was born on 23 September 1900 in Albany. Their third child . . .

Citing Sources

8. **Base everything you write on some kind of research and cite some kind of source for it.** Treat even personal recollections as a serious source. Remember that artifacts, photographs, interviews, and letters are serious sources, as are songs, poems, and even comic books. If you obtain a piece of information from a comic book such as what superheroes your father liked as a child, cite the comic book. Footnoting your own recollections is a good example of how you can attribute every piece of information to some source. As long as you cite where something comes from, and cite it in a professional manner, you will have few naysayers.

9. Write in your own words unless you are quoting and properly citing sources. Quote minimally. Especially avoid long, indented quotations. Quoting original (primary) sources is particularly acceptable. Perhaps you do not have an ancestor's quote to describe something, but a description from another account will suffice. Try to limit quotations from authoritative secondary history sources to phrases within your own sentences. Strictly avoid plagiarism and heavy paraphrasing.

For example, in this passage from *A Scattered People: An American Family Moves West*, Gerald McFarland has worked quotes from an unrelated writer's firsthand account into his family history narrative to enhance his own words.

> Orramel Hinckley Fitch, a traveler to the Western Reserve in 1827, found most Ohio communities 'new and dreary,' but he described Hudson as 'a pleasant village,' albeit one without 'much business.'[2]

10. Examine which part(s) of your family history might make the best narratives. Consider writing shorter articles about those or making your book an in-depth narrative about just a portion of your family history. If your

goal is to write the narrative of the entire family, with all of its branches, from earliest records to the present, more power to you. It is a daunting task. There will always be holes in your information that leave gaps in the narrative. You will always find more information to fit in somewhere—especially after you have published and it is too late. The tangled threads of the lineage and collateral lines will confuse any reader. The lack of a uniting theme, other than "here are all of my ancestors," will bore readers. Break it all down to the separate lines, at least. Also consider that there may be a whole book in the war experiences, frontier lifestyles, arrival and adjustment of an immigrant group, or one person's career. For purposes of composition, consider limiting your topic to one theme or section at a time, as you would for a student's history paper. Each essay then stands alone with intrinsic value and is more manageable, even if you later string them together.

11. Remember that writing historically means revealing dynamic change over time. By definition, history is not static. It moves. If you try to capture a moment of family history frozen in time, you are either writing fiction or a clinical case study. People, events, and environments change all of the time. If you do not yet have enough information to show that change in your narrative, keep looking. Moving the story along is also good, interesting writing.

12. Maintain chronological order whenever possible, especially within stories and sections. Avoid flashbacks or other potential confusions about time. Experience with family history writing classes has taught me that many people like to experiment with flashbacks, alternating scenes from different periods, nightmarish visions, and mysterious dream sequences. I recommend against such divergence from straightforward, realistic themes and chronological development within those themes. I have seen the experiments work well for perhaps one out of twenty-five family history writers. Sometimes a flashback is a creative way to begin a narrative, but they can be disastrous if scattered throughout. Most of us do not have the skill. The goal is to have authentic historical narrative, to recreate what the events must have seemed like at the time, and to convey their significance.

13. Remember that your ancestors were often typical and part of collective behavior. You can use historical descriptions of what was typical to *infer* your family history. Experiment with including inferences while writing the narrative context. Attempt to use transitional language between the known and the inferred that does not interfere with narrative flow yet makes clear the differences and the sources. Ask yourself again if the inferences are nearly certain, merely possible, or somewhere in between. Tailor the language accordingly. Try stating the information, particular and general together, leaving the inference an obvious one for the reader to make.

14. Define and identify unfamiliar terminology, slang, colloquialisms, obscure events or places, dated names for things, and any other items that might bewilder your readers. If possible, define these within the course of your writing. If this is too awkward or interrupts story flow, then use footnotes.

Case Study

TRANSITIONS AND SWITCHBACKS: FROM THE GENERAL TO THE PARTICULAR AND BACK AGAIN

Creating smooth transitions from one topic to another can be one of the subtlest and most difficult tasks in any writing. When writing family history in a social history context, the transitions that seem to be the most challenging are those between general social history and particular family history. Here, the wording that you choose is important to accomplishing two goals.

a. to blend the two types of information into a flowing, cohesive narrative

b. to make it apparent which information is known, specific data on your family and which is general history information that *probably* applies to your family

Of course, you can make the distinction in your footnotes, or you can indicate it by quoting from the historical source and even mentioning that source in your text (see point 9 on page 202). For the sake of your narrative's readability, however, transactions should be subtler, yet still clear. Here are some examples.

> By 1775, the people of Massachusetts were being pulled in two directions—by the patriots who thought that Americans should rebel in response to unfair treatment by the crown, and opposingly by those who wished to avoid war and wanted loyalty to their commonwealth government, with the hope of working out their differences with England peacefully. [Thomas] Cowdin's reaction to the increasing aggressiveness of the dissenters' speech was to speak out in support of the commonwealth government. Thomas had served the crown for many years . . .[3]

> For the slaves in Georgia, including the Butler people at their inland refuge, the labor pains of their birth as free citizens began as General William Tecumseh Sherman and his army of sixty-two thousand men commenced their march to the sea.[4]

Transitioning from general history to particular families and back again is automatic for a social historian because we do it in reverse all the time. When we teach or write, we switch back and forth between generalizations and specific examples to illustrate the generalizations. In the following example, Robert Orsi is telling Italian-American community history by citing one woman in particular in the midst of his otherwise general narrative. Note that the transitional language works the same for family history purposes.

> Rose Marello Tiano immigrated to East Kingston, New York, from Calabria in 1906. By the time of her death in 1939 at the age of one hundred and two, Rose Tiano was presiding over a huge domus, a 'prolific tribe' in the words of one of her grandchildren, which included some three hundred members spanning four generations.[5]

By identifying words that have outlived usage, you are recording some more history for the rest of us.

Sample Terms That Need Identifying and Ways to Do It

He was in his plus fours (long golf knickers).

She was wearing her maryjanes (a popular girl's shoe with a strap across the foot).

He said she was "on the rag."[1]

Dad always came on like gangbusters.[2]

My heroes were Hoppy, Gene, and Roy. Hopalong Cassidy was the earliest cowboy movie star of the three.

---

[1]This was a euphemism for having a menstrual period from the days when women made their own sanitary napkins from rags. Because women might be moody during this time, the phrase also meant being moody, grouchy, or emotional.

[2]*Gangbusters* was a radio program that "came on" (opened on the air) with whistles, gunshots, burglar alarms, police sirens, tires screeching, and glass breaking.

15. In order to include highly experiential descriptions, character typing, and even dreamlike sequences, yet still have a historically authentic narrative, try quoting from literary accounts that do the creative writing for you. No one can capture some times, places, and characters better than the great writers of American literature can.

Ways to Use Literary References and Quotes in Family History Narrative

Technique

- Write about what someone in your family's history read and enjoyed themselves, why, and the circumstances of that reading. For example, my father lived out boyhood fantasies when he was sickly and bedridden by reading about Tom Sawyer and Huckleberry Finn. He wrote and told many stories about his specific reactions to the books that I can quote or retell.

- Write about what was popular reading at that time and how that relates to the family history. Perhaps you do not know whether the ancestor read Horatio Alger stories in his youth, but you found old editions of them in his collection. Your ancestor's name was written in childish hand on the inside covers. Explaining that in your narrative, you can quote or summarize the success-story formula of Horatio Alger and speculate on the influence it may have had on your ancestor's career. If you take care not to assume too much, you can speculate on your historical relatives' reading material based solely on what was popular for people like them, even without direct evidence of what the individuals read. Just honestly state that this literature was popular with people like these.

- Locate a novel, story, or poem that describes the subject—such as a place or event—you want to describe. You may quote that description as truly capturing the subject, better than you can yourself, whether or not your historical relatives would ever have read the same literary piece.

    Quoting literary accounts, when they have acknowledged authenticity, lends their fine prose or poetry to your narrative. It represents their subject from firsthand observations that you might not have the opportunity to

Sources

If you want to locate and read regional literature for the places where your family once lived, there are ways to find it before you know the authors and titles. Of course you may search in library catalogs and ask librarians, but try this, too. Using the AASLH *Directory* or one like it, locate the state historical society in the area you are researching. Write for their catalog of publications. Many of them publish and reprint regional literature along with historical accounts. The same is true of state university presses. Using one of the college directories recommended in the general bibliography, contact a state university to see whether it has a publishing program for regional literature, or search online. See also *Books in Print* for regional subjects and publishers.

make. It also protects you from criticism in those cases where *you* could not get away with it, but Mark Twain always could.

> Maine folks tended to keep a pristine "best room" (one of two parlors) just for company. As author Sarah Orne Jewett observed in *The Country of the Pointed Firs* (Boston: Houghton Mifflin, 1896, 1927), "the best room was too suggestive of serious occasions, and the shades were all pulled down to shut out the summer light and air" (p. 63). Almost every family kept a best room, but that meant the second parlor was cozy.

You can also move all of the source information to a footnote or endnote to make your narrative flow better. As long as the quotation marks and citations are clear, you can legitimately "borrow" the words of other writers.

> Maine folks tended to keep a pristine "best room" (one of two parlors) just for company. The family probably grouped in the second parlor, however, because "the best room was too suggestive of serious occasions, and the shades were all pulled down to shut out the summer light and air."[1]
>
> [1.]Sarah Orne Jewett, *The Country of the Pointed Firs* (Boston: Houghton Mifflin, 1896, 1927, 63.

16. Remember that you can build narrative around family artifacts, photographs, oral tradition, correspondence, and anything else relevant that you can describe or analyze. On page 207 is an example of some family history narrative that accomplishes this.

    Note that the author has created interesting narrative by analyzing artifacts. She has also characterized Helen by showing us the evidence rather than just telling us her opinion. This draws the readers in as we try to analyze Helen along with the writer. Helen is also very much a woman of her own times, her social history context.

17. Avoid *Titanic* Syndrome. Do not insert famous historical events that are irrelevant to the family story. When teaching family history college classes,

Helen Hildebrand, my mother, carefully crafted a bulging Memory Book during her high school years. She reached womanhood during the Roaring Twenties, a time characterized by optimism, high spirits, and experimentation. . . . Helen's book had a strong emphasis on the pleasures of life—parties, dances, and good times. Party invitations covering a wide variety of themes were arranged throughout the book; various gatherings commemorated holidays, school events, wedding showers, birthdays, athletic events, and the changing of the seasons. She attended parties at theaters, restaurants, the Y.W.C.A., the Country Club, parks, church, the high school, and in homes. . . . Often, Helen was accompanied to these parties by young men from her school. Here and there, she had crossed out a man's name or removed his picture, occasionally writing in a derogatory comment where the photo had been pasted. Sometimes the parties were planned for women only. Usually she hand-wrote on the page that she had "had a swell time. . . ."

Studying held little appeal for Helen while she was in high school. Two grade cards from her sophomore and junior years provided evidence for that conclusion. Her grades were nearly all C's. . . . Her cooking teacher wrote this in her memory Book: "I shall always remember you as the little girl who liked to cook but hated 'Book Larnin.' " Helen had a "swell time" in high school, but she was lucky to graduate in four years because of her fervent devotion to her social life.

Quoted with permission from Joanne Ellenberger, "Combined Photo and Artifact Assignments," unpublished paper, c. 1995. Copy in author's possession.

Sharon Carmack and I have noticed **a tendency of uninitiated folks to think that historical context means simply throwing bits of history into their genealogical summaries.** Invariably, these beginners also think that history consisted of famous names, dates, and events. So the historical tidbits that they insert are less connected to their own family histories than social history information—such as fads and fashions—would be.

The sinking of the *Titanic* was the single event we most often saw mentioned irrelevantly in someone's family history. We noticed this several years before the latest film version caused a stir. Many students were senior citizens in the 1990s, and therefore it was likely that the sinking of the *Titanic* made a big impression on their parents. Seeing that this one famous event appeared most often among the irrelevancies, I suggested that we refer to this problem as *Titanic* Syndrome.

Titanic **Syndrome is the unfortunate tendency of some genealogists to believe that placing a family in historical context means mentioning famous historical events or people merely for the sake of mentioning them, even though they have no apparent relevance to that particular family's history. When the relevance is not obvious, the reader imagines it, which can sometimes imply a comical causal relationship.**

\di'fin\ *vb*

Warning

EXAMPLES OF *TITANIC* SYNDROME

Mother was born in 1912. Two days later the *Titanic* sank.

The *Titanic* sank when Robert and Theresa got married.

The teller cashed William's paycheck and then the stock market crashed.

We moved to Colorado Springs when man first walked on the moon. It was one small step for man, one giant leap for mankind.

My baby sister was born 6 May 1945. Two days later, the Nazis surrendered.

Tom celebrated his birthday and then the Japanese bombed Pearl Harbor.

Joseph was born in 1812, when a war with England began and it became the name of a great overture.

I grew up in New Orleans. It was there that in 1815 Andrew Jackson defeated the British. We left there when I finished high school.

After they were married, James and Margaret moved to Alexandria in 1965. George Washington slept there many times. Their first child was born on 4 July 1966.

If you read the examples sympathetically, you realize that some of the writers had method in their madness. Probably the birthday or other event will always be memorable because it fell near a famous historical event. These particular events—the *Titanic*, the 1929 stock market crash, Pearl Harbor, and the moon walk—are events about which people say, "I will always remember where I was and what I was doing when I heard about. . . ." In that case, the cure for *Titanic* Syndrome is simply to explain the relevance within your narrative.

Unfortunately, some writers do not mention events because they were legitmately significant to the family. Some are trying to include historical background, and they mistakenly think that famous facts—no matter how irrelevant to the who, when and where of their narrative—are what that means. **The inoculation to prevent the disease is to start using social history for historical context and concentrate on keeping it directly relevant to your family's lives.**

Important

18. Document sources properly. Remember that scholarly history includes voluminous footnotes or endnotes, and advanced genealogy makes some of those source citations even more specific to the records used. If your documentation is inadequate, other researchers cannot follow your trail in their own research and readers cannot trust your conclusions. See examples throughout this book and sources in the general bibliography.

EXAMPLE OF A CURE FOR *TITANIC* SYNDROME

The family would never forget that it was 1969 when they moved to Colorado Springs because it was the same year that man first walked on the moon. They watched that event as soon as they plugged in their television set. It was "one small step for man, one giant leap for mankind," and a medium-size step in the lives of the family. Colorado Springs was fascinated with the moon walk; the family was now living in an Air Force community.

WRITING FAMILY HISTORY TECHNICALLY

1. Write all history in past tense consistently. To write "he goes" or "she says," for example, confuses the reader. It is not historically appropriate. Staying with past tense is easier to remember and track than switching back and forth. You are writing history, not journalism.

2. Each story, or even each paragraph, should have a theme or thesis statement. Try to make these historical in nature to emphasize the entire context. For instance, the theme of the Helen Hildebrand example on page 207 is that Helen liked her social life better than anything and that this fit 1920s America. Do not struggle unnaturally with thesis statements, however. Let them come. Each time that you write a paragraph, ask yourself whether it maintains the historical narrative rather than distracting from it or backsliding into trivial genealogical facts. Does it have a theme or thesis statement? Does that thesis statement accurately represent what the paragraph is about?

3. Make your themes and sub-themes historically general rather than genealogically specific. Each time that you develop a subtopic—a next step in the story—try to make it a step through historical experience. Certainly, events in the family line—births, marriages, deaths—are worthy of narration, but only when you have something generally historical to say about them. Meanwhile, connecting the family research with the historical context offers more descriptive information, such as what birth was like then. Why did people marry at that time of year? What causes of death were common? (See the Elements of Social History again.)

4. Make and follow an outline of historical and thematic development. Use standard outline format. Even though you will revise it, it will help you stay organized and focused on your thematic goals.

Sample Outline for an Imaginary Family History Narrative

I.   Introduction
    A. How I came to write this book
    B. What the book is about
    C. My methods and practices
II. Summary of General Family Background and Tradition

    A. The Celtic inheritance

    B. The Scotch-Irish frontier heritage

       1. Conditions in Scotland

       2. Treatment in Ireland

       3. Immigration to America

          a. Conditions onboard ships

    C. The ancestors in the Appalachians

5. Write in a serious style so that historians and genealogists will accept your work seriously. Use the accepted style guides: *The Chicago Manual of Style* and Strunk and White's *Elements of Style*. Use third-person voice for objectivity, unless there is a very strong reason to use first-person voice, such as in an autobiography. Use your computer checking features, proofread carefully, and ask fellow professionals to read your drafts to make the best impressions on readers, future researchers, and would-be publishers.

6. Consider what you write to be a historical essay. It should have an introduction and a conclusion. Set the scene and state the theme. Do not leave loose threads at the end. Give the book a deeper meaning than just your family history. Reiterate that meaning and your major themes in both introduction and conclusion, the former as though you are setting out to make your point and the latter as though you have successfully made it. Ease the reader into and out of the narrative, but decide what you want to leave as a single, most lasting impression.

7. Give each story a title that is clever, intriguing, or meaningful. One way to do this is to suggest the most significant historical theme of the story. The title sets or suggests the theme. If you have a theme, you have a more interesting account. The theme should genuinely fit, rather than feel forced. You may change your title as you go and some of the best titles do not become apparent until the work is finished. By using creative titles, you are also borrowing from good fiction-writing techniques. Notice that creative titles tend to be shorter and thus more memorable. You can always add explanatory subtitles that also help maintain credibility. Is there a single theme, symbol, or name in your family narrative? If not, look harder as you learn more.

TRADITIONAL, FLAT TITLES	THEMATIC, CREATIVE, INTRIGUING TITLES
My Family History	*Proud Shoes*
Our Life in Poverty	*Angela's Ashes*
Our Family Moves West	*A Scattered People*
An Italian-American Family	*Unto the Sons*
The Search for My Grandmother	*Halfway Home*
From Poverty to Middle Class	*Homelands and Waterways*
Life During the Civil War	*Defend the Valley*
A Japanese-American Memoir	*Stubborn Twig*
Exploring My Genealogy	*Cottonwood Roots*
The Slave Side of Our Family	*Slaves in the Family*
The Life of Scarlett O'Hara	*Gone With the Wind*
An African-American Family Saga	*Roots*

DEVELOPING CHARACTER IN FAMILY HISTORY NARRATIVE

To follow standards acceptable to scholarly history, you could characterize historical figures by using

- their own words, as found in original sources or oral tradition;

- their actions and physical appearance, as found in sources;

- how others described them, from sources;

- the context of their cultural, ethnic, religious, economic, and social groups, from sources;

- the context of their time and place from historical sources;

- hypotheses based on what was average or typical.

It would be ahistorical, fictional, and/or unethical to attempt to characterize historical figures by

- invented dialogue or actions passed off as authentic;

- invented attitudes, ideas, or feelings passed off as authentic;

- imagined physical appearance passed off as known;

- altered historical words or events.

Of course, I have used authentic book titles in the right-hand column. The authors, in order of appearance, are Pauli Murray, Frank McCourt, Gerald McFarland, Gay Talese, Mary Logue, Adele Logan Alexander, Margaretta Barton Colt, Laurel Kessler, Kem Luther, Edward Ball, Margaret Mitchell, and Alex Haley.

8. Use creative nonfiction writing techniques for developing your "characters." Even though you are not fictionalizing, you can present the individuals in your family history in some of the ways that novelists present their characters.

9. Watch particularly for evidence of dramatic devices and sensory perception in your sources that you can use in your narrative. You should not fictionalize what someone said, thought, heard, saw, touched, tasted, or smelled, but if you discover such evidence, as in an oral history interview, it will bring the history alive. Again, you can also quote from historical sources on what someone like your ancestor typically thought, heard, etc.

10. Through sources, especially through material culture, remember that people's lives historically were as rich as ours are. Use surroundings, artifacts, clothing, physical appearance, settings, and personalities as you find the information in sources. See chapters two through four for reminders on including artifacts and photographs.

11. Analyze motives and causes, effects and outcomes, as evidence allows. Use

historical research to help you determine what the typical motives were for people in the same situation.

12. Write multiple drafts and revise. Set writing aside to revise it afresh later. None of us are our own best editors, but we can see more to alter in our work after some time has lapsed.

13. Vary and improve your historical vocabulary as it comes naturally.

Definitions

14. Avoid **anachronism—something out of place in the given historical period**. Do not use terminology or references to technology or behaviors that do not fit the time about which you are writing. Do not assume that you know how great-grandmother would have ironed a shirt until you find out what was available. Do not describe a historical person as "into" something, "cool," or a "radical feminist," when those terms either did not exist or meant something else. Do not judge earlier people's attitudes or behavior by modern values. For example, an abolitionist (activist against slavery) may have been an extremely radical and daring person for a noble cause, but would probably not have believed in integration of the races the way we do today. To believe so then would have been exceptionally far-sighted. So, as I advise my students, see historical characters more by their past and present than by our hindsight.

15. Avoid author intrusion (mentioning or referring to yourself) unless there is a special reason. Be the historian writing in third person. If you want to tell stories about how you obtained specific information for your narrative, save most of that for the introduction or footnotes or endnotes unless it is important to moving the narrative along.

16. Illustrate your family history narrative creatively from family, genealogical, and historical sources. Return to chapters two through four for some suggestions about photographs and artifacts. Many old books contain line drawings and other illustrations that are now in public domain. Where appropriate, consider illustrating your family history with pictures of your family homes, towns, farms, factories, immigrant ships, other people doing that type of work, typical clothing, or any generic historical version of the image that has not survived in your family. Make sure your captions and citations clarify identity and sources.

Citing Sources

17. **Weigh the relative virtues of footnotes and endnotes.** Genealogists and historians want you to cite your sources. Footnotes are handy because they appear at the bottom of the page and one does not have to turn back for the information. Publishers and printers prefer endnotes because it is very expensive to place footnotes at the bottoms of pages. Whichever you use, try to minimize their number. Historical publishers say to condense citations to one per paragraph, as long as readers can tell which citation goes with which piece of information in that paragraph. If the sources that you need to cite are identical for more than one paragraph in a row, you may also condense citations for multiple paragraphs, as long as you make clear what you are doing. There is no reason to repeat citations or use *Ibid.* over and over. If you have put lengthy, explanatory prose in a citation note, consider whether you could incorporate that information into the text. If you do

something unusual that might be unclear to readers, explain your decisions in your introduction or in the notes themselves.

18. When finished with your book-length family history narrative, please create for it a social history index, not just a name index. This is essential to make a family history useful to other historians. We already use genealogies and family histories in historical research, say, about a town or an ethnic group. We miss much, however, because genealogists tend to index by name only. If, instead, we apply our same social history approach to the index as we do to the research and writing, we have made the social history information in our family histories just as accessible as the genealogical information.

EXAMPLES OF LISTINGS FROM A SOCIAL HISTORY SUBJECT INDEX FOR A FAMILY HISTORY

boarders	land speculation
Boulder, Colorado	marriage
buffalo—chips, wallows	Masonic Lodge, Masons
childbirth	medical care
childhood	mining
Colorado (see also individual places)	music
conventions (see WFM)	newsboys
county commissioners	prairie dogs
county seat elections	rainmaking
deportation (of strikers)	religion
depression of 1893	Scottish heritage
drought	sexual relations
Eastern Star (see Order of)	tornadoes (see also weather)
education, schooling	trains, railroads
elections	tuberculosis
Goodland, Kansas	violence
health	Wales, Welsh
homesteading	weather
housing	Western Federation of Miners
labor unions	women's roles

SKELETONS IN THE CLOSET

Many of my students, when writing family history, have come to me worried about family skeletons. They were not sure whether to include the stories in their narratives and feared offending someone. Events that they viewed as skeletons included

abandonment	divorce
abortion	drug abuse
alcoholism	eating disorders
avoiding military service	extramartial affairs
bad habits	family feuds and their causes
cruelty	fighting in war for the "wrong"
disabilities	side
disease	financial ruin

homosexuality	racism and bigotry
illegitimate conceptions and births	religious extremism
illiteracy or lack of education	running away
imprisonment	secret adoption
interracial relationships	sexual abuse or aberration
mental illness	stupidity
murder	suicide
owning slaves	theft and other crimes
physical or verbal abuse	unemployment
poverty	wartime atrocities
private thoughts	

The list could go on indefinitely because anything could be a family skeleton to someone. What is scandalous in one era—say, divorce—is commonplace in another. There is no need to feel ashamed of your family having a "deep, dark secret." Your family was not unique. If you can understand the personal problem *in historical context*, you can understand it as part of human nature, partially brought about by the times in which the individuals lived.

Reminder

Seeing your family's skeletons in the context of their times and learning habitually to approach families as a social scientist should relieve the sting of shame. I remember a conversation I had with one woman who was writing her family history. A farmer had hanged himself in the barn, and the family had never spoken about it since. When was that? 1932? Had the Great Depression affected them? Yes, he had just received the notice of foreclosure on the farm. Immediately, the importance of historical context became apparent. The farmer was not unique. His behavior was tragic, but understandable. His descendant could research what he had been going through in 1932, see how thousands of others suffered, and understand how he must have felt. She could write the story describing the context of personal crisis in the midst of national crisis.

NO PRIDE, NO SHAME—NO CREDIT, NO BLAME

I have reassured many family historians that they have no reason to feel shame for anything their ancestors did. You had no control over your ancestor's behavior. You are not to blame. This sounds so simple and clear. Yet, remember that some people have had to carry the blame and shame for ancestral or parental sins, real or perceived. Our society, for example, stigmatized some children well into the mid-twentieth century for the "original sin" of being illegitimately conceived. Some people still hold this opinion. But what practical responsibility did the small babe hold for its parents' behavior?

If, however, we bear no responsibility for our ancestors' sins and perceived sins, it is also true that we have no reason to take direct pride in, or credit for, our ancestors' accomplishments. The ancestors were the heroes, not us. Some genealogists may resist me on this. After all, many descendants have proudly joined lineage societies partly as a way to demonstrate that it is special to be the descendant of a presumed hero. Some major lineage societies have traditionally required that you be a genetic descendant, rather than an adopted one, in order to join. Some people believe strongly in bloodlines. Remember, though, that while you may believe there is something wonderful about having a great ancestor's blood coursing through your veins (which, of course, it is not literally doing), you also had nothing to do with whose blood you got! Even genetic engineering has yet to propose a way to retroactively alter our ancestry.

The more family history you research, the more skeletons you will find. Many family historians are thrilled to find their horse-thief ancestors to help liven up the narrative. Sometimes ancestors were simultaneously admirable and wrong. For example, many descendants of the First Families of Virginia (FFV) would take pride in their elite plantation heritage. No matter how kind the master, though, there is no pride in having enslaved other human beings. Of course we will and should critically analyze our ancestors' behavior as part of formulating our own ethics. First, however, we should evaluate people of the past by their own pasts, not by our hindsight. Second, we do not need to attach our self-esteem to how our ancestors fare in this analysis. It can be more fulfilling, anyway, and a still greater tribute to our ancestors, to appreciate and honor them in their own right, for what good they did, in the context of their times.

GENERATING HISTORICAL EMPATHY

Historical empathy (a term I believe I am coining) is the ability to research and understand past lives well enough to walk a mile in their shoes, experience intellectually and emotionally what they must have experienced, and thus deeply understand their behaviors. Empathy does not mean just tolerance for someone or something. It does not mean sympathy or pity. It means imagining what the other person feels so accurately and deeply that you feel it yourself.

\di'fin\ *vb*

Definitions

In Rosalie Keefe's stories about "The Old Timer," she relies on several means to achieve historical empathy. She uses her own perspective as a child, an innocent perspective that can, on one occasion, make a scene more frightening and, on another, allowed her to dismiss the warnings of adults in order to indulge an instinctive fondness. She reminds us to see each individual in the context of his own history, the Old Timer, his son, and even Mike Skelley. She shows us how the outside forces of national history were sometimes only obstacles to circumvent by showing how the Old Timer viewed them and responded to them. Her empathy is so pervasive that she teaches us to appreciate all of the characters in her nonfiction story, even though we might not have liked them all had we met them casually, in passing.

We have discussed many means to generating historical empathy. As you research and write about your family history, remember the Elements of Social History. Everything in life, everything we take for granted, gives life its richness and diversity. Just as we can all heighten our own sensitivity to daily detail by stopping to take it all in, to "smell the roses," we also can heighten our sensitivity to the details of our ancestors' daily lives. Opening our minds to unexplored sources at home and in the library, we can reconstruct those past details. By taking a recipe box seriously, we can extrapolate and imagine Great-Grandma's domestic activities. Take up the old family Bible, hold it and handle it. Read the

Case Study

THE OLD TIMER

The old man with the thick, gray hair wore a long dark coat. He smelled like stale whiskey and his speech was slurred. Tobacco juice stained his mouth and chin. My father [Buddy] reached into the old man's coat and pulled out a whiskey bottle. My father glared at the old man as he held the bottle in front of his face. Like a child getting caught disobeying his father, the old man tried to make excuses. I don't remember what happened after that. The old man was Arthur A. Whyte, Sr., and that was my earliest memory of Grandpa.

>-<

Tragedy struck in Yorkville, Illinois, when [his wife] Margaret "bumped her leg getting out of the car, developed a blood clot and died two weeks later." She was buried the day before [their son] Buddy's sixth birthday. Grandpa was devastated. Unable to cope with his grief, Grandpa found comfort in a whiskey bottle. Buddy lost his mother. Buddy was losing his father. Grandma Jennie and old Mike Skelley took Buddy to live with them. Old Mike Skelley was not a mean man but he had raised nine children on a farm. He expected children to earn their keep. Buddy's life had changed overnight.

Prohibition. Not a problem for Grandpa. He had no trouble supplying himself with his comfort because prohibition laws were generally disregarded and drunkenness among the general public increased every year. Bootlegged beer, whiskey and bathtub gin [were] rampant in the 1930s. Grandpa must have known not only *where* to acquire alcoholic beverages but *how* to make and sell it. Bud remembers . . . Grandpa bottling the contraband in Jennie's basement.

>-<

I wasn't supposed to see him. My parents didn't approve. But I would get on my bike and ride the 8 blocks to the boarding house where he lived in a small room upstairs. Sometimes he would be outside carving a chain of wood. Sometimes he would go up to his room and he would draw for me and I would try to copy what he had done while he drank cold coffee from a jar he kept in the closet. Our relationship was a careful one. I knew there were times when his speech was slurred [and] that I should leave him alone, but other times he would have that twinkle in his blue eyes and we delighted in the conspiracy of our secret meetings. He was my Grandpa Whyte and I was his "Little Dickens."

Quoted with permission from Rosalie Keefe, excerpts from two stories called "The Old Timer," unpublished papers, c. 1997–1998. Copies in the author's possession.

entries and analyze the memorabilia stashed in between its pages. Think of what it meant to the illiterate ancestor who learned to read from it.

Look into the photographed faces of your ancestors. As you research their lives, read their expressions, clothing, and surroundings. They were human beings with fears and dreams, moments of heroism and moments of fear. Listen carefully to the oral traditions that survivors long to share. Make each living relative along the way as important to you as an ancestor. As they talk into your tape recorder or answer your letters, they become characters in the story too. They can share personal recollections so that, together, you can bring your mutual ancestors to life.

Empathizing with the ancestors, we can see what they saw, and think what they thought. The advice in this book will have succeeded if it can take you to that empathetic point from which you can explain your family's past behavior—not necessarily condoning it, but also not necessarily condemning it. You can see the reasons and motives behind the behavior and you can show that to the rest of us. You can engage us with human drama and comedy because knowing the social history—what folks' lives were really like—reveals a multidimensional picture. You can feel close to your deceased family members, even those you never met. You can bring your family history to life as you empathize with its participants, knowing them almost as you know yourself. This is the ultimate gift of social history to the family historian.

CHAPTER BIBLIOGRAPHY
Writing Guides

1. Barnes, Donald R., and Richard S. Lackey. *Write it Right: A Manual for Writing Family Histories and Genealogies*. Ocala, Fla.: Lyon Press, 1983.
2. Cheney, Theodore A. Rees. *Writing Creative Nonfiction*. Berkeley: Ten Speed Press, 1987, 1991.
3. Gerard, Philip. *Creative Nonfiction: Researching and Crafting Stories of Real Life*. Cincinnati: Story Press, 1996.
4. Gouldrup, Lawrence P. *Writing the Family Narrative*. Salt Lake City: Ancestry Publishing, 1987.
5. ———. *Writing the Family Narrative Workbook*. Salt Lake City: Ancestry Publishing, 1993.
6. Gutkind, Lee. *The Art of Creative Nonfiction: Writing and Selling the Literature of Reality*. New York: John Wiley and Sons, Inc., 1997.
7. Hatcher, Patricia Law. *Producing a Quality Family History*. Salt Lake City: Ancestry Publishing, 1996.
8. Kempthorne, Charley. *For All Time: A Complete Guide to Writing Your Family History*. Portsmouth, N.H.: Boynton/Cook Publishers, 1996.
9. Ledoux, Denis. *Turning Memories Into Memoirs: A Handbook for Writing Lifestories*. Lisbon Falls, Maine: Soleil Press, 1993.
10. McCutcheon, Marc. *The Writer's Digest Sourcebook for Building Believable Characters*. Cincinnati: Writer's Digest Books, 1996.
11. Mulvany, Nancy C. *Indexing Books*. Chicago: University of Chicago Press, 1994.
12. Polking, Kirk. *Writing Family Histories and Memoirs*. Cincinnati: Betterway Books, 1995.
13. Selling, Bernard. *Writing From Within: A Guide to Creativity and Life Story Writing*. Alameda, Calif.: Hunting House Publishers, 1988, 1998.

14. Strunk, William, and E.B. White. *The Elements of Style.* 4th ed. Boston: Allyn and Bacon, 1999.
15. University of Chicago Press. *The Chicago Manual of Style.* 14th ed. Chicago: University of Chicago Press, 1993.

SAMPLE COMMUNITY HISTORIES

1. Cronon, William. *Nature's Metropolis: Chicago and the Great West.* New York: W.W. Norton, 1991.
2. Doyle, Don Harrison. *The Social Order of a Frontier Community: Jacksonville, Illinois, 1825–1870.* Urbana: University of Illinois Press, 1978.
3. Goldfield, David R. *Urban Growth in the Age of Sectionalism: Virginia, 1847–1861.* Baton Rouge: Louisiana State University Press, 1977.
4. Hansen, Karen V. *A Very Social Time: Crafting Community in Antebellum New England.* Berkeley: University of California Press, 1994.
5. Haywood, C. Robert. *Victorian West: Class and Culture in Kansas Cattle Towns.* Lawrence: University Press of Kansas, 1991.
6. Hine, Robert V. *Community on the American Frontier: Separate but Not Alone.* Norman: University of Oklahoma Press, 1980.
7. Lingemann, Richard. *Small Town America: A Narrative History, 1620–the Present.* Boston: Houghton Mifflin, 1980.
8. Lockridge, Kenneth A. *A New England Town: The First Hundred Years, Dedham, Massachusetts, 1636–1736.* New York: Norton, 1985.
9. Schultz, Stanley K. *Constructing Urban Culture: American Cities and City Planning, 1800–1920.* Philadelphia: Temple University Press, 1989.
10. Zuckerman, Michael. *Peaceable Kingdoms: New England Towns in the Eighteenth Century.* New York: Alfred A. Knopf, 1970.

Endnotes

Foreword

1 Donald R. Barnes and Richard S. Lackey, *Write It Right: A Manual for Writing Family Histories and Genealogies* (Rockville, Md.: Lyon Press, 1983), 69–71.

2 Lester J. Cappon, "Genealogy, Handmaid of History," *National Genealogical Society Quarterly* 45 (March 1957): 1–9.

3 Samuel P. Hays, "History and Genealogy: Patterns and Change and Prospects for Cooperation," parts 1, 2, and 3, *Prologue*, spring 1975, 39–43; summer 1975, 81–84; fall 1975, 187–191.

4 Elizabeth Shown Mills, "Academia vs. Genealogy: Prospects for Reconciliation and Progress," *National Genealogical Society Quarterly* 71 (1983): 99–106.

5 David Hackett Fischer, "Genealogy and History: The Leah and Rachel of the Learned Disciplines," *The American Genealogist* 287/288 (July/October 1997): 148–157.

Chapter One

1 Gerald McFarland, *A Scattered People: An American Family Moves West* (New York: Pantheon Books, 1985), xxii.

2 Peter N. Stearns, "Toward a Wider Vision: Trends in Social History," in Michael Kammen, ed., *The Past Before Us: Contemporary Historical Writing in the United States* (Ithaca: Cornell University Press, 1980), 4.

3 Peter N. Stearns, *Meaning Over Memory: Recasting the Teaching of Culture and History* (Chapel Hill: University of North Carolina Press, 1993), 124–125.

4 If you care to read the historians' firsthand account of this dispute, see Gary B. Nash, et al., *History on Trial: Culture Wars and the Teaching of the Past* (New York: Alfred A. Knopf, 1997).

5 My doctoral program at the University of California at Santa Barbara was

the Graduate Program in Public Historical Studies. It was through this program that I gained exposure to professional oral history, cultural resource management, historic preservation, and public policy history. My husband, a historian for Air Force Space Command, and I remain public historians.

6 Ralph S. Crandall and Robert M. Taylor Jr., eds., *Generations and Change: Genealogical Perspectives in Social History* (Macon: Mercer University Press, 1986), 25.

7 Lester D. Stephens, *Probing the Past: A Guide to the Study and Teaching of History* (Boston: Allyn and Bacon, 1974), 112–126.

8 Richard Marius, *A Short Guide to Writing About History*. 2nd ed. (New York: HarperCollins, 1995), 43–45.

Chapter Two

1 Jones as quoted in Simon J. Bronner, ed., *American Material Culture and Folklife: A Prologue and Dialogue* (Ann Arbor: UMI Research Press, 1985), 1. Louis C. Jones was a professor of literature who then became director of the New York State Historical Association and its museums.

2 Thomas Schlereth, *Artifacts and the American Past* (Walnut Creek, Calif.: Alta Mira Press, 1996), 3.

3 Susan Strasser, *Never Done: A History of American Housework* (New York: Pantheon Books, 1982), 42, 44.

4 Pat Ferraro et al., *Hearts and Hands; The Influences of Women and Quilts on American Society* (San Francisco: Quilt Digest Press, 1987), 43, 54.

5 For a deeper understanding, see Henry Glassie, "Artifact and Culture, Architecture and Society," in Simon J. Bronner, ed., *American Material Culture and Folklife: A Prologue and Dialogue* (Ann Arbor: UMI Research Press, 1985), 47–62.

6 Emily Croom, *Unpuzzling Your Past: A Basic Guide to Genealogy* (Cincinnati: Betterway Books, 1983), 45–46.

7 Gary Laderman, *The Sacred Remains: American Attitudes Toward Death, 1799–1883* (New Haven: Yale University Press, 1996), 22.

Chapter Three

1 Ralph and Terry Kovel, *Kovels' Know Your Antiques* (New York: Crown Publishers, 1967, 1973, 1981), 208.

2 My definitions are adapted from Henry Glassie, *Pattern in the Material Folk Culture of the Eastern United States* (Philadelphia: University of Pennsylvania Press, 1968), 1–33. I have added my own interpretations and observations.

3 See Jan Harold Brunvald, *The Study of American Folklore: An Introduction*. 2nd ed. (New York: W.W. Norton & Co., 1968, 1978), 302–303; Richard M. Dorson, ed., *Folklore and Folklife: An Introduction* (Chicago: University of Chicago Press, 1972), 233–350; and Robert E. Walls, "Folklife and Material Culture," in George H. Shoemaker, ed., *The Emergence of Folklore in Everyday Life: A Fieldguide and Sourcebook* (Bloomington, Ind.: Trickster Press, 1990), 107.

4 My collection of *Salt* magazines comes from the used-book and magazine sale

shelves at Penrose Public Library in Colorado Springs. The list of topics is the result of scanning the issues from Volume 1, Number 1 in January 1974 through Volume 3, Number 4 in June 1977. See also Pamela Wood, *You and Aunt Arie: A Guide to Cultural Journalism Based on Foxfire and Its Descendants* (Washington, D.C.: Institutional Development and Economic Affairs Service, Inc., 1975).

5 Elizabeth Shown Mills, *Evidence! Citation & Analysis for the Family Historian* (Baltimore: Genealogical Publishing Co., 1997), 18.

6 *Ibid.*, 61.

7 Susan Langley, *Vintage Hats and Bonnets, 1770–1970, Identification and Values* (Paducah, Ky.: Collector Books, 1998), 7.

8 Ilene (Chandler) Miller, *Preserving Family Keepsakes: Do's and Don'ts* (Yorba Linda, Calif.: Shumway Family History Services, 1995), 122.

9 Caleb Sturdevant, handwritten notes, Martinsburg, N.Y., 1827–1837, in Sturdevant Family Bible, New Testament, Cooperstown, N.Y., 1826; original in possession of Nathan A. Allen Jr., Sun City, Ariz.; photocopied pages in author's possession.

10 I owe my better framing experiences and some of my information to Jeanie Sharon, director, Old Town Gallery, Colorado Springs, Colo.

Chapter Four

1 Robert Traill Spence Lowell quoted in John Bartlett, *Familiar Quotations*, 15th ed., Emily Morison Beck, ed., Boston: Little, Brown and Co., 1855, 1980, p. 894:11.

2 The land looks like flat northern plains. It is Cayuga, North Dakota. The town view may be later as there are more buildings and trees, which were not native to the area. People grew grain (stored in silos), had telephones, still used wagons, pumped water with windmills, and attended a Protestant church. (Frank Sturdevant Collection, in author's possession.)

3 This is my grandfather, Archibald Harper. He was an attorney in Globe, Arizona in 1911. I recognize the picture above his desk as of graduating class from the University of Colorado Law School because we found that photograph, and my mother told me that he always hung it above any desk he had. One of his specialties was mining law. (Harper Collection, in author's possession.)

4 The wall portrait in Figure 6 is a charcoal enlargement, an overpainting, of the photograph in Figure 5. This is a boy, not a girl; his hair is not parted in the middle and he is wearing short pants. The boy standing under the wall portrait is the same boy, several years older. The older couple is his grandparents who raised him after his young mother died. They had music in their late-Victorian parlor and the man probably hunted deer at an earlier time. These are, by the way, Lafayette and Sarah Sturdevant with young Frank. (Frank Sturdevant Collection, in author's possession.)

5 Heinz K. Henisch and Bridget A. Henisch, *The Photographic Experience, 1839–1914: Images and Attitudes* (University Park: Pennsylvania State University Press, 1994), 188.

6 Federal Writers' Project, *Vermont: A Guide to the Green Mountain State* (Boston: Houghton Mifflin Co., 1937), 77–81.

7 John Waldsmith, *Stereo Views: An Illustrated History and Price Guide* (Radnor, Pa.: Wallace-Homestead Book Company, 1991), 16, 1, 15.

8 Adele Logan Alexander, *Homelands and Waterways: The American Journey of the Bond Family, 1846–1926* (New York: Pantheon Books, 1999), 246–247.

9 Lise Yasui and Katherine Kline, producers, *A Family Gathering*, WGBH Boston for The American Experience, 1989.

Chapter Five

1 Donald Ritchie, *Doing Oral History* (New York: Twayne Publishers, 1995), 1.

2 Ralph Crandall, *Shaking Your Family Tree: A Basic Guide to Tracing Your Family's Genealogy* (Dublin, N.H.: Yankee Publishing Inc., 1986), 27.

3 Christine Rose and Kay Germain Ingalls, *The Complete Idiot's Guide to Genealogy* (New York: Alpha Books, 1997), 266.

Chapter Six

1 Letter from C.A. Brown to D.A. Keller, 30 January 1884, transcribed in Byrd Gibbens, ed., *This Is a Strange Country: Letters of a Westering Family, 1880–1906* (Albuquerque: University of New Mexico Press, 1988), 190.

2 Val D. Greenwood, *The Researcher's Guide to American Genealogy* (Baltimore: Genealogical Publishing Co., 2000), 132–134.

Chapter Seven

1 Laverne Galeener-Moore, *Collecting Dead Relatives: An Irreverent Romp Through the Field of Genealogy* (Baltimore: Genealogical Publishing Co., 1987), 6.

2 Charles H. Litchman, ed., *Official History of the Improved Order of Red Men* (Boston: the Fraternity Publishing Co., 1893, 1909).

Chapter Eight

1 James Oliver Robinson and Janet C. Robertson, *All Our Yesterdays: A Century of Family Life in an American Small Town* (New York: HarperCollins Publishers, 1993), 458.

2 Gerald McFarland, *A Scattered People: An American Family Moves West* (New York: Pantheon Books, 1985), 77.

3 Joanne Ellenberger, "Thomas Cowdin of Early Massachusetts," unpublished paper, 1997, copy in author's possession, quoted with permission.

4 Malcolm Bell Jr., *Major Butler's Legacy: Five Generations of a Slaveholding Family* (Athens: University of Georgia Press, 1987), 380.

5 Robert Anthony Orsi, *The Madonna of 115th Street: Faith and Community in Italian Harlem, 1880–1950* (New Haven: Yale University Press, 1985), 131. Orsi uses the term *domus* for a family unit among Italian-American peasant immigrants. The unit was simultaneously the family, the building in which they lived, and their kinship network.

General Bibliography

In the interest of saving space so that I could share more sources with you, I have tried not to repeat complete citations from the chapter bibliographies in the general bibliography. So, please also refer to the bibliographies at the ends of the chapters.

Also, these bibliographies are by no means comprehensive. There are literally thousands of books I could have listed. Please remember that these are just starting points. I am considering an annotated bibliography volume for family historians as a companion to this book. So stay in touch and keep your eyes open!

SELECTED GENEALOGICAL, HISTORICAL, AND REFERENCE GUIDES AND DIRECTORIES

American Association for State and Local History. *Directory of Historical Organizations in the United States and Canada*. 14th ed. Nashville: AASLH Press, 1990.

Baird's Manual of American College Fraternities. Menasha, Wis., 1949.

Bentley, Elizabeth Petty. *The Genealogist's Address Book*. 4th ed. Baltimore: Genealogical Publishing Company, 1998.

Bowker, *American Library Directory*. 2 vols. New Providence, N.J. Annual.

Carmack, Sharon DeBartolo. *A Genealogist's Guide to Discovering Your Female Ancestors*. Cincinnati: Betterway Books, 1998.

———. *A Genealogist's Guide to Discovering Your Immigrant and Ethnic Ancestors*. Cincinnati: Betterway Books, 2000.

———. *The Genealogy Sourcebook*. Los Angeles: Lowell House, 1997.

———. *Organizing Your Family History Search*. Cincinnati: Betterway Books, 1999.

Crandall, Ralph. *Shaking Your Family Tree: A Basic Guide to Tracing Your Family's Genealogy*. Dublin, N.H.: Yankee Publishing Company, 1986.

Croom, Emily Anne. *Unpuzzling Your Past: A Basic Guide to Genealogy*. 3rd ed. Cincinnati: Betterway Books, 1995.

Dollarhide, William. *Managing a Genealogical Project: A Complete Manual for the Management and Organization of Genealogical Materials*. Rev. ed. Baltimore: Genealogical Publishing Company, 1991.

Eichholz, Alice, ed. *Ancestry's Redbook: American State, County and Town Sources* Rev. ed. Salt Lake City: Ancestry Publishing, 1989, 1992.

Everton, George B. *The Handy Book for Genealogists: United States of America*. 8th ed. Logan, Utah: Everton Publishers, 1991.

Freidel, Frank, ed. *The Harvard Guide to American History*. 2 vols. Cambridge: Harvard University Press, 1974.

Galeener-Moore, Laverne. *Collecting Dead Relatives: An Irreverent Romp Through the Field of Genealogy*. Baltimore: Genealogical Publishing Company, 1987.

Greenwood, Val D. *The Researcher's Guide to American Genealogy*. 3rd ed. Baltimore: Genealogical Publishing Company, 2000.

Hatcher, Patricia Law. *Producing a Quality Family History*. Salt Lake City: Ancestry Publishing, 1996.

Higher Education Publications. *The HEP Higher Education Directory*. Washington, D.C.: 1983–.

Jones, Henry Z. *More Psychic Roots: Further Adventures in Serendipity and Intuition in Genealogy*. Baltimore: Genealogical Publishing Company, 1997.

———. *Psychic Roots: Serendipity and Intuition in Genealogy*. Baltimore: Genealogical Publishing Company, 1993.

Kammen, Michael, ed. *The Past Before Us: Contemporary Historical Writing in the United States*. Ithaca: Cornell University Press, 1980.

Kline, Mary-Jo. *A Guide to Documentary Editing*. Baltimore: Johns Hopkins University Press, 1987.

Kyvig, David E., and Myron Marty. *Nearby History: Exploring the Past Around You*. Nashville: American Association for State and Local History, 1982.

———. *Your Family History: A Handbook for Research and Writing*. Arlington Heights, Illinois: AHM, 1978.

Macmillan Information. *The College Blue Book*. New York: Macmillan Information, 1977–.

Marius, Richard. *A Short Guide to Writing About History*. 2nd ed. New York: HarperCollins, 1995.

Mills, Elizabeth Shown. *Evidence! Citation & Analysis for the Family Historian*. Baltimore: Genealogical Publishing Company, 1997.

Morris, Jeffrey B. and Richard B. Morris, *The Encyclopedia of American History*. 7th ed. New York: HarperCollins, 1996.

Nash, Gary B., Charlotte Crabtree, and Ross E. Dunn. *History on Trial: Culture Wars and the Teaching of the Past*. New York: Alfred A. Knopf, 1997.

Rose, Christine, and Kay Germain Ingalls. *The Complete Idiot's Guide to Genealogy*. New York: Alpha Books, 1997.

Smith, Juliana Szucs. *The Ancestry Family Historian's Address Book*. Salt Lake City: Ancestry Publishing, 1997.

Stearns, Peter Yuen. *Meaning Over Memory: Recasting the Teaching of Culture and History*. Chapel Hill: University of North Carolina Press, 1993.

Stephens, Lester D. *Probing the Past: A Guide to the Study and Teaching of History*. Boston: Allyn and Bacon, 1974.

Stevens, Michael E. and Steven B. Burg. *Editing Historical Documents: A Handbook of Practice*. Walnut Creek, Calif.: Alta Mira Press, 1997.

Sturdevant, Katherine Scott. "Documentary Editing for Family Historians," *Association for Professional Genealogists Quarterly* 5:3 (Spring 1990) 51–57.

Szucs, Loretto Dennis, and Sandra Hargreaves Luebking, eds. *The Source: A Guidebook of American Genealogy*. Salt Lake City: Ancestry Publishing, 1997.

Taylor, Robert M., Jr., and Ralph J. Crandall, eds. *Generations and Change: Genealogical Perspectives in Social History*. Macon: Mercer University Press, 1986.

Trask, David F., and Robert W. Pomeroy III. *The Craft of Public History: An Annotated Bibliography*. Westport, Conn.: Greenwood Press, 1983.

University of Chicago Press. *The Chicago Manual of Style*. 14th ed. Chicago: University of Chicago Press, 1993.

Watts, Jim and Allen F. Davis. *Your Family in Modern American History*. New York: Alfred A. Knopf, 1974.

SELECTED SOCIAL HISTORY SOURCES

Anderson, William L. *Cherokee Removal: Before and After*. Athens: University of Georgia Press, 1991.

Bacon, Margaret Hope. *Mothers of Feminism: The Story of Quaker Women in America*. San Francisco: Harper and Row, 1986.

———. *The Quiet Rebels: The Story of the Quakers in America*. New York: Basic Books, 1969.

Bailey, Beth L. *From Front Porch to Back Seat: Courtship in Twentieth-Century America*. Baltimore: Johns Hopkins University Press, 1988.

Berrol, Selma Cantor. *Growing Up American: Immigrant Children in America Then and Now*. New York: Twayne Publishers, 1995.

Blassingame, John. *The Slave Community: Plantation Life in the Antebellum South*. New York: Oxford University Press, 1979.

Bleser, Carol. *In Joy and in Sorrow: Women, Family, and Marriage in the Victorian South*. New York: Oxford University Press, 1991.

Bremner, Robert H., ed. *Children and Youth in America: A Documentary History*. 3 vols. Cambridge: Harvard University Press, 1970.

Bremner, Robert. *From the Depths: The Discovery of Poverty in the United States*. New York: New York University Press, 1956.

Brown, Kathleen M. *Good Wives, Nasty Wenches, and Anxious Patriarchs: Gender, Race, and Power in Colonial Virginia*. Chapel Hill: University of North Carolina Press, 1996.

Bushman, Richard L. *From Puritan to Yankee: Character and the Social Order in Connecticut, 1690–1765*. Cambridge: Harvard University Press, 1967.

Calhoun, Arthur W. *A Social History of the American Family, From Colonial Times to the Present*. 3 vols. Cleveland: Arthur H. Clark Co., 1917.

Carp, E. Wayne. *Family Matters: Secrecy and Disclosure in the History of Adoption*. Cambridge: Harvard University Press, 1998.

Censer, Jane Turner. *North Carolina Planters and Their Children, 1800–1860*. Baton Rouge: Louisiana State University Press, 1984.

Chudacoff, Howard. *The Age of the Bachelor: Creating an American Subculture*. Princeton: Princeton University Press, 1999.

Clinton, Catherine. *The Plantation Mistress: Woman's World in the Old South*. New York: Pantheon Books, 1982.

Coontz, Stephanie. *The Social Origins of Private Life: A History of American Families, 1600–1900*. London: Verso, 1988.

———. *The Way We Never Were: American Families and the Nostalgia Trap*. New York: Basic Books, 1992.

Cornish, Dudley Taylor. *The Sable Arm: Negro Troops in the Union Army, 1861–1865*. New York: W.W. Norton and Co., 1966.

Cowan, Ruth Schwartz. *More Work for Mother: The Ironies of Household Technology From the Open Hearth to the Microwave*. New York: Basic Books, 1983.

Cremin, Lawrence. *American Education; The Colonial Experience, 1607–1783*. New York: Harper & Row, 1970.

———. *American Education; The Metropolitan Experience, 1876–1980*. New York: Harper & Row, 1988.

———. *American Education; The National Experience, 1783–1876*. New York: Harper & Row, 1980.

Daniels, Roger. *Coming to America: A History of Immigration and Ethnicity in American Life*. New York: HarperCollins Publishers, 1990.

Demos, John. *A Little Commonwealth: Family Life in Plymouth Colony*. New York: Oxford University Press, 1970.

Fass, Paula S., and Mary Ann Mason, eds. *Childhood in America*. New York: New York University Press, 2000.

Finger, John. *Cherokee Americans: The Eastern Band of Cherokees in the Twentieth Century*. Lincoln: University of Nebraska Press, 1991.

Fink, Deborah. *Agrarian Women: Wives and Mothers in Rural Nebraska, 1880–1940*. Chapel Hill: University of North Carolina Press, 1992.

Fischer, David Hackett. *Albion's Seed: Four British Folkways in America*. New York: Oxford University Press, 1989.

Foster, Morris. *Being Comanche: A Social History of an American Indian Community*. Tucson: University of Arizona Press, 1991.

Fox-Genovese, Elizabeth. *Within the Plantation Household: Black and White*

Women of the Old South. Chapel Hill: University of North Carolina Press, 1988.

Genovese, Eugene D. *Roll, Jordan, Roll: The World the Slaves Made.* New York: Random House, 1974.

Glatthaar, Joseph T. *Forged in Battle: The Civil War Alliance of Black Soldiers and White Officers.* New York: Free Press, 1990.

Gordon, Michael, ed. *The American Family in Social-Historical Perspective.* New York: St. Martin's Press, 1973.

Green, Harvey. *The Uncertainty of Everyday Life, 1915–1945.* New York: HarperCollins, 1992.

Greven, Philip. *Four Generations: Population, Land, and Family in Colonial Andover, Massachusetts.* Ithaca: Cornell University Press, 1970.

———. *The Protestant Temperament: Patterns of Child-Rearing, Religious Experience, and the Self in Early America.* New York: Alfred A. Knopf, 1977.

Gross, Robert A. *Minutemen and Their World.* New York: Hill and Wang, 1976.

Gulliford, Andrew. *America's Country Schools.* Washington, D.C.: Preservation Press, 1984.

Gutman, Herbert. *The Black Family in Slavery and Freedom, 1750–1925.* New York: Pantheon Books, 1976.

Hawke, David Freeman. *Everyday Life in Early America.* New York: Harper and Row, 1988.

Hodes, Martha. *White Women, Black Men: Illicit Sex in the Nineteenth-Century South.* New Haven: Yale University Press, 1997.

Hickey, Damon D. *Sojourners No More: The Quakers in the New South, 1865–1920.* Greensboro: North Carolina Friends Historical Society, 1997.

Jameson, Elizabeth. *All That Glitters: Class, Conflict, and Community in Cripple Creek.* Urbana: University of Illinois Press, 1998.

Jones, Jacqueline. *The Dispossessed: America's Underclasses From the Civil War to the Present.* New York: Basic Books, 1992.

Jordan, Terry G. and Matti Kaups. *The American Backwoods Frontier: An Ethnic and Ecological Interpretation.* Baltimore: Johns Hopkins University Press, 1989.

Kelley, Robert. *The Cultural Pattern in American Politics.* New York: Alfred A. Knopf, 1979.

Larkin, Jack. *The Reshaping of Everyday Life, 1790–1840.* New York: Harper and Row, 1988.

Leach, Robert J., and Peter Gow. *Quaker Nantucket: The Religious Community Behind the Whaling Empire.* Nantucket: Mill Hill Press, 1997.

Lemon, James T. *Best Poor Man's Country: A Geographic Study of Early Southeastern Pennsylvania.* Baltimore: Johns Hopkins University Press, 1972.

Levy, Barry. *Quakers and the American Family: British Quakers in the Delaware Valley, 1650–1765.* New York: Oxford University Press, 1988.

Leyburn, James G. *The Scotch-Irish: A Social History*. Chapel Hill: University of North Carolina Press, 1962.

May, Elaine Tyler. *Homeward Bound: American Families in the Cold War Era*. New York: Basic Books, 1988.

McMillen, Sally G. *Motherhood in the Old South: Pregnancy, Childbirth, and Infant Rearing*. Baton Rouge: Louisiana State University Press, 1990.

McNall, Scott G., and Sally Allen McNall. *Plains Families: Exploring Sociology Through Social History*. New York: St. Martin's Press, 1983.

McPherson, James. *For Cause and Comrades: Why Men Fought in the Civil War*. New York: Oxford University Press, 1997.

McWhiney, Grady. *Cracker Culture: Celtic Ways in the Old South*. Tuscaloosa: University of Alabama Press, 1988.

Mintz, Steven. *A Prison of Expectations: The Family in Victorian Culture*. New York: New York University Press, 1983.

Mintz, Steven, and Susan Kellogg. *Domestic Revolutions: A Social History of American Family Life*. New York: Free Press, 1988.

Mitchell, Reid. *Civil War Soldiers: Their Expectations and Their Experiences*. New York: Simon and Schuster, 1988.

———. *The Vacant Chair: The Northern Soldier Leaves Home*. New York: Oxford University Press, 1993.

Morgan, Edmund S. *The Puritan Family: Essays on Religion and Domestic Relations in Seventeenth-Century New England*. Boston: Trustees of the Public Library, 1944.

Riley, Glenda. *Building and Breaking Families in the American West*. Albuquerque: University of New Mexico Press, 1996.

———. *Divorce: An American Tradition*. New York: Oxford University Press, 1991.

———. *The Female Frontier: A Comparative View of Women on the Prairie and Plains*. Lawrence: University Press of Kansas, 1988.

Robertson, James I., Jr. *Soldiers Blue and Gray*. Columbia: University of South Carolina Press, 1988.

Rothman, Ellen K. *Hands and Hearts: A History of Courtship in America*. New York: Basic Books, 1984.

Rushforth, Scott, and Steadman Upham. *A Hopi Social History*. Austin: University of Texas Press, 1992.

Russell, Howard S. *A Long, Deep Furrow: Three Centuries of Farming in New England*. Hanover, N.H.: University Press of New England, 1976, 1982.

Schlereth, Thomas. *Victorian America: Transformations in Everyday Life, 1876–1915*. New York: HarperCollins, 1991.

Scott, Donald M., and Bernard Wishy, eds. *America's Families: A Documentary History*. New York: Harper and Row, 1982.

Spruill, Julia Cherry. *Women's Life and Work in the Southern Colonies*. Chapel Hill: University of North Carolina Press, 1938.

Stevenson, Brenda E. *Life in Black and White: Family and Community in the Slave South*. New York: Oxford University Press, 1996.

Sutherland, Daniel E. *The Expansion of Everyday Life, 1860–1876.* New York: Harper and Row, 1989.

Thernstrom, Stephan, ed. *The Harvard Encyclopedia of American Ethnic Groups.* Cambridge: Harvard University Press, 1980.

Tucker, Susan. *Telling Memories Among Southern Women: Domestic Workers and Their Employers in the Segregated South.* New York: Schocken Books, 1988.

Ulrich, Laurel Thatcher. *Good Wives: Image and Reality in the Lives of Women in Northern New England, 1650–1750.* New York: Oxford University Press, 1980.

Wall, Helena M. *Fierce Communion: Family and Community in Early America.* New York: Alfred A. Knopf, 1974.

West, Elliott. *Growing Up With the Country: Childhood in the Far Western Frontier.* Albuquerque: University of New Mexico Press, 1989.

White, Deborah G. *Ar'n't I a Woman? Female Slaves in the Plantation South.* New York: W.W. Norton, 1999.

Wiley, Bell Irvin. *The Life of Billy Yank: The Common Soldier of the Union.* Baton Rouge: Lousiana State University Press, 1952.

———. *The Life of Johnny Reb: The Common Soldier of the Confederacy.* Baton Rouge: Louisiana State University Press, 1943.

Wolf, Stephanie Grauman. *As Various as Their Land: The Everyday Lives of Eighteenth-Century Americans.* New York: Harper Perennial, 1993.

Woodward, C. Vann, ed. *Mary Chesnut's Civil War.* New Haven, Conn.: Yale University Press, 1981.

FAMILY HISTORY NARRATIVE IN SOCIAL HISTORY CONTEXT

Alexander, Adele Logan. *Homelands and Waterways: The American Journey of the Bond Family, 1846–1926.* New York: Pantheon Books, 1999.

Ball, Edward. *Slaves in the Family.* New York: Farrar, Straus, and Giroux, 1998.

Bell, Malcolm, Jr. *Major Butler's Legacy: Five Generations of a Slaveholding Family.* Athens: University of Georgia Press, 1987.

Berry, Mary Clay. *Voices From the Century Before: The Odyssey of a Nineteenth-Century Kentucky Family.* New York: Arcade Publishing, 1997.

Colt, Margaretta Barton. *Defend the Valley: A Shenandoah Family in the Civil War.* New York: Orion Books, 1994.

Gibbens, Byrd, ed. *This Is a Strange Country: Letters of a Westering Family, 1880–1906.* Albuquerque: University of New Mexico Press, 1988.

Harrell, Carolyn L. *Kith and Kin: A Portrait of a Southern Family, 1630–1934.* Macon: Mercer University Press, 1984.

Kessler, Lauren. *Stubborn Twig: Three Generations in the Life of a Japanese American Family.* New York: Random House, 1993.

McFarland, Gerald. *A Scattered People: An American Family Moves West.* New York: Pantheon Books, 1985.

Myers, Robert Manson. *The Children of Pride: A True Story of Georgia and the Civil War*. New Haven: Yale University Press, 1972.

Murray, Pauli. *Proud Shoes: The Story of an American Family*. New York: Harper and Row, 1956.

Robertson, James Oliver, and Janet C. Robertson. *All Our Yesterdays: A Century of Family Life in an American Small Town*. New York: HarperCollins, 1993.

Schlissel, Lillian, et al. *Far From Home: Families of the Westward Journey*. New York: Schocken Books, 1989.

Forms for Family Historians

Following are blank copies of forms referred to throughout *Bringing Your Family History to Life Through Social History*:

- Artifact Identification, Analysis, and Cataloging Form
- Cemetery Analysis Form for Family History
- Family Photograph Inventory and Analysis
- Oral History Release Form

These forms are copyright © 2000 by Katherine Scott Sturdevant, but you are free to photocopy them for your *personal* use. No use in a printed work is permitted without permission.

ARTIFACT IDENTIFICATION, ANALYSIS, AND CATALOGING FORM

Cataloger's Name and Address _____

_____

Date _____

Name(s) of Artifact (family, popular, or generic) _____

_____

Description and Identifying Features (material, construction, measurements, color, function)

_____

_____

_____

_____

_____

_____

Inventory Number _____

Estimated Year of Origin _____

Original Location and Date Found_____

Current Location and Ownership _____

_____

History of Ownership _____

_____

_____

Identifying Source Citations, Cultural Analysis, and Interpretive Information

_____

_____

Checklist for Future Investigation _____

_____

CEMETERY ANALYSIS FORM FOR FAMILY HISTORY

Name of Cemetery _____

Date Cemetery Opened _____

Date of Visit _____

Location (Quarter Section, Town or Township, Nearest Roads, County, State)

_____

_____

Family Graves Sought _____

Family Graves Found _____

Transcribe Tombstone Inscriptions Exactly on Separate Sheet _____

Location of Tombstone in Cemetery (Section, Lot, and Block Numbers) _____

_____

Material, Construction, Design of Tombstone _____

_____

Relevant Nearby Graves _____

Relevant Nearby Foliage or Decoration _____

Clues in Nearby Graves to Common Cause of Deaths _____

_____

Unmarked Vacancies Nearby That May Have Been Graves _____

Surnames of Cemetery Neighbors Who May Be Relevant _____

_____

Other Historical Clues (Fraternal Symbols, Metal Markers) _____

_____

Condition of Tombstone _____

Condition of Grounds _____

Photograph Taken? _____ Rubbing or Cast Taken? _____

FAMILY PHOTOGRAPH INVENTORY AND ANALYSIS

Inventory Number (in Soft Pencil or on Archival Label on Back) _____

Date of This Record _____

Recorder _____

Location of Original Photograph _____

Condition of Original _____

Location of Negatives and Copies _____

Original Location _____

Notations on the Photograph _____

_____

Description of the Photograph (Type and Image) _____

_____

Photographer, if Known _____

Setting of Photograph _____

Identifying Features (Artifacts, Clothing, Signage) _____

_____

People Appearing in Photograph (Identified and Unidentified) _____

Analysis of Historical Significance _____

Unsolved Mysteries to Research _____

ORAL HISTORY RELEASE FORM

I _____ (interviewee) hereby give to _____

(interviewer) the original tape recordings and transcripts of our interview conducted on _____

(date) at _____ (place).

I authorize _____ (interviewer) to utilize this interview, in whole or in

part, for history or family history projects, including the possible pubication of history or family history books

and articles.

I further authorize _____ (interviewer) to donate said interview, tapes,

transcripts, or materials derived therefrom, to a historical archive (to be determined) for future educational and

scholarly purposes.

I voluntarily relinquish any rights to this interview, tape, transcript, or material derived therefrom.

Signed _____   Signed _____
       (interviewee and donor)   (interviewer and recipient)

Date _____   Date _____

NOTE: You and your interviewee may negotiate alterations to this form as you see fit.

You are free to copy this form for personal use. For an example of how to fill in, see page 137. © 2000 Katherine Scott Sturdevant, *Bringing Your Family History to Life Through Social History.*

Index